GLANVILLE WILLIAMS:
LEARNING THE LAW

GLANVILLE WILLIAMS: LEARNING THE LAW

BY

GLANVILLE WILLIAMS, QC, LL.D., F.B.A.
Honorary and Emeritus Fellow of Jesus College, Cambridge:
Honorary Bencher of the Middle Temple:
formerly Professor of Public Law and Quain
Professor of Jurisprudence in the University of London,
and Rouse Ball Professor of English Law
in the University of Cambridge

"A man has but one youth, and considering the
consequences of employing that well, he has reason to
think himself very rich, for that gone, all the wealth in
the world will not purchase another."
Sir R. North, *On the Study of the Laws.*

SIXTEENTH EDITION

EDITED BY

A.T.H. SMITH, LL.D.
Fellow of Gonville and Caius College, Cambridge
Honorary Bencher, Middle Temple
formerly Pro Vice-Chancellor and Dean of Law at Victoria University
of Wellington and Professor of Criminal and Public Laws at
Cambridge University

SWEET & MAXWELL   **THOMSON REUTERS**

First Edition	1945	Sixth Impression	1990
Second Edition	1945	Seventh Impression	1992
Second Impression Revised	1946	Eighth Impression	1993
Third Impression	1948	Ninth Impression	1994
Fourth Edition	1950	Tenth Impression	1995
Fifth Edition	1953	Eleventh Impression	1996
Sixth Edition	1957	Twelfth Impression	1997
Seventh Edition	1963	Thirteenth Impression	1998
Second Impression	1966	Fourteenth Impression	1999
Third Impression	1967	Fifteenth Impression	2001
Fourth Impression	1968	Twelfth Edition	2002
Eighth Edition	1969	Second Impression	2002
Ninth Edition	1973	Third Impression	2003
Second Impression	1974	Fourth Impression	2004
Tenth Edition	1978	Fifth Impression	2005
Eleventh Edition	1982	Thirteenth Edition	2006
Second Impression	1984	Fourteenth Edition	2010
Third Impression	1986	Fifteenth Edition	2013
Fourth Impression	1986	Sixteenth Edition	2016
Fifth Impression	1988		

Published in 2016 by Thomson Reuters, trading as Sweet & Maxwell. Registered in England & Wales, Company No.1679046. Registered Office and address for service: 5 Canada Square, Canary Wharf, London, E14 5AQ.

For further information on our products and services, visit *www.sweetandmaxwell.co.uk*

Typeset by Servis Filmsetting Ltd, Stockport, Cheshire, SK2 5AJ
Printed and bound by CPI Group (UK) Ltd, Croydon, CR0 4YY

No natural forests were destroyed to make this product; only farmed timber was used and replanted.

A CIP catalogue record of this book is available for the British Library.

ISBN: 978-0-414-05193-5

Thomson Reuters, the Thomson Reuters Logo and Sweet & Maxwell ® are trademarks of Thomson Reuters.

Crown copyright material is reproduced with the permission of the Controller of HMSO and the Queen's Printer for Scotland.

Preface

One of the purposes of this book is to give law students and those who are thinking of studying the law a flavour of what the experience might be like. It gives general guidance and answers to some of the questions that arise in the minds of law students, particularly in such matters as writing legal essays and preparing answers to problem questions. As such, it is not a book that should be approached as though it were a novel, a work that must be read from cover to cover, starting at page one and ploughing remorselessly through. Chapter 1 gives an overview of some of the building blocks of the law, explaining the language in which they are described by lawyers, and should be used by non lawyers (journalists in particular) who have interests in discussing matters legal. Some of the later chapters on employment prospects (chapter 13) and suggestions for further reading (chapter 14), for example might with profit and interest be dipped into well before you start formal study. But chapter 2 will probably not mean a great deal to you until the time comes, shortly after the beginning of the first term, when the law student will have to come to grips with the law at close quarters for the first time.

One of the most significant developments that has occurred in the last decade or so is the extent to which the processes of legal decision-making have become far more accessible and visible to the public—including those who are subject to it, those who might wish to comment upon it and those who might wish to study it (into which category most of my readers probably fall). The proceedings of the highest court in the land, the Supreme Court, are now available on line at *https://www.supremecourt.uk/,* both live and in archived versions. Whereas earlier editions of this work have suggested to readers that they might like to go to Westminster and walk in to the Court to watch what is happening, now, you can follow what is going on simply by logging on.

In the light of these developments, I am going to suggest that you might like to conduct an experiment. In chapter 6 of the book, I discuss at some length the rather ancient case of *Wilkinson v Downton* (1897) in which a man was sued when (in what was described in the Supreme Court as a "misconceived practical joke") he told a woman (falsely) that her husband had been seriously injured in an accident, as a result of which she suffered nervous shock, for which she successfully sued for damages. That earlier decision was recently considered and in part relied upon by the Supreme Court in 2015 in a case called *O (A Child) v Rhodes* [2015] UKSC 32, in which a man was prevented by the lower courts from publishing a book about his own childhood on the grounds that it might, in effect, cause nervous shock to his own son.

The "experiment" envisaged is that you might like to have a look at the decision. You can simply put "[2015] UKSC 32" in to Google, and you will have the judgment of the Supreme Court on your screen. The main judgment is given by Baroness Hale. In the opening paragraphs, she explains the legal background and the facts. What she has to say is truly shocking, not only because of (be warned) the graphic language that Lady Hale quotes from the book, but also because as Lady Hale says, "the author's life has been a shocking one". What I hope you might get out of such an exercise is some appreciation of the fact that the study of law does not consist in the rote learning of large numbers of rules, but involves instead the careful consideration of conflicting principles (the father's right to freedom of speech was at stake, because he wanted to tell his own story in the book) and interests that have to be balanced in coming to the decision whether or not the father should be allowed to publish his book. Could it be said, for example, that he was intending to cause damage to his own son? There is a brief further analysis of the decision and the issues to which it gives rise on pages 106-107 below.

This edition was prepared at a time when there were significant changes afoot in the relationship between the United Kingdom and Europe (of which the United Kingdom forms an integral part). A referendum on 23 June 2016 determined that the United Kingdom is to withdraw from membership of the European Union. This will throw into reverse over four decades of legal and constitutional development. But the legal and political integration that has occurred during that period will not be easily unpicked, and the process that will be initiated when notice of withdrawal is given under Article 50 of the

Treaty of Lisbon is likely to be protracted, lasting several years. For that reason, I have left in place the first part of chapter three of the book, dealing with the European Union dimension. And although the Conservative Government has pledged itself to withdraw from the European Convention on Human Rights (with which the second part of chapter 3 is concerned), it seems doubtful that this will be very high on the legislative agenda in the years to come.

As with the last edition of this work, the revisions have been undertaken in Cambridge where I have had the pleasure of spending the year as the Arthur Goodhart Visiting Professor at the Cambridge Faculty of Law. Professor A.L. Goodhart's own work, dating from the 1930s, was discussed by Glanville Williams in the first edition of this book published in 1945. It remains pertinent today, and forms a basis for the discussion in chapter six. I express my grateful thanks to the Faculty for doing me the honour of appointing me to the position.

A.T.H. Smith
July 2016

Contents

1 THE DIVISIONS OF THE LAW

> But in these nice sharp quillets of the law,
> Good faith, I am no wiser than a daw.
>
> —Shakespeare, *King Henry the Sixth*, Part I, II, iv.

This book aims to help principally those who have decided to study law—whether in a University, College or other institution, or as a professional qualification.

From time to time I have been told of some who have read the book before making the decision to study law, and have been sufficiently attracted by the taste it has given them of legal studies to make up their minds to continue. I did not, however, intend to proselytise when I wrote. As you will see when you look at Chapter 13, there are quite enough people trying to enter the legal profession without adding to the number. If you are uncertain about your career there may be strong personal and social reasons why you should take up something else: entering the world of commerce or industry, or becoming a technologist or research scientist. In the foreseeable future there is likely be a much greater shortage of IT professionals, electronics specialists, good business managers (not overlooking areas such as banking and management consultancy) and people who combine linguistic skills with other abilities than there will be of lawyers. I assume, however, that you have decided to study the law or that you are giving the possibility serious thought.

On the question whether you should study law as opposed to some other discipline during your time at university, with a view to qualifying to practise law later (assuming, that is, that you have decided that you wish to practise law), it is difficult to be seen to offer objective advice. The former course offers a quicker and cheaper route to employment, and the opportunity to assess for yourself at an early stage whether the law is a discipline to which you wish to attach yourself. But there are some legal practitioners (who may themselves have studied something other than law at university) who would claim that too early a specialisation in the law can narrow rather than broaden the mind by depriving the student of the opportunity to be exposed to other disciplines.[1]

That is not a view that I share.[2] On the contrary, I would wish to argue that a university law course offers a chance to acquire both a necessary legal framework and a deeper understanding of the law. Even if you are only at the stage where you have narrowed your immediate options to obtaining higher education in one of the humanities, I would certainly wish to bring to your notice the attraction of law as compared with the traditional arts subjects.

Law is the cement of society, and an essential medium of change. Its study at a university enables you to explore how and why this is so. A common misunderstanding is that the study of law involves little more than the rote learning of legal rules. Closer acquaintance will show that it is more complex and challenging than that. Far better to think of the law as forming an integral part of a constantly evolving social landscape. Knowledge of law increases one's understanding of public affairs, as well as affording some understanding of social values. At a more practical level, its study promotes accuracy of expression, facility in argument and skill in interpreting the written word. It is of wider vocational relevance than most arts subjects. Its practice does, however, also call for much routine, careful, unexciting work, and it is for you to decide whether you think you are temperamentally suited to that.

In this book I offer an introduction to English law and its study at university or college. A word or two about the term English law. The use of "England" is taken generally to include both England and Wales. Without at this stage wishing to trouble you with the constitutional niceties, you should know that the Scottish legal system is in detail very different from the English. When England, Wales and Scotland are intended to be referred to as a single entity, the correct term is "Great Britain", and when Northern Ireland is added,

---

[1] A debate on the issue between Lord Sumption SCJ and Professor G. Virgo of Cambridge is available on line at *http://www.law.cam.ac.uk/press/news/2013/03/those-who-wish-to-practise-law-should-not-study-law-at-university/2190*

[2] For a passionate defence of the importance of the study of law in the university, see Professor P. Birks, "The Academic and the Practitioner" [1998] L.S. 397.

it becomes the "United Kingdom". The reason why the law emanating from these islands is worthy of study is that it is the home of the common law; the place where a family of law was born, quite different from the civil law that underlies much German, Italian and French law, and very different from Islamic law. The system of law that was historically developed in the courts of Westminster spread with the growth of the British Empire throughout much of the western world—to the United States of America, to the Commonwealth countries of Canada, Australia and New Zealand, to the African continent and to parts of the far east—India, Singapore, Malaysia and many more besides. Ideally, perhaps, a university would offer the chance to study at least some of the elements of these other legal systems—comparative law. But that would place a great burden upon the already crowded curriculum, and the ideal is rarely achieved.

CRIMES AND CIVIL WRONGS

One of the non-lawyer's inveterate errors is to suppose that the law is largely—even exclusively—concerned with the criminal law. In fact the law is divided into two great branches, the criminal and the civil,[3] and of these much the greater is the civil. An old chestnut that the reader beginning legal studies is likely to hear recounted (so why not by me?) concerns the visitor who was being given a glimpse of the Court of Chancery. He peered round and asked where was the prisoner?[4] It is important to grasp the nature of the division at the outset to understand the structure of the English legal system; the terminology is different, the procedure is different and the outcome is different. I shall, therefore, try to give a simple explanation of it.

The distinction between a crime and a civil wrong, though capable of giving rise to some difficult legal problems, is in essence quite simple. The first thing to understand is that the distinction does not reside in the nature of the wrongful act itself. This can be proved quite

---

[3] "Civil law" is a phrase used in several meanings. It may mean, as in the above context, the law that is not criminal law. It may also mean the law of a state as opposed to other sorts of law like international law; or it may mean Roman law. A "civilian" is a person learned in Roman law.

[4] According to a gloss on the tale, someone then explained that a Chancery judge does not try anything except counsel's patience.

simply by pointing out that the same act may be both a crime and a civil wrong. If I entrust my bag to a person working in the left-luggage office at a railway station, and that person then runs off with it, he or she commits the crime of theft and also two civil wrongs—the tort[5] of interference with goods and breach of a contract with me to keep the bag safe. The result is that two sorts of legal proceedings can be taken: a prosecution for the crime, and a civil action for the tort and for the breach of contract. (The claimant in the latter action will not get damages twice over merely because there are two causes of action; there will be only one set of damages.)

To take another illustration. If a railway signaller, in the words of the poet "to dumb forgetfulness a prey", fails to press the button at the right moment so that a fatal accident occurs, this carelessness may be regarded as sufficiently gross to amount to the crime of manslaughter. It is also the tort of negligence towards the victims of the accident and their dependants, and a breach of contract with the employer to take due care whilst at work. It will be noticed that, this time, the right to bring an action in tort and the right of action in contract are vested in different parties.

These examples show that the distinction between a crime and civil wrong cannot be stated as depending upon *what is done*, because what is done (or not done) is the same in each case. The true distinction resides, therefore, not in the nature of the wrongful act but in *the legal consequences that may follow it*.[6] If the wrongful act (or omission) is capable of being followed by what are called criminal proceedings, that means that it is regarded as a crime (otherwise called an *offence*). If it is capable of being followed by civil proceedings, that means that it is regarded as a civil wrong. If it is capable of being followed by both, it is both a crime and a civil wrong.

THE COURTS

Civil and criminal courts in England and Wales are largely but not entirely distinct. *Magistrates* are chiefly concerned with criminal

---

[5] The meaning of which will be explained in due course: see p.19. For now, it is enough to know that it is a civil wrong, as opposed to a criminal offence.

[6] *cf. per* Lord Esher M.R. in *Seaman v Burley* [1896] 2 Q.B. 344 at 346.

cases, but they have important civil jurisdiction over licensing and family matters. The *Crown Court* has almost exclusively criminal jurisdiction. On the other hand, the jurisdiction of the *County Court* is only civil, and so is the *High Court*, apart from appeals.

Over most of the country, magistrates are lay justices of the peace sitting with a clerk. The *clerk to the justices*, whose function is to advise on matters of law, is legally qualified. But he or she is often occupied with administration, and is in practice supported by assistant clerks who may be legally unqualified.[7] In the large cities magistrates' courts are now presided over by full-time *district judges (magistrates' courts)*[8] who are legally qualified, and who until relatively recently were known as *stipendiary magistrates*, or colloquially as "stipes". Since the Access to Justice Act 1999 requires that professional, full-time magistrates are to be known as District Judges (Magistrates' Courts), the expressions "justices of the peace"[9] and "magistrates" have effectively become synonymous.

Courts with civil jurisdiction

Before looking more closely at the courts by which civil cases are tried, the general point might be made that justice in this country is conducted in public. With a few exceptions (particularly relating to the welfare of young people and matters of family law), all courts are open to public view. An intending student should take the opportunity to visit one court of each level[10] operating in the locality to see the process of justice in operation.

Neglecting magistrates' courts, the English system of civil judicature about to be explained may be represented thus:

---

[7] See Penny Derbyshire, "Raising Concerns about Magistrates' Clerks" in S. Doran and J.D. Jackson ed., *The Judicial Role in Criminal Proceedings* (2000).

[8] Not to be confused with district judges of the Family Division of the High Court, or with district judges who sit in the county courts and District Registries of the High Court; see (2001) 151 N.L.J. 505.

[9] Justices of the Peace Act 1997.

[10] Addresses of all courts can be found online at *https://courttribunalfinder.service.gov. uk/search/*. Those for Magistrates' Courts, Crown Courts and county courts can also be found on the Court Service website, *www.hmcourts-service.gov.uk*.

Figure 1

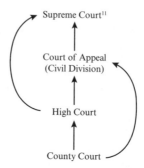

The courts with original[12] civil jurisdiction are chiefly the High Court and county courts. The High Court is divided into three divisions: the *Queen's Bench Division*[13] (commonly referred to as the *Divisional Court*), the *Chancery Division*, and the *Family Division*. The first administers primarily the *common law*, the second primarily *equity*.[14] More will be said about this particular distinction later in the chapter. The Family Division was created by the Administration of Justice Act 1970 in place of the previous Probate, Divorce and Admiralty Division—a curious miscellany of jurisdictions (over "wills, wives and wrecks" was the jocular reference) which were lumped together for no better reason than they were all founded (to some extent) on Roman and canon law. In 1970, wills went to the Chancery Division and wrecks to the Queen's Bench Division. For administrative purposes, the head of the Divisional Court is the Lord Chief Justice of England, assisted by a President of the Queen's Bench Division. The Chancellor of the High Court presides in practice over

[11] Formerly, the highest court in the land was the House of Lords, but it was replaced by a Supreme Court as from October 2009. See p.9 below.

[12] i.e. jurisdiction as a court of first instance, conducting trials as opposed to appeals.

[13] There has been a proliferation of separately created parts of the Queen's Bench Division dealing with specialist areas of the law. Thus, an Administrative Court was established in 2000 dealing with matters of administrative law (principally judicial review) and made part of the Queen's Bench Division, joining there the Admiralty Court, the Commercial Court and the Technology and Construction Court.

[14] In 1977 a Patents Court was set up and made part of the Chancery Division.

the Chancery Division (technically, the Lord High Chancellor is the head of Chancery) and the most senior judge of the Family Division is known as the President.

A civil trial in the High Court is held before a judge, sometimes called a *puisne* (pronounced "puny") judge, generally sitting without a jury. The judge may sit in London or in one of the other major legal centres.[15] In practice, the sheer volume of work is such that High Court cases are often taken by deputy High Court judges. By contrast, certain applications to the High Court are made to the Queen's Bench Division consisting of a Lord Justice and a judge of the High Court.

Court of Appeal (Civil Division)

There is almost always the possibility of an appeal *from* (i.e. against) the decision of a court of trial, providing permission is given by the trial judge or by the Court of Appeal itself. The party who appeals is the *appellant*,[16] the other is the *respondent*. For the High Court the appropriate appellate court is the *Court of Appeal (Civil Division)*. This may be presided over by one of the following: the *Master of the Rolls*, the *Lord Chief Justice*, one of the *Heads of Division* of the Court of Appeal or a *Lord Justice of Appeal*—there are currently nearly 40 members of the Court of Appeal who are Lords (or Lady[17]) Justices. The Court of Appeal generally sits with three members but sometimes with two (depending on the importance of the case), and there will be several such courts in action at the same time.

Other courts and tribunals

There are many courts and tribunals of special jurisdiction, dealing in particular with disputes between citizens and the state, that arise in relation to disputes over such matters as benefit entitlements and other aspects of the state's regulatory framework. The tribunal system developed historically in a rather piecemeal and haphazard

---

[15] The peregrinating High Court was formerly called the *Assize Court*, but this was abolished upon the creation of the Crown Court in 1972.

[16] Emphasis on the second syllable; so also in "appellate."

[17] There are currently 8 women members of the Court.

way from the early part of the 20th century, and is in the process of substantial reorganisation and development following the enactment of the Tribunals, Courts and Enforcement Act 2007.

There is now an Upper Tribunal consisting of four "Chambers". To give you an idea of their scope, they deal with such matters as "Administrative Appeals", "Tax and Chancery", "Immigration and Asylum" and "Lands". Under this body is the "First Tier Tribunal", whose seven chambers deal with such matters as "War Pensions and Armed Forces Compensation", "Social Entitlement", "Health, Education and Social Care", "Tax", "Immigration and Asylum" and "Property".

It is an indication of the seniority of these tribunals that the Upper Tribunal is not bound by decisions of the High Court.[18]

Appeals lie from the decisions of the First Tier to the Upper Tribunal with possible further appeals to the Court of Appeal and Supreme Court.

Still lying outside this system is the Employment Tribunal, which is yet to become a Chamber of the First Tier, and from which appeals are still made to the *Employment Appeals Tribunal*.

County courts

Going down the ladder again, the less important civil cases are tried in the county courts, with appeals to the High Court if permission is given.[19] If the High Court or county court judge when granting permission considers the matter to be of sufficient general importance, the case may be referred directly to the Court of Appeal.

Magistrates' courts

Magistrates also have some civil jurisdiction, chiefly in matrimonial matters, guardianship, adoption, and child support cases. There are

---

[18] *Gilchrist v Revenue and Customs Commissioners* [2014] UKUT 169 (TCC), [2015] Ch 183.

[19] Until 2 May 2000, appeals from the county courts lay directly to the Court of Appeal. By virtue of regulations made under the Access to Justice Act 1999, most appeals are now to the High Court, but with the possibility of an appeal to the Court of Appeal still available in limited situations.

approximately 350 magistrates' courts (numbers have been declining rapidly in recent years as the court system is "rationalised"), staffed by 18,857[20] lay magistrates and approximately 132 District Judges and 135 Deputy District Judges (magistrates' courts). Appeals from magistrates' courts (by means of what is called a "case stated") go to a Divisional Court—which in family matters will be composed of judges of the Family Division.[21]

Together the Crown Court, High Court and Court of Appeal (but for reasons to be explained, not the House of Lords) make up the Supreme Court of Judicature. The present High Court, and the Court of Appeal on its civil side (but not yet criminal) were set up by the Judicature Act 1873.[22]

Appeals to the Supreme Court

Parliament enacted a Constitutional Reform Act 2005 which, when it came in to operation in 2009 created for the United Kingdom a new Supreme Court to replace the Appellate Committee of the House of Lords. The driving force behind the reform was the idea that it was no longer constitutionally appropriate for the most senior judges to be simultaneously members of the legislature.[23] The existing members of the Appellate Committee of the House became Justices of the Supreme Court but, since they retain their Peerages, are still referred to by the former titles. As further members are appointed, they are known as Justices of the Supreme Court, but they are still accorded the courtesy title as "Lord" or "Lady". The Head of the Court is known as the President.

Now the position is as follows: When an appeal is taken to the Court of Appeal (either from the High Court or from a Divisional Court),

[20] In 2013, the number was 23,244.

[21] Another mode of appeal from magistrates is to the Crown Court; this is a full rehearing, unlike the appeal by case stated which is theoretically only on points of law. When an appeal is taken from magistrates to the Crown Court, a further appeal lies from the Crown Court to a Divisional Court on case stated.

[22] The High Court superseded the old courts of Queen's Bench, Common Pleas, Exchequer, Chancery, Probate, Divorce and Admiralty, and a few minor courts. The Court of Appeal superseded the old Court of Exchequer Chamber and Court of Appeal in Chancery.

[23] This view was shared by some of the members of the House, such as the senior Law Lord (Lord Bingham) "The Evolving Constitution" [2002] E.H.R.L.R. 1, 15.

a further appeal lies (with permission) to the Supreme Court. Why two appeals should be allowed can be explained only by reference to history. "The institution of one court of appeal may be considered a reasonable precaution; but two suggest panic", said A.P. Herbert. It is a panic that pays little regard to the resources of the parties to the proceedings who must bear the costs.

The Judicature Act 1873, which was passed by a Liberal Government, would have abolished the appellate jurisdiction of the House of Lords; but the Conservatives took office before it came into force, and repealed this provision fearing that the abolition of the Lords as a judicial body might be the thin end of the wedge leading ultimately to their abolition as a legislative body.[24] Such fears have nothing to do with the question whether a double appeal is justifiable. From time to time there have suggestions that we should dispense with our top-heavy system.

Despite its undoubted expense, however, the balance of opinion is clearly in favour of a further appeal, for a number of reasons.[25] The sheer volume of work undertaken by the Court of Appeal (particularly the Criminal Division) is such that it does not have the opportunity for detached reflection that should characterise the work of a final court. Both Divisions of the Court of Appeal (i.e. civil and criminal) operate in several courts simultaneously, giving rise to the possibility (admittedly rare) that the courts will decide the same point in different directions. Should that happen, it is open to a later Court of Appeal to choose between the two, but the decision of a higher court is more definitive. In those circumstances, with the consent of the parties and on certificate from the judge, a civil case may go on appeal direct from the High Court to the Supreme Court under the "leap-frogging" procedure introduced by the Administration of Justice Act 1969. This can happen if the case turns on the construction of legislation, or is governed by a previous decision of the Court of Appeal, House of

---

[24] See Robert Stevens, *Law and Politics* (1977), pp.52 *et seq.* The Royal Commission on the Reform of the House of Lords, *A House for the Future* which reported in January 2000 (Cm. 4534) took the view that, as long as certain conventions were observed, it was appropriate that the judicial functions of the House should be preserved. But this was overtaken by subsequent events.

[25] See A. Le Sueur, "What Do the Top Courts Do?" (2000) 53 C.L.P. 53 and A. Le Sueur and R. Cornes, *The Future of the United Kingdom's Highest Courts* (UCL, Constitution Unit, 2001).

Lords or Supreme Court which one of the parties wishes the Supreme Court to overturn.

It will have been understood from what has gone before that "the House of Lords" was an ambiguous expression. It referred (1) to all the peers who choose to sit[26] as the Upper House of the legislature (Parliament), which continues to be the case, and also (2) to a court consisting of the highest level of the judiciary. The House of Lords no longer performs the latter function. Originally the House of Lords was a single body, but a convention (understanding) developed that only peers with senior judicial experience should decide appeals. This was finally established in 1844. Because they were regarded as being a part of Parliament, the House of Lords was not part of the Supreme Court of Judicature.

The "Law Lords" (the "Lords of Appeal in Ordinary" and peers who held or had held high judicial office such as former Lords Chancellors), as the *Judicial Committee* of the House of Lords, exercised its judicial function. The Lords of Appeal in Ordinary (like Lord Mance and Lord Carnwath) were (and still are) salaried life peers appointed by the Crown. Generally, this was by way of promotion from the Court of Appeal, but it was not unknown for a member of the Bar to be appointed directly to the House.[27] Members of the Court of Appeal are appointed by promotion from the High Court. Even after the Supreme Court had been created, those remaining members of the old body as Law Lords are truly peers, and can take part in debates and vote in the House, though by custom the Lords of Appeal in Ordinary do so only on legal matters. It has been the practice since the creation of the Court to accord the courtesy title of "Lord" to members who were appointed subsequently to the Court's creation,. The "Lords Justices" of the Court of Appeal, by contrast, are not peers and cannot sit in Parliament. We refer, for example, to "Lord Justice Elias", not "Lord Elias".

Although, when exercising its appellate jurisdiction, the House of Lords consisted exclusively of the Law Lords, it nevertheless sat in the same building as the House of Lords when meeting as a limb

---

[26] Or in the case of hereditary peers, the majority of whom were excluded by the House of Lords Act 1999, those who are still permitted to sit.

[27] Most recently, Lord Sumption, who took office in 2012.

of the legislature; these sittings were in a committee room rather than on the floor of the House itself.[28] This changed when the House became the Supreme Court, but one reason for the delay in implementing the Constitution Act 2005 has been the entirely practical need to find new accommodation for the new Supreme Court. In October 2009, the Justices of the Supreme Court sat for the first time in the new court which is in the former Middlesex Guildhall on Parliament Square. The Court is consequently much easier to visit than was the case when it was housed in Parliament, but if you do not have time to make a visit, you can watch the proceedings of the Court, either live streamed, or archived on the Court's website.

Courts with criminal jurisdiction

The classification of offences

Next, the trial of criminal cases in England. Crimes are divided into *indictable, summary* and offences *triable either way*. Indictable offences are the most serious sorts of crimes, triable by judge and jury in the Crown Court. Summary offences are tried by magistrates in a magistrates' court. Many crimes, though capable of being tried on indictment, can be tried in magistrates' courts if certain conditions are satisfied; these are the intermediate category of offences "triable either way", so called because they might be tried in either the Crown Court or the magistrates' court.

Crown Court

Created by the Courts Act 1971, the Crown Court is now the main criminal court. Theoretically a single court, it is (like the High Court and Court of Appeal) in fact manifold, sitting in nearly 80 centres throughout the country.

A criminal trial in the Crown Court is generally by jury, the exception being where the court is hearing an appeal from magistrates by way of rehearing, in which case the judge will be assisted by two lay

---

[28] For an interesting note on the (surprisingly recent) origins of the present sitting arrangements of the Appellate Committee, see (1968) 118 N.L.J. 1160.

magistrates. The court is normally presided over by a *circuit judge* or *recorder*, who controls the trial and directs the jury; but it may also be constituted with a High Court judge.[29] Notwithstanding their name, circuit judges do not travel a circuit; they are located in one of the six[30] *circuits* into which the country is divided. High Court judges are generally presumed to be more able or more experienced than circuit judges; and the theory is that they therefore try the more serious and difficult cases. But the time of the High Court judge is precious, so having tried any case requiring that level of expertise, the more senior judge will leave lesser cases to be tried by a circuit judge. The old name "recorder" is preserved for part-time judges who are given the same jurisdiction as circuit judges; they continue other occupations such as practice at the Bar or as solicitors, whereas circuit judges are full-time.

The Crown Court sitting in the City of London (off Ludgate Hill) is still known officially as the Central Criminal Court and colloquially (never in court) as the Old Bailey (or, more frequently, the Bailey). Two of its judges (of senior circuit judge rank) are called the Recorder and the Common Serjeant of London. Some of the centres in which the Crown Court sits are served only by circuit judges, but some are also visited from time to time by High Court judges.

Court of Appeal (Criminal Division)

Appeal from the Crown Court in criminal cases lies (with leave) to the *Court of Appeal (Criminal Division)*. This was created in 1966, superseding the Court of Criminal Appeal, which in turn had superseded the Court for Crown Cases Reserved in 1907. The Court of Appeal (Criminal Division) sits in practice in several separate courts. One is often presided over by the Lord Chief Justice, others by a Lord Justice of Appeal, the remaining members of the court being either two High Court judges or one such judge and a circuit judge. Where the appeal is against sentence only (and not conviction), it is not uncommon for only two judges to sit. This court and the Divisional Court normally sit in London, but they very occasionally sit in regional centres. So far

[29] A judge of the Court of Appeal may sit as a High Court judge.
[30] A seventh (European) circuit was created in May 2001, but this is of its nature rather different from the other six, since it does not represent a geographical region of England and Wales as the others do.

as the conviction is concerned, the appeal may be on law or fact, but only the defendant can appeal—not the Crown.[31] On sentence, the Attorney-General can appeal against those considered to be unduly lenient.[32] Where an appeal against conviction is successful, the court will quash[33] the conviction either completely, or substituting a conviction of some other offence of which the jury could have convicted.

From the Court of Appeal a further appeal lies in important cases (with leave)[34] to the Supreme Court. At this stage the appeal is open even to the prosecutor.

In summary cases, the defendant may appeal to the Crown Court, which rehears the whole case; there is no jury, but at least two magistrates sit with the judge or recorder. Or a case may be stated on a point of law for the decision of a Divisional Court of the Queen's Bench Division[35]; and a further appeal may be taken from the Divisional Court (subject to restrictions) to the Supreme Court.

Reverting to the earlier discussion about the wisdom of a further appeal, it might be said that, in criminal cases at least, the principle of a second (qualified) right of appeal is justifiable, if only because the volume of work confronting the Criminal Division of the Court of Appeal is such that the court only rarely has sufficient time to consider and deliver a reserved judgment, and the pressures of time are such

[31] Apart from a purely moot appeal to settle a point of law. When a defendant is acquitted the Attorney-General may ask the Court of Appeal to rule on the law for future cases, the acquittal not being affected by the outcome of the reference: Criminal Justice Act 1972, s.36.

[32] As set out in the Criminal Justice Act 1988, ss.35 and 36. The form of the appeal is an Attorney-General's reference, in appearance similar to the procedure described in the last note. But the sting is that the sentence of the trial court may be quashed and a more severe one imposed on the individual whose case gives rise to the reference.

[33] Note the word and its spelling (neither squash nor quosh). It is cognate with modern French *casser*, as in *Cour de Cassation*. Note also that lawyers speak of *decisions* of lower courts being "reversed", while *convictions* and *sentences* are quashed. The verdict of a jury is "set aside".

[34] This form of appeal lies direct from a magistrates' court and also from a decision of the Crown Court on appeal from the magistrates' court.

[35] The formula is strange. The lower appeal court must certify that a point of law of general public importance is involved; and then it must appear either to that court or to the House of Lords that the point ought to be considered by the House. The Court of Appeal frequently grants its certificate on the first point, and then refuses to grant leave on the second, in effect passing the question to the House itself. But if the matter is of general public importance (and granted that we have a second appeal court to consider it), why should not the appeal be allowed as of right?

that it may be doubted whether that court should be burdened with the role of being the final appeal court.

The scheme of criminal courts can be represented diagrammatically as follows:

Figure 2

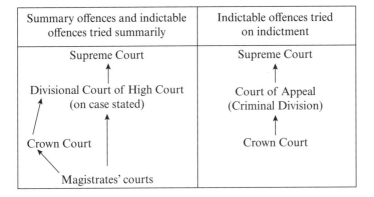

Summary offences and indictable offences tried summarily	Indictable offences tried on indictment
Supreme Court ↑ Divisional Court of High Court (on case stated) ↑ Crown Court ↖ ↑ Magistrates' courts	Supreme Court ↑ Court of Appeal (Criminal Division) ↑ Crown Court

The terminology of criminal procedure

The term *indictment* itself needs a bit more explanation. Originally an indictment (pronounced "inditement") was a *true bill* found by a *grand jury*, i.e. a jury for presenting suspected offenders. The trial upon it at assizes or quarter sessions was by a *petty jury*. Nowadays the grand jury is abolished, but we still retain the word "indictment" for the document commencing criminal proceedings that are to be tried by jury. The present-day indictment may be defined as a document put before the Crown Court by anyone, and signed by the clerk of the court. It may charge different offences in separate *counts*.

Prepositions have come to be used rather sloppily in criminal matters. In good usage, one is charged, tried, acquitted, convicted, or sentenced *on* (or *upon*) an indictment or count or charge. One is indicted *on* a charge of theft (or some other offence) or on two counts of theft. One is indicted or tried *for* theft, and the indictment/count/

information/charge is *for* theft.[36] (An information is a document making a criminal charge before magistrates.) We also speak of a count or charge *of* theft. One is charged (verb) *with* theft. One pleads guilty (or not guilty) *to* a count or charge or indictment of theft, or *to* theft. One is acquitted or convicted (or found guilty) *of* theft.

Formerly there would have been a preliminary investigation (known as *committal proceedings*) of a charge before magistrates; only if the magistrates concluded that there was sufficient evidence to put the accused on trial by jury would they have committed the defendant for trial. But the value of such proceedings has long been doubted and, increasingly, the committal has become an exercise conducted on paper rather than in person. In an increasing number of situations, provision is made for the case to be transferred directly to the Crown Court without preliminary consideration of the evidence by the magistrates.

Other courts

European Court of Justice

For so long as the UK remains a member of the European Union post Brexit, the Supreme Court is no longer the highest court of the United Kingdom, because the European Court of Justice (sitting in Luxembourg) adjudicates upon European Union law, and its decisions can be binding on British courts by reason of the European Communities Act 1972.[37] The impact of Community law grows continually; it is to be seen in company law, trademarks and other "intellectual property", the law of monopolies, employment law, social security, customs, and many other areas. An English court can ask the European Court for a ruling on any doubtful question of Community law.[38]

---

[36] Some writers misguidedly say "indicted with theft", "indicted with counts of theft and robbery", "convicted of three counts", and so on. The horrible expression "summonsed for an offence" (turning the noun "summons" into a verb) has now become accepted usage, but "summoned" remains not only allowable but preferable.

[37] After considerable judicial prevarication, this was eventually settled by the decision of the House of Lords in *Factortame Ltd v Secretary of State for Transport* [1990] 2 A.C. 85.

[38] See further below, Ch.3.

European Court of Human Rights

Any person who claims to be aggrieved by a violation of the provisions of the European Convention on Human Rights, and who is not satisfied with the determinations of the domestic courts, can still complain to the European Court of Human Rights at Strasbourg. If the decision is in favour of the applicant, the Government is under an obligation in international law to take steps to amend our law or practice accordingly. The Human Rights Act 1998 (which incorporated the Convention into United Kingdom law and which is discussed in Chapter 3) should reduce considerably the number of occasions upon which resort to this court should be necessary, since the British court should have taken the European jurisprudence into account in the course of arriving at its own decision.

Judicial Committee of the Privy Council

The Judicial Committee of the Privy Council is the final court of appeal from what remains of the old colonial Empire (with remnants also of its appellate jurisdiction from the self-governing members of the Commonwealth). Its composition is much the same as that of the Supreme Court when exercising appellate jurisdiction, though certain Commonwealth judges (and members of the Court of Appeal, since they are Privy Councillors) may sit in addition. Until the establishment of the Supreme Court, it had jurisdiction to deal with devolution issues arising from the Northern Irish, Scottish and Welsh devolution arrangements but these have been transferred to the new Court. It used to meet in a room in Downing Street, but now there is a separate room set aside for the purpose in the same building as is occupied by the Supreme Court on Parliament Square. In either case, since justice in Britain is normally administered in public, you can (having navigated the security arrangements at the entrance) walk boldly in and listen to its proceedings.[39]

---

[39] Proceedings of the Supreme Court are now also available by live video stream at the Court's website.

ELEMENTARY LEGAL TERMINOLOGY

I am about to consider some elementary matters of English legal terminology, because it is important that the student should become familiar
with legal language at an early stage. A preliminary word of explanation. Many lawyers think that the language of the law is opaque and
difficult for the layperson to understand. Efforts have been made to
alter this by changing the terminology, particularly in the course of
the April 1999 reform[40] of the system of civil procedure. This has the
drawback for those coming new to the law that they need to be familiar
with both the new language and the old, since they will find that much
of the law that they study will be couched in the language of yesteryear.
The beginner may be pleased to know that the language of the criminal
law has not been subjected to the same sorts of changes.

Civil terminology

Turning to civil proceedings, the terminology generally is that a
claimant[41] (known as a *plaintiff* prior to April 1999) *sues* (i.e. brings
an action against) a *defendant*. The proceedings if successful (with the
defendant being found *liable*) result in *judgment for the claimant*, and
the judgment may order the defendant to pay the claimant *damages*
(money), to transfer property, to do or not do something (an *injunction*) or to fulfil obligations under a contract (*specific performance*).
In proceedings against the government or certain public authorities,
known as *applications for judicial review*, whether by means of a *mandatory, prohibiting* or *quashing* order,[42] or otherwise, the parties are
also called *claimant*[43] and *defendant* respectively. In matrimonial cases
in the Family Division the parties are called *petitioner* and *respondent*, the relief sought concerns *dissolution* of the marriage and the
proceedings result in a *decree* of divorce.

---

[40] A new system of civil procedure was introduced on 26 April 1999, giving effect to
Lord Woolf's proposals to be found in the report *Access to Justice* (1996).

[41] Formerly referred to as the "plaintiff". "Complainant" in family proceedings courts
(as magistrates' courts are referred to in dealing with family matters).

[42] Until October 2000 known as orders of *mandamus, prohibition or certiorari*
respectively.

[43] Formerly known as an *applicant*, and in the case of an application for another of the
ancient writs, habeas corpus, is still so known.

Criminal terminology

In English criminal proceedings the terminology is as follows. You have a *prosecutor* prosecuting a *defendant*,[44] the result of the prosecution if successful is a *conviction*, and the defendant who is found guilty may be *punished* by one of a variety of punishments or *sentences* ranging from a fine to life imprisonment, including release on *probation* and other alternatives to custody, or may be discharged without punishment.

The terminology of the one type of proceedings should never be transferred to the other. "Criminal action", for example, is a misnomer; so is "civil offence" (the proper expression is "civil wrong"). One does not speak of a claimant prosecuting or of the criminal defendant being sued. The common announcement "Trespassers will be prosecuted" has been called a "wooden lie", for trespass has traditionally been a civil wrong, not (generally) a crime.[45]

CLASSIFICATION OF CIVIL WRONGS

The more important types of civil wrong may be briefly mentioned. One is the *breach of contract*. This is easy to understand, and all that the student needs to know at the outset of his or her studies is that a contract need not be in a formal document or indeed in any document at all. You make a contract every time you buy a newspaper or a bus ticket.

Another civil wrong is a *tort*. This word conveys little meaning to many outside the legal profession, and its exact definition is a matter of great difficulty even for the lawyer. However, the general idea of it will become clear enough if one says that torts include such wrongs as negligence and nuisance, defamation of character, assault, battery, false imprisonment, trespass to land and interference with goods. It

---

[44] Formerly called "prisoner" in felonies and "defendant" in misdemeanours; felonies were abolished as a separate class in 1967. The term "prisoner" is invidious for one who has not yet been convicted, and is now rarely used. Instead of "the defendant" the expression "the accused" is very commonly encountered.

[45] There are some statutory offences of trespass, such as trespass on a railway line, and *aggravated trespass* where the trespasser has the purpose of disrupting the lawful activities of others (Criminal Justice and Public Order Act 1994, ss.68 and 69).

is a civil wrong independent of contract: that is to say, it gives rise to
an action for damages irrespective of any agreement not to do the act
complained of. Etymologically the word comes to us from the French
tort, signifying any wrong, and itself derived from the Latin *tortus*,
meaning "twisted" or "wrung", the latter term having the same origin
as "wrong".[46] Nowadays, however, a tort is not any wrong but only
a particular kind of wrong that the law recognises as such, of which
examples were given above.[47] The adjective from tort is "tortious":
thus one speaks of a tortious act.

A third civil wrong is a *breach of trust*. A "trust" is not a mere obligation of honour, as the word may seem to suggest, but an obligation
enforced by the courts. It occurs where a person, called technically a
settlor, transfers property (such as land or shares) to another, called
a *trustee*, on trust for yet another, called a *beneficiary*. Where the
trust is created by will the *settlor* is also called a *testator* (the name
for anyone who makes a will); and an alternative name for the beneficiary is *cestui que trust*, an elliptical phrase meaning "the person
[for] whose [benefit the] trust [was created]". In this phrase *cestui* is
pronounced "settee" (with the accent on the first syllable),[48] *que* is
pronounced "kee", and *trust* as in English. Grammatically the plural
should be *cestuis que trust* (pronounced like the singular); but by an
understandable mistake it is sometimes written *cestuis que trustent*,
as if trust were a verb.[49] The beginner will perceive by this time that
several law-French words survive in our law from the time when
French was the language of the legal class. In the case of a charitable
trust there need be no definite beneficiary but the property is held
on trust for the public as a whole or for some section of it. Thus the
heritage organisation "National Trust" preserves beautiful places for
the public enjoyment, and there are many trusts for educational and
religious purposes.

---

[46] It is strange how the notion of wrong is wrapped up with that of twisting: the
opposite of wrong is right, which is the Latin *rectus*, straight.

[47] For a further discussion of the nature of tortious liability, see *Clerk and Lindsell on
Torts* (20th edn, 2010), Ch.1.

[48] The *Oxford English Dictionary* gives the pronunciation "sestwee", but this is not
common among lawyers. Sir Percy Winfield told Glanville Williams that F.W. Maitland's
pronunciation was the one preferred here, and that should be good enough authority for
anyone.

[49] See Sweet, "Cestui Que Use: Cestui Que Trust" (1942) 26 L.Q.R. 196.

The only other type of civil obligation (it is not thought of as a wrong) that the beginner need hear about is the *restitutionary* obligation. Suppose that I pay you £5, mistakenly thinking that I owe it to you: I can generally recover it back[50] in the law of restitution. You have not agreed to pay it back and so are not liable to me in contract; but in justice you ought to pay it back. There are various other heads of unjust enrichment besides the particular example just given,[51] such as the obligation to repay money paid on a consideration that has totally failed.

PUBLIC AND PRIVATE LAW[52]

Another distinction that needs to be considered is that between public and private law. Until relatively recently, it was widely believed (or at any rate conventionally asserted) that the United Kingdom knew no system of public law regulating the citizen and the state separate from ordinary private law that governs the relationships between citizen and citizen. Professor A.V. Dicey in his *Introduction to the Study of the Constitution* (1885) had insisted that it was a feature of the rule of law itself that it was undesirable to seek to control the state other than through the ordinary law of the land, as developed for private citizens. The development in the course of the twentieth century of the doctrines of judicial review of administrative action made this perspective quite unrealistic by the beginning of the twenty-first century. "Judicial review" refers to a body of doctrine and legal rules whereby the courts have ensured that government ministers and other public authorities act within the bounds of the legal powers conferred upon them by Parliament, and that they do so in accordance with appropriate procedural practices. The result is that there is undoubtedly a distinctive body of public law, frequently studied as such in universities, sometimes called by a name such as "constitutional and administrative law".

---

[50] "Recover back", is not, in legal usage, pleonastic; i.e. the word "back" is not superfluous. You "recover" damages, a sum of money that you never had before. You "recover back" a certain sum of money corresponding to one that you did have at some time in the past.
[51] See G. Virgo, *Principles of the Law of Restitution* (3rd edn, 2015), Ch.1.
[52] Lord Woolf, "Public Law—Private Law: Why the Divide?" [1996] P.L. 220 and "Droit Publique—English Style" [1995] P.L. 57.

The distinction between public and private law is not hard and fast, but the dividing line can sometimes be a crucial one. The public law remedies of judicial review are not available against a purely private body,[53] for example, and different procedures are adopted for proceeding against a public as opposed to a private concern. For a time, this dichotomy threatened to return the legal system to the abysmal wrangling portrayed in Charles Dickens' novel *Bleak House*.[54] The position was rectified by the House of Lords after a decade of confusion[55]; now the applicant will lose only if the chosen course (chosen let it be said by the legal advisers, since the client will rarely have expertise in these matters) is manifestly wrong. Similarly, the notion that the validity of a byelaw could be challenged only by bringing separate proceedings for judicial review and not by way of (for example) a defence in a criminal trial was eradicated by the House of Lords before it could gain too entrenched a foothold.[56]

COMMON LAW AND EQUITY

Two technical terms of great importance that are likely to puzzle the novice are "common law" and "equity".

The law of England may be said to be composed of three great elements: legislation, common law and equity. To this must be added the directly applicable law emanating from Europe, which will be explained in Chapter 3.

Legislation

The most important kind of legislation is the Act of Parliament (otherwise called a *statute*), through which the government of the

---

[53] See *R. v Panel on Takeovers and Mergers, ex p. Datafin* [1987] Q.B. 815.

[54] *O'Reilly v Mackman* [1983] 2 A.C. 237 sent the law in the wrong direction, by requiring that the applicant must select the correct of the two available procedural paths, at the risk of losing the case (possibly at the end of lengthy legal proceedings) should the wrong one prove to have been adopted.

[55] *Roy v Kensington and Chelsea and Westminster Family Practitioner Committee* [1992] 1 A.C. 617.

[56] *Boddington v British Transport Police* [1999] 2 A.C. 143, where the defendant to a criminal charge of smoking on a train was permitted on appeal to challenge the British Rail byelaws imposing the prohibition. Initially, it was held, the proper procedure was for the smoker to bring a civil action.

day carries into effect its principal policies. This is known as *primary legislation*. What is called *delegated legislation*, like the many government orders generally known as *statutory instruments*, has come to be of great importance as well. About 3,800 such instruments are promulgated every year, adding detail to the legislative framework created by the Act of Parliament.

A non-lawyer (or layman) is not likely to experience difficulty in understanding what constitutes primary legislation. Not so, however, with common law and equity, which need fuller discussion.

Common law

The phrase "the common law" seems a little bewildering at first, because it is always used to point a contrast and its precise meaning depends upon the contrast that is being pointed. An analogy may perhaps make this clearer. Take the word "layman". In the preceding paragraph the word was used to mean *a person who is not a lawyer*. But when we speak of ecclesiastics and laymen, we mean by "laymen" non-ecclesiastics. When we speak of doctors and laymen, we mean by "laymen" non-doctors. "Laymen", in short, are people who do not belong to the particular profession of which we are speaking. It is somewhat similar with *the common law*. Originally this meant *the law that was not local law*, that is, the law that was *common to the whole of England*. This use may occasionally be encountered, but it is no longer the usual meaning.

More usually the phrase will signify *the law that is not the result of legislation*, that is, the law created by the *decisions of the judges*. The decisions of the courts which create and lay down the law are called *precedents*.

A third use to which the phrase may be put is to denote *the law that is not equity* (i.e. that developed by the old Court of Chancery). In this sense it may even include statutory modifications of the common law, though in the previous sense it does not.[57]

Finally, it may mean *the law that is not foreign law*; in other words, the law of England, or of other countries (such as America) that have

---

[57] Lawyers sometimes use the term to mean only the civil law part of the common law in sense three, to the exclusion of the criminal law.

adopted English law as a starting-point. In this sense it is contrasted with (say) Roman, Islamic or French law, and here it includes the whole of English law; even local customs, legislation and equity.

It will thus be seen that the precise shade of meaning in which this chameleon phrase is used depends upon the particular context, and upon the contrast that is being made. In contrasting common law with legislation and equity I am making particular reference to the distinctions set out in the second and third senses of the phrase.

Equity

The term *equity* is an illustration of the proposition that some words have a legal meaning very unlike their ordinary one. In ordinary language "equity" means natural justice; but the beginner must get that idea out of mind when dealing with the system that lawyers call equity. Originally, indeed, this system was inspired by ideas of natural justice, and that is why it acquired its name; but nowadays equity is no more (and no less) natural justice than the common law, and it is in fact nothing other than a particular branch of the law of England.

Equity, therefore, is law. Students should not allow themselves to be confused by the lawyer's habit of contrasting "law" and "equity", for in this context "law" is simply an abbreviation for the common law. Equity is law in the sense that it is part of the law of England; it is *not* law *only in the sense that it is not part of the common law*.

The process whereby equity came into being may be briefly described as follows. In the Middle Ages, the courts of common law failed to give redress in certain types of case where redress was needed. Disappointed litigants petitioned the King, who was the "fountain of justice", for extraordinary relief and the King, through the Chancellor, eventually set up a special court, the Court of Chancery, to deal with these petitions. Eventually the rules applied by the Court of Chancery hardened into law and became a regular part of the law of the land. The most important branch of equity is the law of *trusts*, but equitable remedies such as *specific performance* and *injunction* are also much used.

The student will learn how, in case of *conflict or variance* between the rules of common law and the rules of equity, equity came to prevail. This was by means of what was called a *common injunction*. Suppose that A brought an action against B in one of the non-Chancery courts and, in the view of the Court of Chancery, the action was inequitable. B's proper course was to apply to the Court of Chancery for an order, called a common injunction, directed to A and ordering him not to continue the action. If A defied the injunction the Court of Chancery would put him in prison for contempt of court. Equity thus worked "behind the scenes" of the common law action; the common law principles were theoretically left intact, but by means of this intricate mechanism they were superseded by equitable rules in all cases of conflict or variance.[58] The result justified the sarcasm of the critic who said that in England one court was set up to do injustice and another to stop it.

This system went on until 1875, when as a result of the Judicature Act 1873 the old courts of common law and the Court of Chancery were abolished. In their place was established a single Supreme Court of Judicature, each branch of which had full power to administer both law and equity. Also, common injunctions were abolished and instead it was enacted that, in cases of conflict or variance between the rules of equity and the rules of common law, the rules of equity should prevail.

Common law as made by the judges

When the term "common law" is used in contrast to statutory law, it may mean either of two things, though they are closely related. It generally means the body of law produced by decided cases without the aid of legislation.[59] Occasionally, however, the invocation of the common law refers not to previously existing law but to the power of the judges to create new law under the guise of interpreting it. Nearly all the common law in the first sense is created by the common law in the second sense, that is to say by the judges in the exercise of their discretion. How much discretion a judge has to expand the law is a complex question. Part of the answer to it will appear in Chapter 6.

---

[58] The common law courts, after a famous struggle in the seventeenth century, lay passive under this process; they did not help but they did not hinder. In some cases they even took account positively of equitable doctrines. See *Master v Miller* (1791) 4 T.R. at 341, 100 E.R. at 1053; *Legh v Legh* (1799) 1 Bos. & Pul. 447, 126 E.R. 1002; *Bosanquet v Wray* (1815) 6 Taunt. 597, 128 E.R. 1166; *International Factors Ltd v Rodriguez* [1979] Q.B. 351.

[59] The expression is used in this sense in Professor J. Beatson's "Has the Common Law a Future?" (1997) 56 C.L.J. 291.

FURTHER READING

A number of works give a description and evaluation of our courts and their workings: Catherine Elliott and Francis Quinn, *English Legal System* (16th edn, 2015). Martin Partington's *Introduction to the English Legal System 2015–16* provides a panoramic perspective. The book is now published annually, and a new edition is pending at the time of writing.

If you have a taste for history, you will derive much pleasure and profit from J.H. Baker's *An Introduction to English Legal History* (4th edn, 2002). A shorter and less ambitious treatment, confined to the history of the courts, but very readable, is H.G. Hanbury and D.C.M. Yardley, *English Courts of Law* (5th edn, 1979). Professor S.F.C. Milsom's *Historical Foundations of the Common Law* (2nd edn, 1981) is the best treatment of the subject, but is perhaps too difficult for a beginner.

2 THE MECHANISM OF SCHOLARSHIP

> "I hold him not discreet that will *sectari rivulos*, when he may *petere fontes*."[1]
>
> —Coke, Preface to 4th part of Reports.

The person who wants to become a lawyer, and not merely to pass law exams (which is not at all the same thing), must learn to use legal materials. A complaint met with increasing frequency is that too many modern (twenty-first century) graduates are unable to conduct "research", by which is meant amongst other things that the student has not been taught (or at any rate has not learnt) how to handle legal materials. To acquire proficiency in this, students must get to know their way about the law library,[2] and must acquire the habit of first-hand work among what lawyers call the sources. It must be said, however, that much modern legal education overlooks this aspect of the process. So keen are most lecturers that the student should engage with the doctrines and principles inherent in the law that they simplify the process by making available large amounts of pre-digested material extracted from cases, statutes, regulations, official publications and other sources. Students are then left to pick up lawyerly skills such as finding the relevant materials for themselves as best they can. One of the purposes of this book is to remedy that deficiency.

The great campaigner among teachers of law for exposure to primary materials at first hand was Sir Frederick Pollock, affectionately known to his own generation as "F.P."; no apology is necessary for repeating his thoughts, since they are difficult to better (though the language in which they are couched may seem aggressively masculine to the modern reader):

[1] "Why chase after little streams when you can go straight to the source?"
[2] More detailed and extremely valuable guidance is contained in J. Knowles and P Thomas, *Effective Legal Research* (4th edn, 2016) and P. Clinch and J. Beaumont, *Legal Research: A Practitioner's Handbook* (2nd edn, 2013).

"We no longer make and transcribe notes and extracts, with infinite manual labour, in a huge 'commonplace book', as former generations were compelled to do by the dearth of printed works of reference. But, since the law is a living science, no facilities of publishing and printing can ever perfectly keep pace with it. A student who intends to be a lawyer cannot realise this too soon. There is no need for him to make voluminous notes (indeed there is a great deal of vain superstition about lecture notes)[3]; but those he does take and use ought to be made by him for himself, and always verified with the actual authorities at the first opportunity. Another man's notes may be better in themselves, but they will be worse for the learner. As for attempts to dispense with first-hand reading and digesting by printed summaries and other like devices, they are absolutely to be rejected. No man ever became a lawyer by putting his trust in such things; and if men can pass examinations by them so much the worse for the examinations."[4]

Some may think that put a trifle too exuberantly[5] but in essentials the advice is sound. The great disadvantage of confining oneself to textbooks and lecture notes is that it means taking all one's law at second hand. The law of England is contained in statutes and judicial decisions; what the text writer thinks is not, in itself, law. The author may have misinterpreted the authorities, whereas the reader who goes to the authorities directly goes to the fountainhead. Besides becoming familiar with the law reports and statute book, the lawyer-to-be should get to know the way about the library, together with its apparatus of catalogues and books of reference, even in days when so much legal material is to be found electronically. To quote Pollock again:

---

[3] To this I would add the modern hazards of mindless photocopying and the downloading of voluminous quantities of undigested electronic material.

[4] Pollock, *Oxford Lectures* (1890), pp.104–105.

[5] It is not entirely clear what Pollock meant by "printed summaries and other like devices", which are thus absolutely to be rejected. He could not have meant textbooks, because he himself wrote several. He did not mean case books, because after writing the above passage he went on to approve them. He was probably referring to books written for the purpose of assisting exam revision, and, so understood, any teacher would agree, since they inevitably oversimplify to the point of distortion.

"Facility in such things may seem a small matter, but much toil may be wasted and much precious time lost for want of it. To the working lawyer these things are the very tools of his trade. He depends on them for that whole region of potential knowledge which must bear a large proportion to the actual."[6]

But this is preaching; and I do not want to preach, but only to give practical advice to those who wish to hear it. Let us therefore pass at once to:

NAVIGATING THE LAW LIBRARY

The Law Library

Near the entrance to the library (or possibly scattered throughout), there will probably be computer terminals giving access to the catalogue of the contents of the library. In some libraries, this may also still be in the form of printed volumes or a card index, though these are increasingly rare. Each entry contains a number of figures or letters or a combination of the two. This is known as the *class mark*, and it should be accurately noted, since it enables the volume to be traced in the library. You should make a point of discovering the system adopted in your library, by wandering round the shelves. Some classifications use what may be called a *decimal* system, even though no decimal point appears. For example, volumes next to each other on the shelf may be marked AF 1, AF 2, AF 22 and AF 7. If you imagine a decimal point before these numbers you will see that they are not out of order. The system enables the library staff to insert new sub-groups without altering the main order.

One has to use common sense in consulting a catalogue. Suppose you want a book by an author called Bowen-Rowlands. You should first try "Bowen", but if it is not there try "Rowlands". Libraries vary in their treatment of these hyphenated names. Anonymous books are usually included in the author catalogues under their titles. Thus, *Every Man's Own Lawyer*, by A Barrister, will probably be in the author catalogue under "Every", though it may be under "Barrister"

---

[6] Pollock, *Oxford Lectures* (1890), p.106.

or "A Barrister" or "Anonymous". Periodicals may be in the author catalogue either under their titles or grouped under the general heading of "Periodicals".

Near the catalogues there will probably be works of reference, such as dictionaries and bibliographies. The law reports, statutes and periodicals will probably be found in special sections of the library. Usually, too, there will be special sections devoted to individual subjects such as criminal law, international law, jurisprudence and legal history. Most of the rest of the library will be taken up with law textbooks and periodicals. The texts may be arranged alphabetically under authors, or they may be classified by subject, and arranged alphabetically under authors within each subject. Where there is no subject arrangement, and it is desired to find books relating to a particular subject, it will usually be necessary to consult the subject catalogue in the library, or else one of the works mentioned later (Chapter 12). Periodicals may be arranged alphabetically, or by jurisdiction (Commonwealth being separated from American, for example) or by some other set of classification.

During the vacation it may be worthwhile to locate a library near your home. You should be able to obtain permission to use the library of a local university or college, or (if you are going to be a solicitor) of the local Law Society; and the larger public libraries have some law books.

LAW REPORTS

Now to look more closely at the law reports, statutes and periodicals. A good deal of the material about to be considered is now available in electronic form, either over the internet (Westlaw, LexisNexis Professional and Context Justis, to name but a few of the databases), or in CD-Rom form. When available, they greatly facilitate access to the material; learning how to use these tools is one further skill now required of the competent lawyer, and they will be further discussed in Chapter 12. Even with their advent, however, the lawyer needs to know the basic structure of the system of law reports.

The practice of law reporting is at a critical juncture. It was formerly possible to say that law reports are reports of the more important cases decided by the superior courts, and that not all cases are reported: only those of legal interest. The advent of the internet has changed that state of affairs, since so many law reports, many of them of trivial significance, are now readily accessible. In order to avoid over-citation of these unimportant decisions, the courts are anxious to limit the citation of authorities to those which are "relevant and useful".[7]

The criteria according to which decisions are selected for reporting by the semi-official reports[8] published by the Incorporated Council of Law Reporting are known as the "Lindley principles" which were first set out in 1863, based on a paper prepared by Nathaniel Lindley (later Master of the Rolls and Law Lord). He said that care should be taken to exclude (i) cases which pass without discussion or consideration, and which are valueless as precedents; and (ii) cases which are substantially repetitions of what is reported already, but to include (i) cases which introduce, or appear to introduce, a new principle or a new rule; (ii) cases which materially modify an existing principle or rule; (iii) cases which settle, or materially tend to settle, a question upon which the law is doubtful; and (iv) cases which for any reason are peculiarly instructive.

Whilst the Incorporated Council no doubt still adheres to these principles,[9] other reporters do not, particularly those whose coverage is specialist, relating to (for example) housing law, media law, the environment or road traffic. Experts in these relatively limited fields may well appreciate the significance of a decision that has escaped the more general reporter. The result is that there are many more reported cases than hitherto. The availability of material on the internet undoubtedly increases enormously the problem of over-citation of authorities by legal practitioners.

---

[7] In consequence of which a *Practice Direction (Citation of Authorities)* [2001] 1 W.L.R. 1001; 2 All E.R. 510 was issued governing the citation of authorities which requires counsel (amongst other things) to " . . . state . . . the proposition of law that the authority demonstrates", and the courts themselves to make an express statement to the effect that the case "purports to establish a new principle or to extend the present law". *Practice Direction (Citation of Authorities)* [2012] 1 W.L.R. 780. For a judicial reminder, see the remarks of the Chief Justice, Lord Judge C.J. in *Erskine* [2010] EWCA Crim 1425, [2010] Crim. L.R. 48, who also drew attention to the relevant provisions of the Consolidated Criminal Practice Directions. See now CPD 2015, XII, General Application D.

[8] See R.J.C. Munday, "The 'Official' Law Reports" (2001) 165 J.P.N. 162 for discussion as to the status of these reports.

[9] Although the series of reports published by the Incorporated Council has also expanded to include "The Public and Third Sector Law Reports" and the "Business Law Reports", which are available online only.

The reports may be divided very roughly into the old and the new. The old run from the time of Henry VIII[10] to 1865, and the new since that date.

Pre-1865 reports were produced chiefly by private reporters under their own names (and are known as the "nominate reports"). Altogether there were some hundreds of different series, though many of them ran only for a short time. Most, but not all, were reprinted in a series known as the *English Reports* (abbreviated E.R.).[11] You are not likely to have to consult them a great deal in the course of your studies, but you should know about them; they are discussed further below (see p.36).

In 1865 there commenced the semi-official "Law Reports" (with capital letters) published by the Incorporated Council of Law Reporting. At present[12] they are published in four series. There is one for each Division of the High Court. They are:

- *Queen's Bench Division* (cited e.g. as [2016] 2 Q.B. 600, meaning the second volume for the year 2016 at p.600);

- *Chancery Division* (cited e.g. as [2016] 1 Ch. 600);

- *Family Division* (cited e.g. as [2016] Fam. 600).

These series contain judgments at first instance in the three Divisions, and they also contain the judgments on appeal to the Court of Appeal. If a further appeal is taken from the Court of Appeal to the Supreme Court, that decision will be reported in a separate series called the *Appeal Cases* (cited e.g. as [2016] A.C. 600).[13] The *Appeal Cases* volumes also contain cases decided in the Judicial Committee of the Privy Council.

[10] Before Henry VIII's time there were the Year Books, but it is highly unlikely that you will ever need to consult them.

[11] These Reports are discussed more fully below (p.36). If your library does not possess the English Reports (which are now available online through Justis and Westlaw), the case you want may possibly be included in the selection called the Revised Reports.

[12] The historical development of these reports may be found in earlier editions of this work.

[13] Sometimes the Appeal Cases contain a report of the decision in the Court of Appeal as well as the House of Lords or now, it may be supposed the Supreme Court. Another trick—the loose parts of the Chancery Reports and the Family cases are issued bound together, but subsequently appear bound as separate volumes.

Neutral citation

If you consult any recent volume of the reports, you will notice that the judgments have paragraph numberings which continue sequentially throughout the judgment.[14] This practice was introduced (on 11 January 2001) to facilitate the publication of judgments on the internet and their subsequent consultation by electronic database users. In addition, a form of neutral citation was introduced for both divisions of the Court of Appeal and the practice was subsequently extended to the High Court; these judgments are numbered in the following way:

Court of Appeal

Court of Appeal (Civil Division)	[2016] EWCA[15] Civ 1, 2, 3
Court of Appeal (Criminal Division)	[2016] EWCA Crim 1, 2, 3

High Court

Queen's Bench Division	[2016] EWHC *number* (QB)
Chancery Division	[2016] EWHC *number* (Ch)
Family Division	[2016] EWHC *number* (Fam)
Administrative Court	[2016] EWHC *number* (Admin)
Admiralty Court	[2016] EWHC *number* (Admlty)
Technology and Construction Court	[2016] EWHC *number* (TCC)
Patents Court	[2016] EWHC *number* (Pat)

---

[14] Judges were required to do this by the *Practice Direction (Judgments: Form and Citation)* [2001] 1 W.L.R. 194. See now *Practice Direction (Citation of Authorities)* [2012] 1 W.L.R. 780 For comment as to the difficulties that this causes in law reporting, see the remarks by the editor of the Justice of the Peace Reports, Dr. R.J.C. Munday, (2001) 165 J.P.N. 342.

[15] The first two letters referring to England and Wales; Scotland and Northern Ireland have adopted similar arrangements. The system was also adopted by the House of Lords (shortly before it was abolished) and Privy Council, which are cited as [2010] UKHL 1, 2, 3 and UKPC respectively, and now UKSC for the Supreme Court.

The number mentioned at the end of each citation is a unique number assigned by the official shorthand writers to each approved judgment, and there are no page numbers in the judgments themselves. *Williams v Davies*, the tenth numbered judgment of the year in the Civil Division of the Court of Appeal should now be cited thus: *Williams v Davies* [2016] EWCA Civ 10 at [59] (or whatever paragraph is being cited).[16]

In the High Court, the citation would be, for example, [2016] EWHC 123 (Fam); or [2016] EWHC 124 (QB); or [2016] EWHC 125 (Ch).

The structure of a law report

Take down any volume of the published law reports and look at the beginning of a case. At the top are what are called the *catchwords*, indicating briefly what the case is about. They enable the reader to make sure at a glance that the case is relevant to the point of current concern. Then comes the *headnote*, which is again not part of the report but simply a summary written by the reporter. Occasionally inaccurate, the headnote is nevertheless useful as a guide to the content of the judgments. Sometimes the first judgment is delivered by the senior member of the court when *dissenting*; if the student reads it without having consulted the headnote, the reader will for quite a time labour under a misapprehension as to what was decided. Obviously it is better to read the judgments of the majority first, though dissenting judgments may be valuable because they may find favour in a higher court if the point is carried further, or because the dissenter may express a particular point upon which he is not dissenting in a particularly illuminating way. It should also be noted that there is a trend in the Court of Appeal to deliver "the judgment of the court" and speak with a single voice. The House of Lords was also tending to adopt the same approach shortly before its abolition, but it is too early to say what its successor, the Supreme Court, will do.

Generally the headnote states the short facts of the case. If they appear to be adequately summarised, it is quite permissible in ordinary cases to skip the facts as stated in detail by the judge, and go

---

[16] *Practice Direction (Citation of Authorities)* [2012] 1 W.L.R. 780. The extension of the system was initially effected by *Practice Direction (Judgments: Neutral Citations)* [2002] 1 W.L.R. 346.

forthwith to the part of the judgment that deals with the law. Except as above it is unwise to rely on the headnote. At the very least, one of the (majority) judgments should be read, in whole or in part. It is also very improving to read the argument for the side that lost, or a dissenting judgment if there is one, in order to appreciate that there were two sides to the question, as there usually are respectable arguments on both sides in cases that get into the law reports.

The Incorporated Council of Law Reporting also publishes a weekly series known as the *Weekly Law Reports* (W.L.R.), which in 1953 replaced the earlier *Weekly Notes* (W.N.). The W.L.R. are bound in three volumes, the first containing cases that are not afterwards included in the Law Reports, and the second and third comprising those cases that are expected to be published in and superseded by the version in the Law Reports. As from 2000, Volume 1 is bound in two separate parts, such is the quantity of material that is now regarded as reportable. Very occasionally, a case reported in Volume 2 or 3 is not eventually reported in the Official Reports.

The commercially published and specialist law reports

In addition to the official Law Reports various privately owned series are also published. These usually reproduce the decisions of the courts *verbatim*. A major advantage for the user of the library of having these collateral reports is that if the reader wants a volume of the Law Reports and finds that it is being used by another reader, it is very often more convenient to turn up the case in one of the collateral series than to wait for the Law Reports version. For citation in court the Law Reports (when available) are required, because the judgments they print have been revised by the judges.[17] The Law Reports have the further advantage that counsels' arguments are summarised. But neither of these points are usually very relevant to the student in a hurry, and you should develop at an early stage the ability to find the case that you want to consult, irrespective of wherever it is reported.

---

[17] The endorsement accorded to this particular series of reports in the *Practice Direction (Law Reports: Citation)* [1991] 1 W.L.R. 1 was reiterated subsequently in *Practice Direction (Citation of Authorities)* [2012] 1 W.L.R. 780 and *Practice Direction (Citation of Authorities)* [2012] 1 W.L.R. 780.

The most important is probably the *All England Law Reports* (All E.R.). (Both the *All England Reports* and the *Weekly Law Reports* offer considerable discounts to students, newly-called barristers and newly-admitted solicitors.) The *Times Law Reports* (T.L.R.) ceased at the end of 1952. In 1991, the series restarted, and bound volumes of cases reported in the daily newspaper, *The Times*, appear annually. These reports must be approached with some caution, since they are edited versions of the actual judgments, and their brevity is such that sometimes, they do not convey the full import of the decision. The All E.R. Reprint includes selected cases from the *Law Times Reports* and other earlier reports.

The student of criminal law should seek out in the library two series of reports of particular interest: *Cox's Criminal Cases* (Cox), and the *Criminal Appeal Reports* (C.A.R. or Cr.App.R.). These are supplemented by the *Criminal Appeal Reports (Sentencing)* (Cr. App.R. (S)), though these reports are of greater interest to the practitioner than to the student. Then there are the *Justice of the Peace Reports* (J.P.). Before Volume 96, these are usually bound at the end of the *Justice of the Peace* newspaper (abbreviated J.P.N.: note the independent pagination after Volume 67); from Volume 96 onwards they are separate. Distinguish, therefore, between (say) 96 J.P. 261, which is a reference to a reported case (the small volume), and 96 J.P.N. 261, which is a reference to the journal (the big volume).

Brief reports of cases are also given in the *Criminal Law Review* (Crim.L.R.). These reports are accompanied in each case by learned commentary. Employment lawyers will need to consult the *Industrial Cases Reports*, and the *Industrial Relations Law Reports*. Note also the existence (proliferation perhaps) of the specialist series of reports that have been published in recent years—the *Road Traffic Reports*, the *Housing Law Reports, Entertainment and Media Law Reports*, and so forth. The student is unlikely to need to have much recourse to these, since the really important decisions should eventually be reported in the mainstream series.

The English Reports

If you are looking in to the history of a legal point, you may need to become familiar with the English Reports. The pre-1865 reports are, for the most part, to be found reprinted in the volumes of the *English Reports*. A chart supplied with the *English Reports* indicates the volume in which a particular volume of the old reports is to be found reprinted—the chart will either be found hanging in the library (as a wall-chart), or in a slim volume at the end of the series of *English Reports*. For instance, if your reference is to 1 B. & Ad. 289 (which means Volume 1 of the *Reports of Barnewall and Adolphus*, at page 289); the chart will tell you that the corresponding volume of the *English Reports* reprint is Volume 109. As you take down the volume from the shelf, notice the names in gilt letters at the bottom of the spine. These will tell you the order in which the old reports are reprinted in the particular volume. Volume 109 bears the legend "Barnewall & Cresswell 9–10; Barnewall & Adolphus 1–2". This indicates that 1 B. & Ad. will probably be found just beyond the middle of the book. Open the book, and you will find your page reference in heavy type at the top centre of the open pages (top outside corner in the first 20 volumes). If something goes wrong and your case eludes you, try the index at the end of the volume. Failing that, Volumes 177–178 contain a complete index of all cases in the reprint.

The chart just referred to is not quite complete, because it indexes each of the old reports under one title only, whereas in fact many of the old reports were known under various titles or under various abbreviations of the title. If you are having difficulty in locating one of the reports, consult the full chart published by Professional Books. If this is not available, use the chart in Donald Raistrick, *Index of Legal Abbreviations and Citations* (4th edn, 2013) supplemented if necessary by the chart in 7 C.L.J. 261.

These old reports were of uneven quality, at least in the period before 1757, and need to be handled with some care. Of the worst of them many stories are told. In *Slater v May* (1704)[18] a case was cited from 4 Modern, then a comparatively recent volume of reports. Upon search of the roll (that is, the official record of the case) it was found that the report in 4 Modern had omitted a material fact. Upon this Holt C.J. burst out: "See the inconveniences of these scambling reports, they will make us to appear to posterity for a parcel of blockheads". When another of the early reporters, Barnardiston, was cited before Lord

[18] 2 Ld.Raym. 1071; 92 E.R. 210.

Lyndhurst, the latter exclaimed: "Barnardiston, Mr. Preston! I fear that is a book of no great authority; I recollect, in my younger days, it was said of Barnardiston, that he was accustomed to slumber over his notebook, and wags in the rear took the opportunity of scribbling nonsense in it."[19] Reporters even of the nineteenth century did not always escape judicial condemnation. The one who got most kicks of all was Espinasse, who reported Nisi Prius cases between 1793 and 1807. Pollock C.B. said of him that he heard only half of what went on in court and reported *the other half*.[20] And Maule J., when a case in Espinasse was referred to, said with some emphasis that he did not care for Espinasse "or any other ass".[21] Denman C.J.'s response when a case from Espinasse was cited was:

"I am tempted to remark, for the benefit of the profession, that Espinasse's Reports, in days nearer their own time, when their want of accuracy was better known than it is now, were never quoted without doubt and hesitation; and a special reason was often given as an apology for citing that particular case. Now they are often cited as if counsel thought them of equal authority with Lord Coke's Reports."[22]

---

[19] J.W. Wallace, *The Reporters* (4th edn, 1882), p.424.

[20] Anon., *A Lawyer's Notebook*, p.43; (1938) 54 L.Q.R. 368.

[21] Biron, *Without Prejudice* (1936), p.88.

[22] *Small v Nairne* (1849) 13 Q.B. at 844; 116 E.R. at 1486. Some further comments may be added from A.J. Ashton's *As I Went on my Way* (1924), pp.27–28: "More decorous, though not more learned, judges than Maule always insisted that the fifth Espinasse must not be cited, and would hardly admit even the earlier volumes. Lowndes, who reported on the northern Circuit, would barely be tolerated. It is in his rare and amusing volume that the head note is to be found, 'Carlisle. Possession of trousers in Scotland evidence of larceny in England.' It was not desirable to quote the Modern Reports if you could find Lord Mansfield in any other report. Carrington and Payne depended a good deal on the number of the volume. The later it was, the less it was attended to. It would seem that Carrington, like Espinasse, went down the hill, and I have myself heard a judge refuse to hear Carrington and Kirwan cited. These reports follow Carrington and Payne in date; and the judge said he didn't believe the reporter could at that date be trusted. This was a bold commercial judge, now dead. Of Price's Reports in the Exchequer it used to be said that you could find in them anything you wanted, if you looked long enough. He was the Beavan of the common law reporters. I once looked a long time and thought I found something in Price which seemed authority worth citing in a case in which Sir Horace Davey led me. At two or three consultations running, I brought this case forward after the second leader had finished, and Sir Horace always let me read the passage to him and murmured, 'Yes that seems some authority.' I should point out to my American friends that Sir Horace did not mean what they mean by these words. But I never got him to take the book into his hands until he was arguing in court. He suddenly swerved round

I relate these tales only to put the researcher on guard when dealing with some of the old reports, not to discountenance their use altogether. It sometimes happens that even poor maligned Espinasse is the only reporter to give us an important case. *Wilkinson v Coverdale*,[23] which the student may perhaps come across in tort or in contract, is an example—and, as Denman C.J. indicated, he and others of like stamp are not altogether unusable, though usable only with caution. Also, this sort of condemnation does not apply by any means to all the old reports, many of which are of outstanding quality.

The student wishing to know more about these old reporters may read Pollock's chapter in the *First Book of Jurisprudence* (6th edn, 1929), pp.292 *et seq.*, or Veeder's article in (1901) 15 *Harvard Law Review* 1, 109, partly reprinted in *2 Select Essays in Anglo-American Legal History* 123, or C.G. Moran's *The Heralds of the Law* (1948). Detailed monographs are J.W. Wallace, *The Reporters* (4th edn, 1882) and Sir J.C. Fox, *Handbook of English Law Reports* (1913).

How to find a reference

In your student days you will probably be given clear references to all the cases you need to read, either in a textbook or by your lecturer. However, you may sometimes know the name of a case but not its reference. Or you may have a reference to the case but find that the report is not on the shelf, so you want a reference to the same case in another series of reports. If you have access to and know how to use an electronic database, you will probably be able to find that quite simply.

If the case is since 1865, start your hunt with the *Law Reports Index*, which, for cases up to 1949, was called the *Law Reports Digest*. This gives the references to the case at all its stages through the courts;

---

and said, 'Give me that case of yours,' and began turning the pages with a listless and indifferent hand—for he was very tired—and glancing at them in a lack-lustre way, said, 'Then there is a case, my Lord, in the fourth Price'—looking at the number on the back of the volume—'which decides a number of interesting matters, including, I see'—pausing at a particular page, 'the ownership of a pond in Hertfordshire, and there is somewhere', turning a few more pages, 'something that seems to bear on this matter. But, however,' ceasing to turn any more pages from sheer inanition, 'I don't think I'll cite it', handing the book back to me with a smile." (The author is mistaken as to Lowndes—the report of the case referred to is in 1 Lewin 113; 168 E.R. 980—and it was a horse, not a pair of trousers.)

[23] (1793) 1 Esp. 75; 170 E.R. 284.

you will probably be looking for the reference to the last appeal, so start by looking at the references at the end of the list. The *Index* is particularly useful because it gives references not only to the Law Reports and *Weekly Law Reports*, but to the *All England Reports, Criminal Appeal Reports*, and a good many other series. (Distinguish between the Table of Cases *Reported* and the Table of Cases *Judicially Considered*.) The large red index volumes cover a span of years, the latest being the *Index* for 1991–2000. Cases thereafter are listed in separate indexes for each year and then in additional cumulative parts of the current year. For more recent cases still, look at the cumulative index in the *Weekly Law Reports*, starting with the current number (which will tell you when the previous cumulative index was included). Cases that are too recent even for the *Weekly Law Reports*, being published only in some place like *The Times* newspaper or the *Criminal Law Review*, will be noted in the monthly publication called *Current Law*.[24] The annual volumes of *Current Law* in your library may be called *Scottish Current Law*; this is the same as the English law version except that it includes Scottish cases in addition.

Other methods can be used if for any reason this one fails. The *All England Reports Consolidated Tables and Index* is useful, but it gives only the *All England Reports*. The *Current Law Case Citators 1947–1977* and *1977–1997* cover all cases for the periods specified, and later cases will be found in the annual volumes and the monthly parts of *Current Law* for the current year. For the current year start with the latest monthly number, which contains a cumulative list to date.

Current Law is helpful, but it does not always give all the reports of the case. Failing all else, use *The Digest* (formerly called the *English and Empire Digest*), which in any event you will need for the older cases. The procedure is simple: consult the table of cases at the front of the annual Cumulative Supplement. This gives a reference to the volume, subject and *case number*. Take down the appropriate (green band)[25] volume from the shelf and look up the case again in the

---

[24] If your need to have the full transcript of a case is particularly urgent and you are not fortunate enough to have access to a subscription to an electronic source (such as Westlaw, LexisNexis, Smith Bernal) you should be able to find what you want on *www. bailii.org*.

[25] The previous edition (the 2nd edn) was marked with blue bands, but this edition has been entirely replaced and superseded.

table of cases at the front of the volume. This will give you the case number within the subject. The official instructions on how to use *The Digest* are to be found at the front of the Cumulative Supplement.

If you are looking up a case in the index to a volume of the *Criminal Appeal Reports*, it is worth knowing that the "Table of Cases" is a snare and delusion; the true table of cases (for the Court of Appeal) is headed "Appellants and Applicants", while the table of cases decided in other courts is idiotically separated from this and concealed overleaf.

Other indexes for the older cases are the index to the *English Reports* (cases before 1865) and the index to the *All England Law Reports Reprint* (cases before 1935).

Abbreviations: law reports and periodicals

At the beginning of your studies, you will frequently come across abbreviations that you do not recognise. There are a number of places where you can look to dispel the puzzlement. Raistrick's *Index of Legal Abbreviations and Citations* (4th edn, 2013) will decipher the multitudinous abbreviated names of law reports, as will the (online) *Cardiff Index to Legal Abbreviations*. If both of these works are unavailable, you might look in one of the following: Volume 1 of *Halsbury's Laws of England* (updating if necessary with the *Current Service*); *Current Law* (both the *Monthly Digest* and the *Yearbook*); the *Index to Legal Periodicals*; "Where to Look for your Law", reprinted in Osborn's *Concise Law Dictionary* (12th edn, 2013); *Mozley and Whiteley's Law Dictionary* (12th edn, 2001); Volume 1(1) of the *Digest* (formerly *English and Empire Digest*); Stroud's *Judicial Dictionary of Words and Phrases* (8th edn, 2013) Vol.1; *Civil Procedure*, Vol.1 (known as "the White Book", which is published annually). If you think that the reference that has you stumped might be from an overseas jurisdiction, there is a four-volume looseleaf series, *World Dictionary of Legal Abbreviations*.

Scottish decisions

The current Scottish law reports known as *Sessions Cases* are divided into three series all bound into one volume for the year: Supreme

Court (and to 2009 House of Lords) and Privy Council, Court of Justiciary and Court of Session. They are cited as, for example, 2016 S.C. (H.L. or P.C.) 100, 2016 S.C. (J.) 100 and 2016 S.C. 100; note that there are three different page runs in each volume. Where cases are reported in this series, they should be cited in preference to reports of the same case in the *Scots Law Times* (1893–), which in turn is preferred to the *Scottish Criminal Case Reports* (SCCR) or the *Scottish Civil Law Reports* (SCLR), both of which commenced publication in the 1980s.

Two references given

Sometimes the reader's reference will contain two page references, thus "[1892] 1 Q.B. 273, 291" or "[1892] 1 Q.B. 273 at 291". Here the first page mentioned contains the beginning of the case and the second page the particular passage (often a pithy statement of principle) to which the real reference is being made. Beginners have been known to spend many hours reading a case to which they were referred only for a single passage in the middle of it. Generally speaking, if a case is quoted for these limited purposes, there is no need to read the whole of the case. As the neutral citation mode became more widespread, we have become accustomed to the use of square brackets [**] to denote the particular paragraphs of the judgment to which attention is being called.

Square and round brackets

The use of square and round brackets surrounding the dates of cases requires a word of explanation. Compare the following two references:

Stanley v Powell (1890) 60 L.J.Q.B. 52.
Stanley v Powell [1891] 1 Q.B. 86.

Why are the dates different, and why the two different sorts of brackets? To answer the second question first, the custom is to use square brackets where the date is an indispensable part of the reference to the case, round brackets where it is not. The report first cited has a volume number (60), so the date is not necessary to trace the case; the second report has no volume number, so the date is in square brackets. As to the first question, the judgment in the case was pronounced in 1890, which is therefore its true date. But some time elapses before the cases are reported in the Law Reports, and this case did not get in until 1891, which is the date in the second reference. Where cases are reported in the Law Reports it is customary to adopt the date of publication of the Law Reports version as the date of the case. The reader should be spared this pedantry; it is explained here simply to save bewilderment.

Electronic searching

It should be mentioned at this stage that many of the reports that you will require are available electronically, either as a CD-Rom version or, more recently, over the internet. Some of these services are available free. The decisions of the Supreme Court, for example, are placed on the internet within hours of their being delivered in the Court itself, and can be viewed at the Supreme Court website *http://www.supremecourt.gov.uk/*. You will note when you consult a judgment of this sort that it lacks the editorial additions such as a headnote and catch words. Other services such as Westlaw, Smith Bernal and LexisNexis are subscription only services, and require a password. The librarians in your university library will no doubt give guidance as to which is available, and further guidance in their use.

Titles of cases

It is helpful to know certain rules for the naming of cases. Trials on indictment are in the name of the Queen (as representing the State); thus a criminal case is generally called *Reg. v* [whomever it is]—*Reg.* being short for *Regina* (pronounced "Rejyna"), and *v* being short for *versus*. When there is a king on the throne, *Rex* is used instead of *Reg. Regina* and *Rex* both conveniently abbreviate to *R.*, which saves having to remember which is which. Thus *Reg. v Sikes* or *Rex v Sikes* may both be written *R. v Sikes*. Some textbooks on criminal law even print simply *Sikes*. This last is a convenient usage for the student of criminal law.

In some types of criminal case the title of the case will not contain

Rex or *Reg.* before the *v*, but will contain the name of a private person. This happens when the case is tried summarily before magistrates (i.e. justices of the peace); here the name of the actual prosecutor appears instead of the nominal prosecutor, the Queen. Again, when an appeal was taken to the House of Lords, the practice was formerly that the name of an official or private prosecutor, usually the Director of Public Prosecutions or a government department, was substituted for the word *Reg.* Having two names for a case was a nuisance, particularly because when the appeal was by the defendant the names of the parties became reversed. Eventually it was decided that as from 1979 criminal cases in the House of Lords should be reported under the same title as in the court below.

Civil cases will usually be cited by the names of the parties, thus: *Rylands v Fletcher*. If the Queen (as representing the Crown) is a party she is, in civil cases, usually called "The Queen", and similarly with the King, thus: *British Coal Corporation v The King;* but *R.* may also be used.

In order to make life more difficult for us all, the name of the appellant is put first when an appeal is taken to the Divisional Court, even though the appellant was the defendant in the court below; this means that the names may become reversed. Nattrass, an inspector of weights and measures, instituted a summary prosecution entitled *Nattrass v Tesco Supermarkets Ltd*; on appeal by the defendant company to the Divisional Court this became *Tesco Supermarkets Ltd v Nattrass*,[26] and the title stayed the same on further appeal by Tesco to the House of Lords. We need an edict saying that the titles of cases shall never change.

Pronouncing case names

There are peculiar conventions in pronouncing the names of cases. For example, the criminal case *R. v Sikes* is sometimes (though loosely) referred to thus (pronounced as written), or more correctly as *Regina* (or *Rex*) v *Sikes* (again pronounced as written). In court, however, the proper method of referring to the case is "*The Queen* [*or The King*] *against Sikes*". In civil cases the "*v*" coupling the

[26] [1972] 1 A.C. 153.

names of the parties is pronounced "and", both in court and out of it. Thus *Smith v Hughes* should always be pronounced (but never written) "Smith and Hughes", and similarly *British Coal Corporation v The King* (which was a civil proceeding against the Crown) is pronounced with an "and". Lawyers thus write one thing and say another.

In some cases, as where a will is being interpreted, the name of the case is "*In re*" (in the matter of) somebody or something; for instance, *In re Smith*. It is permissible to shorten this to *Re Smith* (*Re* is pronounced "*ree*"). Certain applications to the courts are labelled "*Ex parte*": *Ex p. Smith* means "on the application of Smith" and you will find this spelled out in full in the most recent cases in the Administrative Court, in particular. In probate cases (that is, cases concerned with the proof of a will) the title *In Bonis* (i.e. in the goods of) *Smith* may be met with in the older reports, and in Admiralty cases the name of a ship (for example, *The Satanita*). Other possible ways of naming cases need not be considered here, but, in order to prevent the student from being puzzled, one oddity may be mentioned. The Supreme Court is often the final court of appeal for Scotland (and Northern Ireland) as well as England, and a Scots case that goes to the Supreme Court may become important in English as well as Scots law. Two such important cases are *McAlister (or Donoghue) v Stevenson*[27] and *Hay (or Bourhill) v Young*.[28] The oddity is the alternative name in brackets, for which the explanation is as follows. In Scotland a married woman, though she takes her husband's name, does not cease for legal purposes to go also by her maiden name. When she figures in litigation, her maiden name is placed first, and her married name is given as an alternative afterwards. Nevertheless, the correct mode of citation, when brevity is desired or when the proceedings are in the Supreme Court,[29] is by the married name.[30] The two cases above are, for brevity, cited as *Donoghue v Stevenson* and *Bourhill v Young*, but not as *McAlister v Stevenson* or *Hay v Young*.

---

[27] [1932] A.C. 562.
[28] [1943] A.C. 92.
[29] See 1972 S.L.T. (News) 149.
[30] See Lord Macmillan, "The Citation of Scottish Cases" (1933) 49 L.Q. R. 1; P.H.W. (1945) 61 L.Q.R. 109.

STATUTES

The state of the statute book

In theory there is nothing to prevent the whole of the law being
set out clearly and logically in statutory form. In practice, human
sloth, indifference and perversity have combined to keep the statute
book in a state far short of perfection until comparatively recently.
Even now, statutes are not arranged on a rational plan, since the
same subject may be divided between many statutes and the same
statute may contain bits of several subjects. Statutes are amended
from time to time, so that often the law has to be gathered by
reading two or more statutes side by side. Relief is at hand when
a statute and its amending Acts are gathered together into a single
"consolidating" Act. This makes for convenience, but even a consolidation statute is unlikely to state the whole law on the subject
with which it deals—partly because there may well be other statutes
bearing on the subject, and partly because a consolidation statute
does not attempt to set out the common law. The process of setting out both statute law and common law as a single, well-ordered
body of law is called codification, but for reasons that it would not
be flattering to examine in detail English lawyers were historically
hostile (or, at best, indifferent) to this. So far as the criminal law
is concerned, the position is much changed, with the senior judges
such as Lord Bingham taking the lead in calling publicly for the
enactment of a criminal code.[31]

The situation has been greatly improved by the advent of the electronic databases. Prior to this development, legislation in the United
Kingdom was in a deplorable state because of its inaccessibility.
Lawyers frequently need to know what the law was as originally
enacted, what amendments have been made affecting the law in force
as at the current date, and what the state of the law was in between

---

[31] When he was Chief Justice, in "A Criminal Code: Must We Wait Forever?" [1998]
Crim. L.R. 694, the text of which formed part of his speech at a dinner for H.M. judges at
the Mansion House, London, on 22 July 1998. Lord Bingham returned to the question in
his book, *The Business of Judging* (2000) saying that he regarded "the absence of a comprehensive criminal code as a critical deficit in the democratic provision of our country"
(p.387). See also Dame Mary Arden (now Arden L.J.) in [1999] Crim.L.R. 439.

times. Having to make all these inquiries through a process of manual search was extremely time consuming, and the commercial providers Westlaw and LexisNexis began to make the texts of Public General statutes in force (as amended) available in electronic form. This has subsequently been supplemented by the UK Statute Law Database, which is the official revised edition of the primary legislation of the United Kingdom. In addition, Justis and Lawtel provide historical versions (in the case of Justis and Westlaw including all statutes as far back as Magna Carta, and including Statutory Instruments) with cross references to amendments and repeals.

As a student you will probably have all the extracts from statutes you need in your textbook or in a book of cases, statutes and materials specially produced for your subject. If you do need to look up a statute (and you will certainly have to as a practitioner) read the advice on this in Chapter 12. In particular, there may be relevant statutes passed since your book was written. These can be traced by consulting the appropriate title in *Halsbury's Statutes*. If you are lucky enough to have access to online services, you can short-circuit the process by going directly to the up-to-date version.

The citation of statutes

Statutes are cited in three ways: by the short title, which includes the calendar year (for example, the Fatal Accidents Act 1846,[32] by the regnal year or years and the chapter (for example, 9 & 10 Vict. c.93[33]), or by a compromise of the two (for example, the Fatal Accidents Act 1846 (c.93)). Two regnal years are given (as in the foregoing example) when the session of Parliament in which the statute was passed did not fall within a single regnal year. The chapter indicates the number of the statute—formerly, the number in the session. It will be seen that "9 & 10 Vict. c.93" means an Act that received the royal assent in the session of Parliament beginning in the ninth year of Queen Victoria's reign and concluding in her tenth year, being the ninety-third statute

---

[32] Acts passed before 1963 had a comma in the short title before the date; in 1969 a change was made and the comma was omitted. It seems sensible now to drop the comma in pre-1963 Acts as well.

[33] Pronounced as "the statute nine and ten Victoria, chapter 93", or "the ninth and tenth Victoria, chapter 93".

passed in that session. Since 1962, chapter numbers have referred to the calendar year.[34]

The parts of a statute

The main body of a statute is divided into sections, and sections may be divided into subsections. Where there are subsections they comprise the whole of the section—there is no opening part of the section before the subsections. A subdivision following an opening part is called a paragraph. Subsections have a number in brackets while paragraphs have a letter in brackets.[35] Here is an example drawn from the Theft Act 1968, s.21, which establishes the crime of blackmail. Section 21 opens immediately with subsection (1).

> "(1) A person is guilty of blackmail if, with a view to gain for himself or another or with intent to cause loss to another, he makes any unwarranted demand with menaces; and for this purpose a demand with menaces is unwarranted unless the person making it does so in the belief—
>
>   (a) that he has reasonable grounds for making the demand; and
>   (b) that the use of the menaces is a proper means of reinforcing the demand."

You would cite this as subsection (1), and the paragraphs as paragraph (a) and paragraph (b) respectively, abbreviated in writing as section 1(1)(a). In informal speech lawyers sometimes refer to "section 1 subsection (1)" as "section 1 sub (1)", and so on. When the Bill is still before Parliament, the segments are called "clauses" and "sub-clauses".

STATUTORY INSTRUMENTS

As a student you are not likely to have much to do with statutory instruments ("SI"—formerly known as statutory rules and orders, "S.R. & O."), though exceptionally you may have to consult them.[36]

---

[34] They do things better in some other parts of the Commonwealth such as the provinces of Canada, which issue current statutes without a number. At the end of the year the statutes are arranged alphabetically and only then given a number.

[35] These were italicised until 1987, when the practice was stopped.

[36] As will be explained in Ch.12.

When referring to statutory instruments, instead of calling the particular provisions of the instrument "section" and "subsection" as with statutes, one calls them "articles" or "rules" and "paragraphs" respectively.

Many statutory instruments are made in order to give effect to European Union law. A substantial part of such law takes effect directly on individuals and affects private rights and duties; this is true for some provisions of the Treaty of Rome and for nearly all *regulations* made under the Treaty. These regulations are expressly incorporated into our law by statutory instruments made under the European Communities Act 1972, but if for any reason a statutory instrument fails to express part of a regulation that is directly applicable to citizens of the Community, the regulation itself retains full effect. The organs of the Community also produce *decisions* and *directives*, which do not generally affect our law directly, but again may be incorporated into statutory instruments.[37]

PERIODICALS

Legal periodicals contain articles of great importance for the lawyer and student. Special mention must be made of the publications that contain material of general interest, ranging across all subject areas. These are: the *Law Quarterly Review* (L.Q.R.), which as its title suggests is published four times a year; the *Modern Law Review* (M.L.R.), published every two months, and the *Cambridge Law Journal* (C.L.J.), published three times a year: students may obtain these journals at greatly reduced rates, though they should be available in any law library of even modest ambition. *Current Legal Problems* (C.L.P.) is another useful publication, which appears annually. Newer entrants on the scene are *Legal Studies* (L.S.) (successor to the *Journal of the Society of Public Teachers of Law*) and the *Oxford Journal of Legal Studies* (O.J.L.S.). Specialist publications include *Public Law* (P.L.), the *Criminal Law Review* (Crim.L.R.), the *Conveyancer* (Conv.), the *Journal of Planning and Environment Law* (J.P.L.), *Family Law* (Fam. Law), the *Industrial Law Journal* (I.L.J.), and the *International and Comparative Law Quarterly* (I.C.L.Q.). Space does not allow

---

[37] See Ch.3.

mention of the numerous periodicals published overseas, or of various others published in the United Kingdom, but you will find them catalogued in the *Index to Legal Periodicals* which is itself produced at regular intervals throughout the year. Further information on the use of a law library will be given in Chapter 12.

The legal weeklies, the *New Law Journal* (N.L.J.), *Solicitors' Journal* (S.J.) and *Justice of the Peace* (J.P.N.) are published chiefly for practitioners; the best coverage is in the *New Law Journal*, which is available to students at a reduced rate (though even then it is not exactly cheap).

Newspapers such as *The Times, Daily Telegraph, The Guardian* and *The Independent*, each of which has a weekly legal section, are available to students at reduced prices. Particulars can be obtained from a newsagent.

I should not need to remind my readers not to deface library books, however urgently the text may seem to need correction, emphasis or comment. It is distracting to have to endure the handiwork of other readers.

3 THE EUROPEAN DIMENSION

> "But when we come to matters with a European element, the Treaty is like an incoming tide. It flows into the estuaries and up the rivers. It cannot be held back. Parliament has decreed that the Treaty is henceforward to be part of our law. It is equal in force to any statute."
>
> —Lord Denning M.R. in *H.P. Bulmer Ltd v Bollinger SA* [1974] Ch. 401 at 418.

As discussed in the preface to this work, the United Kingdom's relationship with Europe is in two senses in a state of flux. On 23 June 2016, a referendum is to be held on its continued membership of the European Union. Depending upon the outcome of that ballot, it is possible that a long process of constitutional change will take place over a number of years as the consequences of a decision to leave manifest themselves. Second, the Conservative Party, which was elected in to power by the general election of 7 May 2015 gave a clear manifesto commitment to repeal "Labour's Human Rights Act" and replace it, ending "the ability of the European Court of Human Rights to force the UK to change the law".[1] Both changes, if they were to come about, would have a significant impact upon the present constitutional arrangements.

For the moment, it is at least arguable that the "European dimension" does not deserve or require a chapter of its own, since the law emanating from Brussels, Luxembourg and Strasbourg now forms (directly and indirectly) part of United Kingdom law, and Europe's legal sources and materials have correspondingly become part of the common lawyer's heritage. Even if either or both of the two developments described in

---

[1] A Commission was established in March 2011, to investigate the possibility of a Bill of Rights that "incorporates and builds on Britain's obligations under the European Convention on Human Rights" In December 2012 the Report showed that the members of the Commission were divided on many of the issues involved. In October 2014, The Conservative Party Published "Protecting Human Rights in the UK" setting out the arguments in more detail.

the previous paragraph were to transpire, it is important that common lawyers should know about the sources and the institutions from which European law emanates. Since they are so different from the common lawyer's stock in trade, they continue to be given separate treatment here. The sheer volume of material (much of it available in electronic form) is daunting, and the need for accurate translations of the official sources into several different languages means that official publication of the sources can be extremely slow; so the student in hot pursuit of a topical point may be forced to be particularly resourceful.

THE EUROPEAN UNION

The principal purpose of the European Union (known originally as the European Economic Community (EEC) and colloquially as the Common Market) was to create a free market for the provision of goods and services within the Union's borders. No attempt is made here to explain the substantive European law governing such matters as the free movement of persons and goods, competition law and employment matters.[2] This chapter will consider the institutions and legal sources that have been (or are being) embraced by the common law as a result of recent integrational developments. In certain circumstances European law can take priority even over the law enacted by Parliament.[3] The great Victorian constitutional lawyer Dicey would have regarded that as constitutional heresy, but the European Court of Justice had made it plain, by enunciating a principle of the primacy of European law well before the entry of the United Kingdom into the Community, that the Member States have, within certain ever wider fields, limited their own sovereign rights, creating a body of laws which binds both their nationals and themselves.[4]

---

[2] See D. Wyatt and A. Dashwood, *European Union Law* (6th edn, 2011); S. Weatherill, *Cases and Materials on EU Law* (12th edn, 2016); P. Craig and G. de Búrca, *EU Law: Text, Cases and Materials* (6th edn, 2015); D. Chalmers *et al, European Union Law: Text and Materials* (3rd edn, 2015).

[3] As the House of Lords eventually acknowledged at the end of the litigation reported as *R. v Secretary of State for Transport, ex p. Factortame Ltd* [1990] 2 A.C. 85; *R. v Secretary of State for Transport, ex p. Factortame Ltd (No.2)* [1991] 1 A.C. 603, ECJ and HL.

[4] Case C26/62 *Van Gend den Loos v Nederlandse Administratie der Belastingen* [1963] E.C.R. 1 and Case 6/64 *Costa v E.N.E.L.* [1964] E.C.R. 585.

The United Kingdom became part of the European Communities on January 1, 1973 with the coming in to force of the European Communities Act 1972. The "communities" in question were the European Coal and Steel Community (ECSC) (1951), the European Atomic Energy Community (Euratom) (1958) and the European Economic Community which was established under the Treaty of Rome (1958). The initials of this body (EEC) became the name by which the whole was commonly denoted until shortened to the *European Community* (EC) by the Maastricht Treaty (which came into force in November 1993). There has been a progressive harmonisation of laws across all Member States, accomplished through treaties such as the Single European Act 1986 (confusingly so titled, since it really is what we would call a treaty), the Treaty on European Union (Maastricht) (1992) which changed the EEC into the EC, and the Treaty of Amsterdam (1997) which, apart from anything else, altered and renumbered the provisions of the earlier treaties.

The wider body brought into being through Maastricht is now referred to as the European Union (EU). The Treaty of Nice, signed on 26 February 2001 was intended to effect further changes, particularly in the enlargement of the Community, extending membership to a number of countries and although its ratification was a matter of some difficulty, it has eventually led to the admission of further member states. With the accession of Croatia as from 1 July 2013, the number is now 28. An attempt to make provision for a new Constitutional Treaty for the enlarged Union was, however, stymied by the electorates of France and the Netherlands, both of which voted against in May 2005, leaving the precise status of the whole institution in a state of some uncertainty. Most recently, the Treaty of Lisbon which entered in to force on 1 December 2009 made a number of changes, including the creation of the office of President of the European Council, elected for a period of two and a half years and a High Representative of the Union for Foreign Affairs and Security Policy.

The principal institutions

There are six principal institutions of the Union, whose functions are as follows:

Council of Ministers

The *Council of Ministers* is more commonly called the *Council*. This body consists of political representatives of each of the Member States, and it is in a sense one of the two legislative bodies of the Community (though its deliberations are not held publicly). Each minister is authorised to commit the government of the Member State to which he or she belongs to a particular decision or policy. The identity of the representative at any particular meeting will depend upon the subject under discussion. If the matter at hand is transport, for example, the United Kingdom representative would be the Secretary of State for Transport. The Council operates according to a system of weighted voting. The Council of Ministers must then approve (or reject) the Commission's legislative initiatives before they can take effect. This body should not be confused with the European Council.

The European Council

The *European Council* consists of the Heads of State (in the United Kingdom, it is the Prime Minister who attends) who meet with increasing frequency—since 2002 at least four times a year in a summit meeting. Its role has changed somewhat as the size of the membership has increased. According to Article 4 of the Treaty on European Union, the primary task is to "provide the Union with the necessary impetus for its development and . . . define the general political guidelines thereof". This includes making decisions about the future institutional direction and shape of the Union itself. Further enlargement, for example, would be first considered by this body. It also takes the lead in setting the agenda for the development of Union policy, taking initiatives in such matters as the protection of fundamental rights within the Union itself and in the Member States and to regulate migration flows and to control the external borders of the Union.

Commission

The *Commission* is a body of 28 Commissioners appointed for renewable periods of five years, with one Commissioner from each Member State. Each Commissioner is responsible for one or more of the Departments (known as Directorates-General—more commonly DG), and specialised services. This body acts as the secretariat of the Union; more particularly, its functions include the instigation of legislative proposals for the approval (or otherwise) of the Council of Ministers. Secondly, it enforces the application of EC law, if necessary by taking steps before the European Court of Justice against a Member State that is believed to be in breach of a treaty obligation, or that has failed to implement Community legislation. Members of the Commission are expected to act in the general interest of the Community as a whole (having taken an oath of independence), and not to take instructions from their governments or any other body.

European Parliament

The *European Parliament* (formerly the Assembly) is not at all like the mother of Parliaments at Westminster and its offspring throughout the common law world. Initially its function was largely advisory, but its powers have greatly increased since its inception in 1957, and it now shares with the Council the power to legislate. Since 1979, its members have been elected by direct universal suffrage throughout the Union (rather than having been appointed, as hitherto), and the numbers of members representing each state vary according to population size.

A second function performed by the Parliament is the approval (or otherwise) of the budget. Here it can adopt amendments and propose modifications which it may ultimately insist upon being carried. It also exercises supervision over the Commission, approves the nomination of Commissioners and has the right to censure the Commission, and exercises political supervision over all the institutions.

European Court of Justice

The *(European) Court of Justice* (sitting in Luxembourg) functions in something the same way as a common law court, but interpreting the EC law. But there are differences as well as similarities. In particular, the role of the court is not an appellate one but an advisory one when it is engaged in giving "preliminary rulings". But the national Member State court making the reference is obliged to follow the advice that is given in making its own determination. The court consists of 28 judges, one from each Member State, who sit in chambers (of three, five and sometimes 13) as well as in plenary session, assisted by eight Advocates-General, whose duty it is to make reasoned submissions on cases brought before the court. The nearest equivalent in the United Kingdom would be the appointment of an *amicus curiae*, a person who is appointed from time to time to assist the court. Decisions of the European Court of Justice (which was founded in 1952) come in two parts[5]: (a) the Opinion of the Advocate-General, being an impartial review of the decisions, a review of the previous case law and the view (Opinion) of the Advocate-General as to the correct solution of the case; followed by (b) the (single) judgment of the court itself. Normally, there are at least three judges, and no dissent is permitted. To reduce some of the pressure on the court itself, there has also been (since 1989) a *General Court* now called the *Court of First Instance*, from which there is an appeal to the European Court of Justice. The court is concerned mainly with competition and anti-dumping. Until late in 2005, it was also concerned with cases related to staffing, i.e. disputes between the Community and its officials and servants, but that jurisdiction is now exercised by a Civil Service Tribunal, from which appeals go to the Court of First Instance.

The role of the court: the preliminary ruling procedure

The development of the Community legal order has largely been achieved through the co-operation between the Court of Justice and the national courts and tribunals through what is known as the *preliminary ruling* procedure. Under Article 234 (formerly 177) of the Treaty, the court has jurisdiction to give *preliminary rulings* concerning the interpretation of the Treaty, the validity and interpretation of acts of the institutions and certain other matters. In some situations, the law of the Community obliges the national courts to refer questions. In other situations, the matter is for the discretion of the national tribunal.[6] The rulings may be requested by national courts

---

[5] Before 1 January 1994, the Report also included a "Report for the Hearing" which was a statement made to the court by a reporting judge outlining the facts and giving a summary of the legal argument.

[6] The Court of Justice of the European Communities has given guidance as to when

which consider that a decision is "necessary" to enable them to give judgment, the national court then presenting a series of questions for the Court of Justice to answer. The nomenclature is really a bit misleading, since the preliminary procedure is in truth the principal mechanism through which the court offers guidance to national tribunals as to the meaning and effect of Community law. Questions referred must be limited to the interpretation or validity of a provision of Community law, since the court does not have jurisdiction to interpret national law or assess its validity. The questions posed may well be of Community-wide interest, and the Member States and Community institutions are entitled to submit observations as to the questions submitted. It is left to each Member State to give effect to and enforce the decisions of the court.

Court of Auditors

In spite of its title, this body does not actually have a judicial function. Instead, it conducts an independent examination of the accounts and the income and expenditure of the Community (and certain other bodies managing Community expenditure) and publishes an Annual Report at the end of each financial year, with a view to ensuring sound financial management. It is mentioned here principally for sake of completeness.

Other relevant institutions

Mention should also be made of the Economic and Social Committee and the Committee of the Regions, since they are consulted as part of the legislative process. The former was established in 1957, and consists of 350 members who belong to one of three groups: employers, workers and "various interests", the latter being representatives of farmers' organisations, small businesses, the crafts sector, consumer and environmental organisations, the family, women, disabled people and the scientific community and so forth. The role is principally a consultative one (through "structure co-operation") in the legislation-making

and in what form references are to be made, which is contained in Sch.B to the *Practice Direction (E.C.J. References: Procedure)* [1999] 1 W.L.R. 260.

process. The Committee of the Regions is more recent in origin, created by the Maastricht Treaty in 1992. This too has 350 members, but its remit is to make representations on any proposals that are likely to have an impact at local or regional level, in such areas as economic and social cohesion, trans-European infrastructure networks, health, education and culture, to which were added by the Treaty of Amsterdam in 1999 a further five areas, employment policy, social policy, the environment/vocational training, and transport.

Sources of law

You will have gathered from what you have read so far that the European Union is in origin a creature of *treaties* (Rome, Maastricht, Lisbon etc.) which established the constitutional framework of the Community. There are then several sources of law which set out in particular detail how the general purposes and objectives identified by the treaties are to be accomplished; this legislation consists of *regulations* and *directives*.

Regulations are automatically part of domestic law (directly applicable). Member States do not need to take any further steps to implement them. Regulations operate both as between the individual and the state (*vertical direct effect*) and as between citizen and citizen (*horizontal direct effect*). An example of such a measure is Regulation 1612/68 on free movement for workers within the Community [1968] O.J. Spec. Ed. (II) 475.

Directives are addressed to all Member States. They are not initially directly effective. Instead, they lay down an objective or policy that must be achieved within a specified time, and the individual states are entitled to achieve the objectives by whatever means they see fit. These measures therefore can become law only through national legislative action, either an Act of Parliament or a statutory instrument, whichever is (in the particular context) thought to be the more appropriate. However, the case law of the Community is now such that where a Member State has not adopted the implementing measures required by a directive within the prescribed periods and where the provisions of the directive appear to be "unconditional and sufficiently precise", they are directly applicable. A state is not permitted to rely, as against individuals, upon its own failure to perform the obligations which the directive entails. Furthermore, those provisions may be relied upon directly by the individual, where the national state has not implemented them within the required time.[7] But the directive is not enforceable against a private individual—it being said that the directives have *vertical* but not *horizontal* effect. That is, they can be used against governments, but not against private parties.[8]

An example of such a measure is the so-called "working time" Directive,[9] which regulates the permissible number of working hours in a week to 48 and makes provision for a certain minimum number of weeks' paid holiday.

Decisions[10] are not, as might be supposed, the judgments of the European Court of Justice. Instead, they are generally measures adopted by the Community, or one of its institutions, in the form of administrative action taken by the Commission officials. They are, in effect, legislative measures. An example is the Council Decision 98/256 of 16 March 1998 [1999] O.J. L195/42) as amended by the Commission Decision 98/692 of 25 November 1998 [1998] O.J. L328/28) concerning emergency measures to protect against BSE ("mad cow disease), relating to the export of cattle and produce to the Community and third countries.

Recommendations and opinions are not legally binding and are sometimes referred to as "soft law" as a result; they merely suggest a line of action or give a view on a particular question. They can be taken into account for the purposes of interpreting a measure.[11] They may sometimes, however, be a preliminary to legal action as when the Commission states an opinion (whether of its own initiative, or

---

[7] For an application of these principles in the UK context, see Case 152/84 *Marshall v Southampton and South West Hampshire AHA* [1986] E.C.R. 723.

[8] But see Cases C–6/90 and 9/90 *Francovich and Bonifaci v Italy* [1991] E.C.R. I–5357, in which it was held that an individual may be permitted to sue the state by way of an action for damages for failure to implement a directive. Where this action is available, it compensates for the lack of direct effect. See also Cases C178–179 & 188–190/94 *Dillenkofer v Federal Republic of Germany* [1996] E.C.R. I–4845.

[9] Council Directive 93/104 [1985] O.J. L307/18.

[10] As to the status of these decisions, see R. Greaves, "The Nature and Binding Effect of Decisions under Article 189 EC" (1996) 21 E.L. Rev. 3. For a more recent analysis of the use by the House of Lords of the preliminary ruling procedure, see A. Arnull, "The Law Lords and the European Union: swimming with the incoming Tide" [2010] E. L.Rev. 57.

[11] Case 322/88 *Grimaldi v Fonds des Maladies Professionelles* [1989] E.C.R. 4407.

at the behest of another Member State) upon the question whether a
Member State is in breach of an obligation, having given the state an
opportunity to submit observations. If the Member State should then
fail to comply with the opinion, the Commission may initiate proceedings before the court.

The law-making procedure

When the Commission puts forward proposals for legislation, draft
versions are initially put forward as *Commission documents*, which are
published in the *Official Journal* C series.[12] Proposals are considered
by the European Parliament and the Economic and Social Committee
or the Committee of the Regions which publish *reports* or *opinions*.
Once the various suggestions from these bodies have been considered,
the Council adopts the directive or regulation, which is then published in the *Official Journal* L series. The documents produced at the
various stages of the consultation process are available, and recently
they can be found online through EUR-Lex (see p.64).

Official publications

If the institutions and procedures of the European Community have
not baffled you entirely, the chances are that (at least at first) the many
publications will threaten to engulf you; abbreviations and acronyms
are very much the order of the day. As with United Kingdom publications, the same material is often made available by more than one
provider—commerce is at work here too, supplementing the official
sources.

Although much of the relevant material is available online,
it should be noted at the outset that the online sources EUR-Lex
and Europa both carry a disclaimer to the effect that it cannot be
guaranteed that a document available online exactly reproduces an
officially adopted text. Only European legislation published in the
paper editions of the *Official Journal of the European Communities* is
deemed authentic.

---

[12] They are also available as COM.docs on the Commission website (*http:europa.
eu.int/comm/index—en.htm*).

In short, it is necessary to have a command of where the paper versions are to be found.

Official Journal

The *Official Journal of the European Communities*, abbreviated as *Official Journal* or O.J., is published almost daily, and is found in several parts:

- the "L" series (Legislation) giving the text of the legislation;

- the "C" series (Communications and Information) which contains draft legislation, official announcements and information on EC activities;

- the "S" series, which publishes details of public contracts open to competitive tender;

- the Annex, which contains the full text of debates of the European Parliament.

Since the year 2000, neither the S series nor the Annex has been published in paper format, but they are available in CD-Rom format, and on the websites mentioned below (p.000).

How to cite legislative Acts

The reference to the legislative Act (whatever it may be) is composed from the following elements:

- the origins of the Act (usually the Commission, but it may be the Council);

- the form of the Act (regulation, directive, decision, etc.);

- an Act number;

- the year of enactment;

- the institutional treaty basis (EC, Euratom, etc.);

- the date on which the Act was passed.

Whereas regulation references are given with the number first and the year following, directives and decisions reverse the order. Examples include:

- Council Regulation (EEC) 3820/85 [1985] O.J. L370/1 on the harmonisation of certain social legislation relating to road transport, which regulates maximum driving hours and sets minimum rest periods for drivers of road haulage and passenger transport vehicles.

- Council Directive 93/104 [1985] O.J. L307/18 is the so-called "working time" Directive, which regulates the maximum number of permissible working hours and makes provision for a certain minimum number of weeks' paid holiday.

The O.J. reference given in each case is to the *Official Journal*, the series and the volume and page numbers.

Citation of court reports

There are two courts, the most important being the European Court of Justice. *Official Reports of Cases Before the Court*, but more generally referred to as the *European Court Reports* (E.C.R.), contain the decisions of the European Court of Justice and the Court of First Instance. The reports are split into two parts, which contain the judgments of each court respectively. The case citation is now composed as follows:

- case number;

- year;

- name of the parties;

- citation indicating where the case is to be found.

Where the judgment is one delivered by the European Court, it is cited in the following form:

- Case C–106/89 *Marleasing SA v La Comercial Internacionale de Alimentacion SA* [1990] E.C.R. I–4235.

In the case of a decision of the Court of First Instance, the citation will read:

- Case T–72/99 *Meyer v Commission of the European Communities* [2000] E.C.R. II–2521.

Some points to note about the citations: The *C* in "Case C" indicates that this is a decision of the Court of Justice itself ("Cours"), whereas the *T* denotes the Court of First Instance ("Tribunal"). The Roman numerals I and II are volume numbers—again the decisions are split as between the Court of Justice (I) and the Court of First Instance (II).

Once you know the number of the case in question, it is easy to find by looking at one of the databases referred to below, and using the "Numerical access to the case law" section of the database. For very recent cases, you should go to the website of the Court of Justice itself (*www.curia.europa.eu*).

The most widely used of the commercial paper based reports are the *Common Market Law Reports* and the *All England Reports European Cases*.

Other publications

Other sources of information about current developments in EU law include:

- *General Report on the Activities of the European Union*—annual survey;

- *Bulletin of the European Union*—which appears monthly; and

- *Directory of Community Legislation in Force*.

There are a number of specialist journals: the *Common Market Law Review; European Law Review; European Business Law Review; European Competition Law Review*.

Databases

EUROPA (*http://europa.eu*). The main internet site of the European Union, affording access to other official databases. It contains general details of the European Union, links to the home pages of its institutions (such as the Parliament, the Council, the Commission and the Court) and its policy.

EUR-Lex Started by the European Union in 1998 as a daily update service at *www.EUR-LEX.EUROPA.EU*, this site (in 2004) became the first gateway into EU law.

CELEX This is the official multilingual legal database of the European Union. It contains the full text of the treaties, and the *Official Journal* L series, and the *European Court Reports*. It is intended to add the C series progressively in the coming years. CELEX can be accessed through EUROPA and EUR-Lex (by subscription) and online from a number of commercial publishers such as Westlaw, Justis, CELEX and LexisNexis Library, where there accessibility and usability is enhanced by easy-to-use cross links.

EUROPEAN CONVENTION ON HUMAN RIGHTS[13] AND THE HUMAN RIGHTS ACT 1998

After many years of dithering and foot drag, Parliament eventually "incorporated" the European Convention of Human Rights and Freedoms through the enactment of the Human Rights Act 1998, which came into force on 2 October 2000. The United Kingdom had been a party to the European Convention on Human Rights since 1953, but until the enactment of the Human Rights Act 1998, the Government had made no provision for the Convention to be enforced by our courts. On 2 October 2000, the Act came into force, with the result that United Kingdom courts were required, at a stroke, to "take account of" the sizable and rapidly developing body of Strasbourg jurisprudence. They were also required to interpret legislation "so far as possible" in accordance with the terms of the Convention and, in the event that an interpretation that was inconsistent with the

---

[13] An excellent introductory work on this is Karen Reid's *A Practitioner's Guide to the European Convention on Human Rights* (5th edn, 2015).

terms of the Convention was unavoidable, to make a "declaration of incompatibility".[14] The development is likely to have a profound effect upon the way in which law approaches such fundamental rights as the right to life, freedom from arbitrary arrest, freedom of speech and freedom of assembly. You should note at once that, institutionally, this has nothing to do with the European Community or the European Union. It is a creature of the Council of Europe, based in Strasbourg, and is an entirely separate legal regime.

The European Convention on Human Rights was promulgated by the Council of Europe, a body established immediately after the end of the Second World War. Its principal objective was to prevent any repetition of the wholesale violations of human rights that had occurred during the war and in the period leading up to it. It was signed in Rome in 1950, ratified by the United Kingdom in 1951 and came into force in 1953. A great many states are now party to the Convention; 47 by the year 2016, with other nations having "guest" status. It was a part of the post-war movement for international co-operation giving rise to the creation of the Council of Europe in 1949, and was in part inspired by the United Nations Declaration of Human Rights (1948).

Technically the Convention is a treaty in international law, and as such was not a part of United Kingdom municipal law until made so by the United Kingdom Parliament. Treaties usually regulate relationships between nation states, and do not confer enforceable rights directly upon citizens of those states. Unusually, however, the Convention accords (with the consent of the Member State) a right of *individual* petition, and, since 1966, that right has been available to citizens of the United Kingdom. This has meant that a citizen, aggrieved by the remedy or lack of it afforded by the United Kingdom courts, may go to Strasbourg to complain. Technically, such an

---

[14] The Act has spawned a vast literature. See e.g. R. Clayton and H. Tomlinson, *The Law of Human Rights* (2nd edn, 2009); S. Grosz, J. Beatson *et al, Human Rights: Judicial Protection in the United Kingdom*, (2nd edn, 2008). Lord Lester Q.C. and D. Pannick, *Human Rights Law and Practice* (3rd edn, 2009) is another leading work. These are all excellent works, but they have inevitably become somewhat dated, in an area where the law is very fast moving. J. Simor and B. Emmerson have produced a looseleaf publication, *Human Rights and Civil Liberties*, a format that realistically anticipates the extent of potential development in this field of law. See also the *European Human Rights Law Review*, a periodical journal.

action is not an "appeal", since the European Court of Human Rights forms no part of the system of courts of which complaint was to be made. Furthermore, the road to Strasbourg has typically been long, correspondingly slow and expensive. The court has no jurisdiction unless the local remedies have been exhausted, which might entail a journey to the national Supreme Court first. In the event of an adverse finding, the particular law or governmental practice must be altered to bring it into line with the Convention. The Contempt of Court Act 1981 was an early example of this, following a ruling of the European Court[15] that the law of contempt as stated by the House of Lords[16] inadequately respected freedom of speech and was therefore at variance with Article 10 of the Convention.

European Court of Human Rights

The grievance machinery established in 1959 consisted of a Court of Human Rights and a Commission which exercised a filtering and conciliatory role. Both were abolished in November 1998, and a new single Court of Human Rights was created. The court now consists of a hierarchy of committees and chambers with a plenary court at the apex. Questions of admissibility, previously determined by the Commission, are now decided by the judges in committee. Notoriously the Court has had a dreadful backlog of cases, and it is not unknown for cases to be decided up to seven years after proceedings have been lodged.

Publications

European Court

Until 1995, decisions of the court were published in *Publications of the European Court of Human Rights, Series A: Judgments and Decisions.* Series B contained such matters as pleadings, oral arguments and other documents. Since 1996, there has been a series entitled *Reports of Judgments and Decisions.* Sweet and Maxwell publish the *European*

---

[15] *Sunday Times v United Kingdom* (1979) 2 E.H.R.R. 245.
[16] *Att.-Gen. v Times Newspapers Ltd* [1974] A.C. 273.

Human Rights Reports, which are commonly cited in the English courts, and these are available through Westlaw. A case such as *Handyside v United Kingdom* would be cited as Series A, No.24; (1976) 1 E.H.R.R. 737.

The court has its own website at *www.echr.coe.int*. This gives free access to the full text of the judgments, as well as to a list of cases pending and basic texts (the European Convention itself, together with the Rules of Court). There is a useful section of the site offering help on how to use the system to search for the document that you seek.

Commission

You will occasionally see references in the earlier law cases to the "Commission", which ceased to function in October 1998. It acted as a preliminary filter of cases seeking leave to bring proceedings before the Court. Starting in 1955, there is a *Collection of Decisions of the European Commission of Human Rights*. This consisted of 46 volumes of the decisions made by the Commission from the commencement of the series until 1973, the text being in English and French. The series *Decisions and Reports* was commenced in 1974, and follows on from the previous publication. From Volume 76 onwards, two versions have been published: in Volume A the text is in the original language and in Volume B will be found the translation into the other official language.

Human Rights Act 1998

Successive United Kingdom governments having declined to incorporate the European Convention on Human Rights, the "New Labour" government finally took the plunge. When the decision had been taken, the reform process was rapid. A consultation paper was published on December 1996, setting out the Labour Party's plans (the party being still in opposition) to incorporate the Convention, and a White Paper was published very shortly after the Government took office on 1 May 1997. The Bill to accomplish this objective, the Human Rights Bill 1998, was introduced into the House of Lords on 23 October 1997, only months after the election in May of that year, and received its Royal Assent on 9 November 1998. There was very little time, then, to discuss and debate in any serious way any of the longer-term implications of the form of incorporation proposed; very little change could be made to the package as contemplated in the White Paper, and very few concessions—none of them structural—were made as the Bill made its way through Parliament. The Act then came into force in October 2000.

The Act contains certain constitutional novelties. When Ministers introduce legislation into Parliament, they must certify that the Bill is compliant with the Human Rights Act 1998. More significantly, the Act gives the judges of the superior courts the power to make a declaration of incompatibility[17] when it is found that an Act of Parliament (whether passed before or after the Act) is at variance with the rights identified in the Schedule to the 1998 Act itself, the Schedule being the text of most of the European Convention. The Act does not give to courts the power to declare legislation invalid after the fashion of the United States Supreme Court—that would have represented too great a break with constitutional tradition. But it does represent a considerable advance on the pre-Act situation where the Convention was treated as being little more than an aid to interpretation,[18] and a guide as to the direction in which the common law might be developed.

The influence of Europe—a preliminary assessment

The legendary Chinese leader Chairman Mao is reputed to have replied, when asked (by the then American Secretary of State, Henry Kissinger) about the impact of the French Revolution, "it is still too early to tell". He might have made the same remark had he been seeking to assess the significance of the impact of European legal thought upon the common law. In some areas of the law, the change has been minimal. The details and the basic principles of the substantive criminal law, for example, remain largely untouched. But it is undoubtedly the case that different methods and modes of thought are necessary

---

[17] Although such measures should be seen as of last resort, a number of declarations have been made by the Court of Appeal; 00000

[18] *R. v Secretary of State for the Home Department, ex p. Brind* [1991] A.C. 696.

to an understanding of European law, and that some of these may in time migrate into the common law way of thinking. The following general points may perhaps be made.

1. The style of legislative drafting is different, and the practices of interpretation are correspondingly different. Whereas the common law draftsman values certainty and precision and adopts a correspondingly detailed legislative style, the European lawyer is content to paint with a relatively broad brush, leaving the detail to be worked out by others, including the courts. The European courts in turn adopt a contextual and purposive approach to the legislation. What matters is not so much what the legislature may or may not have intended. As will be seen in Chapter 7, the purposive approach to statutory interpretation has become more or less the standard approach here; whether as a result of exposure to European method, it is impossible to be sure.

2. Attitudes to precedent are different. In the common law, there is a strict system of precedent, in which judgments are binding according to a system of *stare decisis*. In European law there is no strict doctrine of precedent, and a like point could in theory be decided differently on each occasion that it arises. Whereas in the common law there are several judgments, some of which may be dissenting, in EU law there is generally only one judgment and no dissents. Judges in European law can also approach their task in a more openly creative spirit than is available to their common law counterparts, although here too, it is now far more common than it was hitherto for common law judges to abandon the fiction that their role is a non-creative one.

3. Certain concepts may have been imported from the European systems. A good example is the notion of *proportionality*. This is a concept familiar in EU law,[19] and in the constitutional law of countries as diverse as Germany, Canada and South Africa

[19] As in Case C–451/93 *Union Royale Belge des Sociétés de Football Association ASBL v Jean Marc Bosman* [1995] E.C.R. I–4921, para.110.

and Switzerland. The contours of the principle of proportionality are familiar. In *de Freitas v Permanent Secretary of Ministry of Agriculture, Fisheries, Lands and Housing*[20] the Privy Council adopted a three-stage test. Lord Clyde observed that, in determining whether a limitation (by an act, rule or decision) is arbitrary or excessive the court should ask itself:

"whether: (i) the legislative objective is sufficiently important to justify limiting a fundamental right; (ii) the measures designed to meet the legislative objective are rationally connected to it; and (iii) the means used to impair the right or freedom are no more than is necessary to accomplish the objective."[21]

In short, the doctrine of proportionality dictates that where as a result of the action of a public authority, individual rights are curtailed, the effect on the individual should not be disproportionate to the objectives that the measure seeks to achieve. A sledgehammer should not be used to crack a nut. Since it was the obligation of the courts of the Member States to apply the EU jurisprudence locally, the United Kingdom courts soon became familiar with its application.[22] Similarly, since the courts have to apply a proportionality test in appropriate cases in accordance with the jurisprudence of Strasbourg as a result of the Human Rights Act 1998 when a Convention right is being protected,[23] it is now an accepted part of United Kingdom law.

---

[20] [1999] 1 A.C. 69.

[21] At p. 80.

[22] See, e.g. *W.H. Smith Do-it-all Ltd v Peterborough City Council* [1991] 1 Q.B. 304 and *R. v Secretary of State for the Home Department, ex p. McQuillan* [1995] 4 All E.R. 400.

[23] *R. (on the application of Holding & Barnes Plc) v Secretary of State for the Environment, Transport and the Regions* [2003] 2 A.C. 295 [51] *per* Lord Slynn.

4 METHODS OF STUDY

"Learning by study must be won;
'Twas ne'er entailed from son to son."

—Gay, *Fables*, II, ii.

TEXTBOOKS

With the advent of modern electronic media, the task of giving advice as to the best methods of study have undoubtedly become slightly more complicated, since the materials that you require are now likely to be available to you to download, so that you can consult them at times most appropriate to your own routines.[1] But the old question: how is my time better spent: sitting in the library reading cases in the reports, or stewing over a textbook or case book in my own room? is still a pertinent one, is often put by beginners, and it is a hard one to answer. One can, of course, answer it discreetly by saying—*do both*. But then the question is—in what proportion? What is the relative importance of the two modes of study?

Before answering this question let me remind the reader that when studying law there is not one aim but two. The primary and most important aim is to make oneself a lawyer.[2] The secondary (but also very important) aim is to pass the law exams with credit.

Now to a large extent these two aims can be pursued by the same means. For both purposes one must study cases, either in the original law reports or in case books. It is through applying oneself to cases that one gets to understand how legal problems present themselves and how legal argument is conducted. That understanding

---

[1] I am making the assumption that you will not have access to your computer and its materials in the examination room.
[2] That is, a person familiar with and able to employ legal resources and reasoning, not necessarily a legal practitioner.

is important whether one's object is to solve exam problems or to give sound opinions on points of legal practice.

But there is one difference between preparation for practice and preparation for exams. For the practising lawyer, having a large field of what Pollock called potential knowledge is more important than having a small amount of actual knowledge. What the practitioner needs is a grasp of general legal principles, a sound knowledge of practice and procedure, an ability to argue, and a general knowledge of where to find the relevant law. But it is not essential for the practitioner—though, of course, it is a great help—to carry much law in the mind.[3] To shine at exams, on the other hand, one must not only know how to argue, and be able to display a first-hand knowledge of the sources; one must also be able to recite a considerable number of rules and authorities. From the exam point of view there is a danger in discursive reading that is not accompanied by a considerable amount of learning by rote.

Teachers of law regret the amount of memorising that is required, but they have not agreed upon effective counter-measures. Often it seems to smother constructive thought. Some exam scripts are positively shocking for the amount of word-perfect memorising that they display, coupled with lack of individuality. Copies of statutes and other legal materials are allowed to be used in some law exams. The result should not be to lower the standard of the exam but to raise it, for it means that the exam can be made more starkly a test of intelligence and lawyerly ability. But some candidates fall prey to the temptation to recite long passages from the permitted materials, which gives the examiner the impression that they are insufficiently prepared to answer the question (even though the passage cited may be largely in point). There is no reason why case books should not be permitted, or at least lists of names of cases. In some universities, some teachers

---

[3] There is an old tale of a solicitor who won great renown for his deep knowledge of the law. His secret was this. He had had three copies of *Every Man's Own Lawyer* bound to resemble law reports and lettered respectively "3 Meeson and Welsby", "1 Term Reports" and "7 Manning and Granger". When a client propounded a legal question, the solicitor would ring for his clerk and say: "Bring me 3 Meeson and Welsby", or "1 Term Reports", or "7 Manning and Granger". When the volume came he would gravely look up the point and then say triumphantly: "Ah! here it is. I thought so. The very authority we wanted". The solicitor was not such a fraud as a layman hearing this story might think. At least he knew his way about that particular book better than the clients did.

allow pupils to take into the exam all material that they have prepared themselves.

But I must not vex present readers with problems of educational reform. My reason for writing the above was merely to underline the importance, as matters now stand, of some memory work. Students whose schooling has consisted of project work and other forms of continuous assessment might well find that the degree of material that must be committed to memory is rather daunting. It is distressing when a student who has worked industriously and read widely fails to achieve a due place in the exam merely through failure to commit to memory a due proportion of what has been read.

There is another observation to be made about the learning of law through the medium of textbooks. It is an observation that everyone accustomed to learning has already made personally, but it is, perhaps, worth putting on paper for the sake of those whose acquaintance with this discipline has hitherto been slight. It is this. The more often a book is read, the easier and quicker it is to read (which is obvious), and the more it repays the reading (which is, perhaps, not quite so obvious). When a book on an unfamiliar subject is read for the first time (including I should suppose this one) it is rather heavy-going, and one seems not to remember very much of it. The second reading is both easier and more interesting, and more (but still not much) is remembered. Many people take their exam at this point. Had they had the perseverance to read through the book a third, fourth and fifth time, they would have found that each successive reading came more easily and that the residue left in the mind each time went up in geometrical progression.

While on the subject of memory work it is worth pointing out that learning by heart is best performed in short periods distributed over as long a time as possible. For instance, it is better to devote one hour a day to revision than six hours at a stretch once a week. By the same token, you can learn the same amount in less learning time by distributing your learning evenly over term and vacation than by crowding your learning into the term and leaving the vacations an academic blank.[4]

"It has been found", says a psychologist, "that when acts of reading

---

[4] See A. Baddeley, *Human Memory: Theory and Practice* (1997).

and acts of recall alternate, i.e. when every reading is followed by an attempt to recall the items, the efficiency of learning and retention is enormously enhanced."[5] This means that learning is best done by reading a paragraph or page or similar convenient amount, and immediately reciting the gist of it, and it has been found better to recite aloud than to perform the recall in the head. If you find that you cannot remember the passage properly, read it again and then try another recall. The longer the passage that you set yourself for recall the better; in other words, read as much at a time as you will be able to reproduce at the next recall. Heavy footnotes to a book are sometimes distracting, and it is then a good plan to read the book through a first time without looking at the footnotes.

It is a mistake to spend valuable time in digesting a textbook on paper, unless the digest consists of little more than subject headings and names of cases. Mere transcription from a book that one owns oneself is certainly folly.

"Many readers I have found unalterably persuaded", wrote Dr Johnson, "that nothing is certainly remembered but what is transcribed: and they have therefore passed weeks and months in transferring large quotations to a commonplace book. Yet, why any part of a book, which can be consulted at pleasure, should be copied I was never able to discover. The hand has no closer correspondence with the memory than the eye. The act of writing itself distracts the thoughts, and what is twice read is commonly better remembered than what is transcribed."[6]

CASES AND MATERIALS BOOKS

Some teachers of law do not recommend the use of case books, although the numbers who adopt such a high-minded line is undoubtedly dwindling. In their view, the only way to become a proficient lawyer is to sit down and read cases, not contenting oneself with the headnote or any other simplified version of the case, but reading through the whole of the statement of facts and the whole of

[5] C.A. Mace, *The Psychology of Study* (2nd edn), p.38.
[6] *The Idler*, No.74.

the judgments. Faced with such a counsel of perfection the student may well echo from the heart the words of Doderidge J., written when legal literature was but a fraction of its present bulk: "*Vita brevis est, ars longa*, our life is short and full of calamities, and learning is a long time in getting."[7] A teacher must consider, before giving advice like the above, the amount of time actually available to a law student for studies. Taking first those at the universities, their period of residence is only about seven months in the year, and few can work for more than eight months in the year altogether. In that time they have to cover four or five subjects. This means an average of between six and eight weeks for each subject. Into this alarmingly short space they must fit attendance at lectures and tutorials/supervisions, the reading of the textbooks, wider reading in the library, and revision, as well as the manifold activities that very properly occupy the undergraduate outside work. Those studying for professional exams, particularly those engaged in office work during the day, will probably have less rather than more time than undergraduates.

It becomes obvious, then, that time must be carefully managed. Granting that the student must read cases, it is a permissible economy of time to buy a good case book for each department of law that is being studied. Using a case book has two advantages for the learner. First, the case book saves some of the trouble (beneficial, but time-consuming) of making one's own notebook of cases. Secondly, it does something to eliminate immaterial facts, thus helping in the search (again beneficial, but again time-consuming) for the facts that are legally material.

It should be added that the use of case books by no means dispenses with the need for reading at least some of the original reports. For one thing, many of the more important cases in the case book can profitably be read in full in the law reports, using the case book version only for revision. Also, there are bound to be many cases that the keen student will come across and want to read that are not in the case book—among them, cases decided since the case book went to print. And it should be remarked that examiners are prone to set papers in which recent cases figure prominently, if only because they afford such rich material demonstrating the growth points of the law.

---

[7] *The English Lawyer* (1631), p.38.

To the student of modest means the high price of law books is intimidating, but it is false economy to do without basic works. Many are available at reasonable prices in paperback. Money can usually be saved by buying secondhand books (often organised by the student Law Society where you are intending to study), but the beginner who does this should be careful never to buy anything but a latest edition, and to make sure that a new edition is not in preparation at the time of purchase. It can be infuriating to buy in June, only to find when the course starts in late September or early October that a new edition has appeared. As a rule of thumb, I would say, be a bit suspicious of any textbook in its third or fourth year.

The following is a London firm specialising in secondhand and new law books. An email to Wildy & Sons Ltd, Lincoln's Inn Archway, Carey Street, London WC2A 2JD (info@wildys.co.uk) (or a phone call—020 7242 5778) will bring a quotation.

LECTURES AND CLASSES

In the Middle Ages lectures were necessary because of the shortage of books. Now that printing has been with us for some hundreds of years, that many lecturers provide very comprehensive handouts and that lectures are increasingly becoming available electronically, is there any need to continue the lecture system?

Perhaps the only comprehensive answer to this complex question is that it depends upon the particular lecturer and the particular lectures. You should soon appreciate that not all lecturers are seeking to achieve precisely the same objectives in the course of a lecture session. If you start with the assumption that each lecturer is determined to provide you with a set of perfect notes, with the aid of which you will be equipped to sail through the exam, you will be sorely disappointed. But, speaking generally, lectures may be said to possess several merits as a means of instruction. They can quicken interest. To listen to a competent lecturer makes a welcome change from the reading of books. Some lecturers seek to help an audience by giving the "basis and essentials" of the subject, elucidating the broad principles and indicating what is matter of detail. It is possible to dwell on the parts of the subject that experience shows to cause special difficulties. Another point in favour is that by varying the emphasis the lecturer can be more readily understood than can the toneless words of a book. Finally, the lecturer can bring textbooks up to date, and in a smallish class can solve individual difficulties through interaction and discussion.

Taking notes

You will in time develop your own system of note taking, but there are some well-established systems, such as the "Cornell" system for taking notes and subsequent study. This suggests that you should draw a vertical line about 2 inches from the left hand edge of the paper, using the right hand side to "record" the lecture itself, and the left for "recall" purposes subsequently. That is, the lecture is captured in general idea rather than detail and the key ideas can be summarised and reflected upon later in the recall column.

Some lecturers regard it as their sole function to stimulate and inspire; oblivious, perhaps, to the old Chinese proverb that "the palest ink is worth more than the most retentive memory", they do not particularly want notes to be taken. Certainly it is a great waste of time to sit through the average lecture making notes mechanically without thinking what they are about. Either concentrate on the lecture and rely upon your books for acquisition of facts, or form the habit of taking notes (using a laptop if you are sufficiently familiar with the operation of such a machine as not to be distracted by it, and you can do this without distracting others) and at the same time following the line of argument. It may set an edge upon your attention if you imagine that you are due to be tested in the subject immediately after the lecture. Another inestimable habit is of spending a part of each evening reading through all the notes taken in the day. It need hardly be added, after what has already been said about transcription, that the making of a fair copy of one's own lecture notes is a dismal waste of time.

Using shorthand

Some lecturers are blamed for saying too many valuable things in too short a time, making it difficult for the pens of their audiences (particularly those not used to note-taking) to keep pace. Often, you will find that the lecturer is in fact making the same (or a very similar) point but in different language, in order to get the idea across. But if you are not used to taking notes in lectures, and if the lecturer is using a handout and visual aids (such as a Powerpoint presentation), the difficulties of keeping track are compounded. One tip that might help to meet these difficulties is to suggest that you use abbreviations. You can devise your own system, but might find that the following are particularly useful:

H husband	W wife
T tenant	L landlord
Er employer	Ee employee
C claimant	D defendant (in both civil and criminal cases)
A agent	P principal
P purchaser	V vendor

In land law it is customary to refer to imaginary pieces of land as Blackacre, Whiteacre, etc. The conventional abbreviations for these are Bacre, Wacre, etc.

Some traditional abbreviations make use of the stroke, "/". Apart from "a/c" (account), they all represent two words, the stroke being placed between the initial letters of each:

b/e	bill of exchange
b/l	bill of lading
b/n	bank note
b/s	bill of sale
h/p	hire purchase
p/n	promissory note

This method can, of course, be extended to other common legal phrases:

a/b	act of bankruptcy
a/t	abstract of title
A/P	Act of Parliament
b/f	*bona fide*
e/r	equity of redemption
l/a	letters of administration
n/i	negotiable instrument
n/k	next of kin
p/a	power of appointment
p/p	personal property, part performance
p/r	personal representative
r/p	real property
r/c	restrictive covenant
s/g	sale of goods
s/p	specific performance

Alternatively the initial letters may be separated by periods:

b.f. (p)	*bona fide* (purchaser)
c.q.t.	*cestui que trust*
c.q.tt.	*cestuis que trust*
p.f.	*prima facie*

Or they may even be joined up:

CPS	Crown Prosecution Service
DPP	Director of Public Prosecutions

Another traditional method of abbreviation is to write the first pronounceable part of the word and then write the ending. Common examples of this method are *assn* for *association, dept* for *department* and *insce* for *insurance*.

If you fail to catch or understand a particular sentence, most lecturers do not mind being asked to repeat or amplify it. Exercise discretion in the matter. If you have missed the name of a case, and the lecturer has provided a handout, it may be better discreetly to ask a neighbour to point you in the right direction rather than disrupt the flow of the lecture. Some lecturers invite questions and argument; in that case see that you play your part.

Considerably more important than the average lecture is the discussion class, generally called a tutorial, class, seminar or supervision. And of discussion classes, the most beneficial are those in which the discussion is centred on legal problems. With regard to these classes my injunctions are limited to two: first, attend them, and secondly, prepare for them by attempting to work out the problems for yourself before the session. Half the value of the exercise is missed if you sit supinely back and let the instructor or the other members of the class address the problems for you. The larger the group, the less likely it is that you will be pressed to speak, and the more important it is that you should speak—if only in order to cultivate self-possession and to get used to the sound of your own voice in public.

Talking about your work, whether in class or with friends, has the further very important advantage of helping the memory. To quote one of our psychologists again:

"Some form of action or of expression would seem to be essential to unimpaired retention. It seems that good conversationalists and great talkers generally have good memories. It is over-simple to suppose that this is due to the fact that, having good memories, they are well supplied with topics of conversation. The reverse connection would seem to be involved. What is talked about is more firmly impressed upon the mind. Such men when they read a book immediately discuss it with a friend, thus unconsciously employing the potent principle of active repetition."[8]

---

[8] C.A. Mace, *The Psychology of Study* (2nd edn), pp.40–41.

Apart from this necessary conversation, form the habit of working a full morning (which includes making use of the spare time that you have between lectures), because this is the part of the day when you are freshest. Do not do minor chores in the morning. As for the rest of the day, you will wish to make your own choice between the afternoon and evening for work, but at either time you will find that alcohol is inconsistent with study.

In conclusion, a few words on a comparatively humble matter, that of materials. The use of bound lecture notebooks is not to be recommended, because they are cumbersome and inelastic. If you use such notebooks and have three or four lectures to attend in a morning, this means a considerable weight and bulk to be carried about. Also, if you want to expand the lecturer's remarks with notes of your own you will find it difficult to do so within the confines of the notebook. On both counts the looseleaf system is greatly preferable. The student who adopts this system needs to take to lectures only a single looseleaf notebook, the day's work being transferred to larger specialised files in the evening. Notes taken down in this form can be rearranged and expanded at leisure.

THE STUDY OF HISTORY

Some students who have studied English history may be able to recollect the order and the dates of the kings and queens of England. Such knowledge is useful in the study not only of constitutional but of purely legal history, for regnal years are the foundation of legal chronology. Those whose historical knowledge is shaky may possibly be glad of the following mnemonic rhyme, which was once learnt by Victorian children. Even if you do not trouble to learn it, you may find in the course of your studies that you will need to date a piece of legislation, and on the basis that it may come in useful for that purpose, I set it out with the corresponding regnal years at the side:

First William the Norman	1066–1087
Then William his son;	1087–1100
Henry, Stephen, and Henry,	1100–1135, 1135–1154, 1154–1189

Then Richard and John;	1189–1199, 1199–1216
Next Henry the third,	1216–1272
Edwards, one, two and three,	1272–1307, 1307–1327,
	1327–1377
And again after Richard	1377–1399
Three Henrys we see	1399–1413, 1413–1422,
	1422–1461
Two Edwards, third Richard,	1461–1483, 1483, 1483–1485
If rightly I guess;	
Two Henrys, sixth Edward,	1485–1509, 1509–1547,
	1547–1553
Queen Mary, Queen Bess,	1553–1558, 1558–1603
Then Jamie the Scotsman,	1603–1625
Then Charles whom they slew,	1625–1649
Yet received after Cromwell	[1649–1660]
Another Charles too.	1649[9] (1660)–1685
Next James the second	
Ascended the throne;	1685–1688
Then Good William and Mary	
Together came on,	1689–1702
Till, Anne, Georges four,	1702–1714, 1714–1727,
	1727–1760, 1760–1820,
	1820–1830
And fourth William all past,	1830–1837
God sent Queen Victoria:	1837–1901
May she long be the last!	
Perhaps it is time to add to the edifice:	
Edward, George, then	1901–1910, 1910–1936,
Edward 8, George; now Bess	1936, 1936–1952, 1952–
is head of state.	

If the regnal years are not already known and the task of learning them all seems too great, the student should at least notice the sovereigns whose reigns commenced at or shortly after the turn of

---

[9] Although Charles did not become king *de facto* until 1660, his regnal years were computed from the execution of his father in 1649.

each century. Knowledge of this, combined with a knowledge of the order of the sovereigns, will place every sovereign in the proper century. The sovereigns just referred to are:

Henry I	1100
Henry III	1216
Edward II	1307
Henry V	1413
Henry VIII	1509
James I	1603
Anne	1702
George IV	1820
Edward VII	1901

Not only regnal years but dates in general are often a bugbear to students of history. The intelligent way to remember dates is to memorise a few key ones, and then to remember others by working backwards and forwards from these. By relating this in the mind, and noticing the differences in years, the one will become linked to the other, and both can be recalled together. In time the same date can be related to several others, so that all important dates become interlocked in the mind. This method of memorising helps to build up the sense of historical perspective, which is the only rational justification for remembering dates. A useful dictionary is J. Gardiner ed., *The Penguin Dictionary of British History* (2000).

5 TECHNICAL TERMS

> " 'Zounds! I was never so bethump'd with words"
>
> —Shakespeare, *King John*, II, i.

LATIN AND FRENCH

At first the beginner may be rather lost among the many technical terms, especially those used in the older reports, and may find some difficulty with Latin and law-French phrases and maxims.[1]

Examiners are fond of recounting "amusing" mistranslations to which such difficulty can give rise. There was the youth who innocently asked whether the phrase *en ventre sa mere* (unborn child) meant the same thing as *in loco parentis* (in place of the parent). To another candidate belongs the credit of suggesting that *fructus naturales* (perennial plants) means illegitimate children, and that *animus revertendi* (the intention to return) means the transmigration of souls. Weak latinity may also result in ungrammatical constructions. Thus the word "*obiter*" in "*obiter dictum*" (a judge's "saying by the way" or "passing remark") is not a noun but an adjective—one should not write, as another examinee did, that a lawyer in reading cases needs to "hack through the *obiter* to reach the actual decisions."

Differences of view as to the usefulness or otherwise of using Latin and law-French are hardly new. Some phrases and maxims can encapsulate in brief compass a notion or concept that is difficult to express in our native tongue. Equally, however, there is the view

---

[1] The law-French phrases survive from the time when French, or rather Anglo-Norman, was the language of the courts. See J.H. Baker, *Manual of law French* (2nd edn, 1990); Holdsworth, *History of English Law*, Vol.ii, pp.477–484; Theo. Mathew, "Law French" (1938) 54 L.Q.R. 358. Latin was formerly the language for official documents, like writs, and sometimes survives in the names of writs (*habeas corpus*, whose literal translation is according to one authority "you (i.e. the accuser) are to produce the body", which will hardly do for the writ that protects personal security, said to be "the most fundamental legal right").

that their use is cultish and obscurantist and designed to confer a mystique on their users. In 1730 Parliament passed an Act abolishing law-Latin in legal proceedings. But it was found that technical terms like *nisi prius, quare impedit, fieri facias* and *habeas corpus* were (as Blackstone put it) "not capable of an English dress with any degree of seriousness", and so two years later another Act was passed to allow such words to be continued "in the same language as hath been commonly used".

The lessons of that episode have not been wholly absorbed, and there is a movement (running concurrently with the reforms of civil procedure spearheaded by Lord Woolf) to eliminate much Latin from our legal language. An electronic search for "Latin" through the recent law reports suggests that the battle is not yet won.[2] The distinction suggested earlier between the useful and the unnecessary use of Latin finds echo in the work of B.A. Garner who says that we should "distinguish between TERMS OF ART, for which there are no ordinary English equivalents, and those terms that are merely vestigial Latinism with simple English substitutes".[3] Unnecessary use of Latinisms he castigates as serving "no purpose but to give the writer a false sense of erudition. These terms convey no special legal meanings, no delicate nuances apprehended only by lawyers. They are pompous, turgid deadwood." I concur with this view, adding only that it may sometimes be open to argument as to which category best describes any particular expression. The translations offered in the first paragraph of this chapter suggest that most of the expressions used there fall into the pompous category. But *obiter* is entirely blameless in this respect.

As it is, official translation of some of the new terminology associated with the Woolf reforms has led to oddities. *Ex parte*, for example, is now supposed to mean "without notice" (whereas the usual translation would be "on the part of one side only"). But it was (and is) quite common practice to alert the other side to the fact that an *ex parte* application is to be made, in which case we have a "without notice" application being made, notice having been given.

[2] And see R.J.C. Munday (2001) 164 J.P. 995.

[3] *A Dictionary of Modern Legal Usage* (2nd edn, 2001), p.501.

DICTIONARIES

A law dictionary can assist in demystifying some of the secrets of the law. In the library, you should look for *Broom's Legal Maxims* (10th edn, 1937). The age of the work should not deflect you from using it. Maxims are often couched in Latin because they are derived from Roman law or because they were invented by medieval jurists. An excellent guide is B.A. Garner, *A Dictionary of Modern Legal Usage* (2nd edn, 2001). Four dictionaries suitable for students are L.B. Curzon's *The Longman Dictionary of Law* (8th edn, 2011), Osborn's *Concise Law Dictionary* (12th edn, 2013), *Oxford Dictionary of Law* (7th edn, 2009). A magnificent dictionary-encyclopedia is David M. Walker's *The Oxford Companion to Law* (1980). As its name implies, it is not limited to English law but gives a general view of other common law countries and foreign systems, as well as of legal philosophy; legal history is catered for, and there are brief biographies of judges and jurists. A splendid book to have on your shelf, if your funds will reach to it; anyway you will probably find it in the reference section of your law school or public library. *The New Oxford Companion to Law* (2008) eds P. Cane and J. Conaghan is intended to replace and update Walker. Note also Earl Jowitt's *Dictionary of English Law*, which is founded upon earlier works by Wharton and Byrne.

Additionally, a good English dictionary can afford considerable assistance on the meaning of individual English words, though not, of course, on Latin maxims; the good ones include *Collins English Dictionary*; the *Concise Oxford Dictionary*; and *Collins Concise Dictionary*; you might also consider *Chambers Compact Dictionary* or the *New Penguin English Dictionary* —all of these represent an investment for a lifetime, and since these works are regularly updated, it should be possible to pick a good one up second-hand.

PRONUNCIATION

A few words may be said about pronunciation. Latin words and phrases are generally pronounced by lawyers in the same old barbaric way as they were in the Middle Ages,[4] that is to say, as if they were

---

[4] There is a medieval tale, told by an assistant in the Record Office, of some nuns

English. *C* and *g* are soft where they would be in English,[5] and the pronunciation of such syllables as *atio* in ratio *decidendi* is also anglicised ("rayshio deesidendy"). Long vowels are pronounced as in English (the sounds being those in the names of the vowels).[6] Moreover, whether the vowel is to be pronounced long or short depends more upon English rules than upon Roman ones.

(1) In words of two syllables, the first vowel is pronounced long even though it was short in Latin. Examples are bonus, onus, opus, genus ("jeenus"), *capias* ("caypias"), *mens rea* ("mens reeah"), *modus vivendi* ("mohdus vivendy"), *nisi prius* ("nysy[7] pryus"), *ratio decidendi* ("rayshyoh deesidendy"), *sine die* ("synee dyee"), and *vice versa* ("vysee"). This lends point to Mr Punch's translation of *pendente lite*[8] as "a chandelier".

(2) In words of three or more syllables derived from the Latin, vowels are generally pronounced short before the penultimate syllable, whether or not they were short in classical Latin. This is seen in the ordinary English words codicil, general and genera, ominous and operates. (Strictly, we should pronounce "economic" and "devolution" in the same way with a short first

who needed extra help about the convent and who accordingly sent down to the village by word of mouth for *servitia*. The request was understood by the villagers as a request for *cervicia*, an ale-feast, and they acted accordingly. The anecdote shows that the "c" in *cervicia*, and probably also the "t" in *servitia*, were pronounced like "s".

[5] Hence R.H. Barham's lines in allusion to Sir C. Wren's epitaph in St. Paul's Cathedral:

"And, talking of epitaphs, much I admire his,

'Circumspice, si monumentum requiris,'

Which an erudite verger translated to me,

'If you ask for his monument, Sir—come—spy—see!'"

[6] But there are no immutable rules, any more than there are in the pronunciation of English. Thus *si* is pronounced "see" by old and new school alike, though to be consistent the old school should pronounce it "sy", as indeed it does in the world *nisi*.

[7] There is an anecdote of how Lord Hewart C.J. "put down" counsel who applied for a rule *nisi* (pronouncing it "nysy", which was correct). Lord Hewart listened in silence and then said: "The judgment of the court will be short, like the first i in nisi". In this he displayed both his classical education and his ignorance of the rules of English pronunciation. It may be observed that it is most unlikely that a modern judge would seek to discomfort counsel in such a way. The lawyer's traditional pronunciation of "patent" with a short a breaks the rule.

[8] "While the suit is pending."

vowel, but they have become lengthened by usage.) It will be seen that the preferable pronunciation of *obiter*, according to the rule, is with a short *o*.

Law-French words are pronounced much as they were in the Middle Ages; it is a solecism (though not a serious one) to utter them as if they were modern French. The pronunciation is, indeed, much nearer to modern English than it is to French. Thus the town crier quite correctly said "Oy-ez", not "Oy-ay". The following are pronunciations of legal terms deriving from medieval French.

attorn (-er)
attorney
autrefois acquit (oterfoyz, with "acquit and convict" pronounced as usual in English)
autrefois convict
detinue (det-)
distress damage feasant (feezant)
emblements (embliments)
formedon ("e" pronounced indeterminately, as in "added")
feme sole (femm)
feme covert (cuvert)
feoffment (feff-)
laches (laytshiz)
lien (lee-en or leen)
mesne (meen)
misfeasance (-feez-)
nonfeasance
pur autre vie (pur oter vee)
que (in the phrase "in the *que* estate" and in *cestui que trust*: pronounced kee)
seisin (-eez-)
semble (anglicised as written)
venue (accent on the first syllable)
villein (villen)

The old practices whereby lawyers retained the archaic pronunciations of English words has all but disappeared. The noun "record", for example, used to be pronounced like the verb, with the stress on the second syllable,[9] and the term for an insured person, "assured," had the last syllable pronounced like "red" and stressed. To pronounce them in this way in the twenty-first century would be to invite a charge of affectation. Some traces remain however. In pronouncing "recognisance", some lawyers do not acknowledge the intrusive "g", though we do in writing, and generally in "cognisance", and "cognisable". (The "g" comes through latinising the law-French word "conusance").

LEGAL ABBREVIATIONS[10]

Judicial titles

Legal abbreviations are another frequent source of vexation to a beginner. The possession of a law dictionary is again a great help, but something may be said here of the more common abbreviations and short-cut terms seen in print.

First, as to the titles of judges.[11] "Smith J." means "Mr Justice Smith" (or Mrs Justice Smith, as the case may be), and when speaking of the judge in public he or she will be given that full title. Never say "Justice Smith", which is an Americanism, to be avoided on this side of the Atlantic. The plural abbreviation is JJ.: "Smith and Walker JJ.", which is read out as "Mrs Justice Smith and Mr Justice Walker". A circuit judge is referred to as "Judge Smith".

---

[9] "Condemn the fault, and not the actor of it?
Why, every fault's condemn'd ere it be done.
Mine were the very cipher of a function,
To fine the faults whose fine stands in record,
And let go by the actor."
—Shakespeare, *Measure for Measure*, II, ii.
"Then turning to the Judge, he cry's, My Lord,
(And thus runs o'er their Crimes upon record)."
—Edward Ward, *A Journey to H—, or a visit paid to the D—*(or, *The Infernal Vision*), Part I, Canto II (A.D. 1700–1705).

[10] Keys to the abbreviations of law reports and journals are given in Ch.2.

[11] Sometimes called *puisne* (pronounced "pewny"—ew as in few) judges, meaning any judge of the High Court (or the older courts that it replaced) other than the chiefs.

The following letters placed after the names of the judges have the following meanings:,

B.	Baron [of the Exchequer]. A member of the former Court of Exchequer—not to be confused with Barons who are peers. Plural BB. Title now obsolete.
C.	Chancellor of the High Court of England (in use only since 2006)
C.B.	Chief Baron: the head of the former Court of Exchequer. Title now obsolete.
C.J. (or L.C.J.)	Lord Chief Justice. With the coming in to force of the Constitutional Reform Act 2005, this office displaced the Lord Chancellor as the head of the judiciary[12]. But it has in turn been superseded in seniority by the President of the Supreme Court.
J.A.	Justice of Appeal. Title found between 1875 and 1877, and now obsolete.[13]
J.S.C.	Justice of the (newly created) Supreme Court
L.C.	Lord High Chancellor of Great Britain. Until the Constitutional Reform Act 2005, this office was occupied by the Head of the judicial system. He is now a government minister, and is not a member of the House of Lords.
L.J.	Lord Justice or Lady Justice. Member of the Court of Appeal. Plural L.JJ.: Lords Justices, or where the entire bench consists of women, Ladies Justices.
M.R.	Master of the Rolls. Member (and President) of the Court of Appeal (Civil Division).
P.	President, either of the newly established Supreme Court, or of Family Division or Criminal Division of the Court of Appeal.

---

[12] The Lord Chief Justice was formerly also the Head of the Queen's Bench Division and President of the Court of Appeal (Criminal Division), but these are now separate offices.

[13] See R.A. Riches, "A Note on Judicial Titles" (1945) 61 L.Q.R. 231.

| V.-C. | Vice-Chancellor (now obsolete, and - replaced by the "Chancellor of the High Court"). In effect head of the Chancery Division. |
| V-P | Vice President of the Court of Appeal (one each for the Civil and Criminal Divisions) and of the Queen's Bench Division of the High Court |

Do not omit or abbreviate "Lord" before the name of a judge who is a Law Lord or other peer. Thus you will write "Lord Irvine L.C." not "Irvine L.C." and similarly "Lord Judge C.J.". (or "Lord Judge L.C.J."). These are read out as "Lord Irvine, Lord Chancellor" and "Lord Judge, Chief Justice" (or "Lord Chief Justice"). In the case of Chief Justices who were not peers, like Rufus Isaacs and (for a time) Sir Thomas Bingham, the written designation is "Isaacs C.J." (or "L.C.J."), which is read out as "[Lord] Chief Justice Isaacs", "Elias L.J." is read out as "Lord Justice Elias". "Jackson and Elias L.JJ." are "Lords Justices Jackson and Elias".[14] Lord Neuberger M.R. is "Lord Neuberger, Master of the Rolls". Where this last office is not held by a peer the usage is that one has to remember the holder's first name when speaking of him, so "Donaldson M.R." was "Sir John Donaldson, Master of the Rolls", and "Brett M.R." was "Sir Baliol Brett, Master of the Rolls".[15]

Citations and cross-references

Certain abbreviations and shorthand expressions supply a convenient mechanism for referring to authorities. A tale is told of the librarian who received a request form filled in by a reader asking for a supposed book called "*Ibid*". Evidently the reader had seen this referred to many times in footnotes, and thought that it must be an extremely important book, written perhaps by an eminent Persian. "*Ibid.*" is

---

[14] Occasionally, the first name forms a part of the official title (for example Lord Justice Simon Brown), in which case the reference is made to the fuller title.

[15] J.L. Montrose (1963) 79 L.Q.R. 190. It is related that on one occasion, counsel apologised for being unable to provide the court with the first name of the first judge appointed to the Divorce Court. "Creswell", interjected the bench, in an attempt to be helpful. "No, My Lord, his first name", at which point the bench explained that the judge's unlikely name was indeed "Sir Creswell Creswell".

actually short for *ibidem*, meaning "in the same place"; it is simply a way of repeating a reference previously given. Similarly, *op. cit.* means "the book (or work) previously cited", and *loc. cit.* means "the page previously cited in the book previously cited". *Passim* means "everywhere in the book". Other compendious expressions are *per, semble, aliter* (or *secus*) and *contra*. *Per* generally means "statement by": thus "*per* Lord Millett" following a quotation means that the remark quoted is that of Lord Millett. *Per curiam* and *per incuriam* derive from entirely different Latin roots, and are not opposites. *Per curiam* means that the statement is by the whole court. *Per incuriam* means that a judge's remark was made by mistake.

Semble is law-French for "it seems" or "it seems that" (when the authority for a proposition is weak or not completely satisfactory; usually it indicates an *obiter dictum*). *Aliter* and *secus* mean "otherwise" and *contra* refers to an authority contradicting what one has first said. Thus one can write "*Semble* the phrase 'carcass or portion of a carcass' in this statute does not include a sausage—see *per* Tripe L.J., *obiter*, in *Sage v Onions*, CA; *contra, Ham v Eggs*, Div Ct; *aliter* if the sausage meat is not yet minced". This may not be an elegant style but it does represent an economy of effort, which to some minds has a beauty of its own.

6 CASE LAW TECHNIQUE

> "Mastering the lawless science of our law,
> That codeless myriad of precedent,
> That wilderness of single instances,
> Through which a few, by wit or fortune led,
> May beat a pathway out to wealth and fame."
>
> —Tennyson, *Aylmer's Field.*

RATIO DECIDENDI

English courts are obliged to follow previous decisions of English courts[1] within more or less well-defined limits. This is called the doctrine of precedent.[2] The part of a case that is said to possess binding authority is the *ratio decidendi* that is to say, the rule of law upon which the decision is founded. Finding the *ratio decidendi* of a case is an important part of the training of a lawyer. It is not a mechanical process but is an art gradually acquired through practice and study. One can, however, give a general description of the techniques involved.

What the doctrine of precedent declares is that cases must be decided the same way when their material facts are the same. Obviously it does not require that all the facts should be the same. We know that in the flux of life all the facts of a case will never recur; but the legally material facts may recur and it is with these that the doctrine is concerned.

Although there is nothing like universal agreement on the point,[3]

---

[1] But not the European Court of Human Rights. See below (p.115).

[2] Or *stare decisis* (let decided things stand) as it is sometimes called. More detailed studies demonstrate that the picture presented here is, for reasons of space, necessarily somewhat simplistic. See L. Goldstein ed., *Precedent in Law* (1987); R. Cross and J.W. Harris, *Precedent in English Law* (4th edn, 1991); D.N. MacCormick and R.S. Summers, *Interpreting Precedent* (1997). An interesting and readable study is N. Duxbury, *The Nature and Authority of Precedent* (2008).

[3] The Court of Appeal has cited with approval a somewhat different formulation

the *ratio decidendi* of a case can be defined as the material facts of the case plus the decision thereon.[4] The same learned writer who advanced this definition went on to suggest a helpful formula. Suppose that in a certain case facts A, B and C exist; and suppose that the court finds that facts B and C are material and fact A immaterial, and then reaches conclusion X (for example, judgment for the claimant,[5] or judgment for the defendant). Then the doctrine of precedent enables us to say that in any future case in which facts B and C exist, or in which facts A and B and C exist, the conclusion must be X. If in a future case facts A, B, C and D exist, and fact D is held to be material, the first case will not be a direct authority, though it may be of value as an analogy.

What facts are legally material? That depends on the particular case, but take as an illustration a "running down" action, that is to say, an action for injuries sustained through the defendant's negligent driving of a vehicle. The fact that the claimant had red hair and freckles, that her name was Smith, and that the accident happened on a Friday are immaterial, for the rule of law upon which the decision proceeds will apply equally to persons who do not possess these characteristics and to accidents that happen on other days. On the other hand, the fact that the defendant drove negligently, and the fact that in consequence the claimant was injured, are material, and a decision in the claimant's favour on such facts will be an authority for the proposition that a person is liable for causing damage through the negligent driving of a vehicle.

The foregoing is a general explanation of the phrase "the *ratio decidendi* of a case". To get a clearer idea of the way in which a *ratio decidendi* is extracted, let us take a decided case and study it in detail. Set out below is the case of *Wilkinson v Downton*,[6] where the plaintiff

from that adopted here, that of Professor Cross in Cross and Harris, *Precedent in English Law* (4th edn, 1991), p.72: "The ratio decidendi of a case is any rule of law expressly or impliedly treated by the judge as a necessary step in reaching his conclusion, having regard to the line of reasoning adopted by him": *R. on the application of Al-Skeini v Secretary of State for Defence* [2005] EWCA Civ 1609, [2007] 1 Q.B. 140 at [145].

[4] A.L. Goodhart, "Determining the Ratio Decidendi of a Case" in *Essays in Jurisprudence and the Common Law* (1931), p.1.

[5] To remind—the "claimant" used to be known as the "plaintiff" and will be referred to as such in this chapter, where necessary for historical authenticity.

[6] [1897] 2 Q.B. 57.

was awarded damages by a jury for nervous shock, and the trial judge then heard argument on the question whether the verdict could be upheld in law. The first part of the judgment, which is all that needs be considered here, runs as follows.

WRIGHT J.: In this case the defendant, in the execution of what he seems to have regarded as a practical joke, represented to the plaintiff that he was charged by her husband with a message to her to the effect that her husband was smashed up in an accident, and was lying at The Elms at Leytonstone with both legs broken, and that she was to go at once in a cab with two pillows to fetch him home. All this was false. The effect of the statement on the plaintiff was a violent shock to her nervous system, producing vomiting and other serious and permanent physical consequences at one time threatening her reason, and entailing weeks of suffering and incapacity to her as well as expense to her husband for medical attendance. These consequences were not in any way the result of previous ill-health or weakness of constitution; nor was there any evidence of predisposition to nervous shock or any other idiosyncrasy.

In addition to these matters of substance there is a small claim for 1s. 10d. for the cost of railway fares of persons sent by the plaintiff to Leytonstone in obedience to the pretended message. As to this 1s. 10d. expended in railway fares on the faith of the defendant's statement, I think the case is clearly within the decision in *Pasley v Freeman* (1798) 3 T.R. 51. The statement was a misrepresentation intended to be acted on to the damage of the plaintiff.

The real question is as to the £100, the greatest part of which is given as compensation for the female plaintiff's illness and suffering. It was argued for her that she is entitled to recover this as being damages caused by fraud, and therefore within the doctrine established by *Pasley v Freeman* and *Langridge v Levy* (1837) 2 M. & W. 519. I am not sure that this would not be an extension of that doctrine, the real ground of which appears to be that a person who makes a false statement intended to be acted on must make good the damage naturally resulting from its being acted on. Here there is no *injuria* of that kind. I think, however, that the verdict may be supported upon another ground. The defendant has, as I assume for the moment, wilfully done an act calculated to cause physical harm to the plaintiff— that is to say, to infringe her legal right to personal safety, and has in fact thereby caused physical harm to her. That proposition without more appears to me to state a good cause of action, there being no justification alleged for the act. This wilful *injuria* is in law malicious, although no malicious purpose to cause the harm which was caused nor any motive of spite is imputed to the defendant.

It remains to consider whether the assumptions involved in the proposition are made out. One question is whether the defendant's act was so plainly calculated to produce some effect of the kind which was produced that an intention to produce it ought to be imputed to the defendant, regard being had to the fact that the effect was produced on a person proved to be in an ordinary state of health and mind. I think that it was. It is difficult to imagine that such a statement, made suddenly and with apparent seriousness, could fail to produce grave effects under the circumstances upon any but an exceptionally indifferent person, and therefore an intention to produce such an effect must be imputed, and it is no answer in law to say that more harm was done than was anticipated, for that is commonly the case with all wrongs.

The reader will notice that the judge does not cite any authority for his decision that the £100 is recoverable. The only authorities he cites are authorities on which he says he prefers not to rely. The reason is that at the date when the case was decided there was no English authority on the general question whether it was a tort intentionally to inflict bodily harm on another. There was, indeed, the very ancient tort of battery, which is committed when D hits or stabs or shoots P. But Downton committed no battery upon Mrs Wilkinson; nor did he assault her by threatening a battery. Consequently, the case was one "of first impression", and the judge decided it merely on common-sense principles. He took the view that if a person deliberately does an act that can be shown to have caused physical harm to another, that act can give rise to liability in damages as a matter of law. It was clear to him that, even if the person doing the act (in this case telling a lie) did not mean to cause any harm, if harm is in fact caused, there should be liability. It would be a grave reproach to a civilised system of law if it did not give a remedy on such facts.

Let us now see how the *ratio decidendi* is to be extracted. This is done by finding the material facts. The judge has already done much of the work for us, because he has omitted from his judgment many of the facts given in evidence that were obviously irrelevant to the legal issue, for example, the address at which the plaintiff lived. But the judgment mentions the address at which the husband was supposed to be lying, which also is clearly irrelevant. As a first step in boiling it down we may say that the essential facts, and the pith of the judgment, were as follows:

The defendant by way of what was meant to be a joke told the plaintiff that the latter's husband had been smashed up in an accident. The plaintiff, who had previously been of normal health, suffered a shock and serious illness. Wright J. held that the defendant was liable, not perhaps for the tort of deceit but because the defendant had wilfully done an act calculated to cause physical harm to the plaintiff, and had in fact caused such harm.

The above would represent the sort of note that an intelligent student would make of the case. How are we to frame the *ratio decidendi*? There are two main possibilities.

The first would be to take such of the detailed facts as may be deemed to be material, plus the decision on the facts. This would result in the following rule: that where the defendant has wilfully told the plaintiff a lie of a character that is likely (a clearer word than "calculated") to frighten and so cause physical harm to the plaintiff, and it has in fact caused such harm, the defendant is liable, in the absence of some ground of justification.

This *ratio* omits to specify the particular lie told by the defendant, because this was immaterial. What mattered was not the particular lie as to the plaintiff's husband's alleged injury, but the more general fact of lying. The particular lie told by the defendant was material only in the sense that it was the sort of lie that was likely to frighten and cause physical harm to the plaintiff.

But, it may be objected, such a *ratio* would be too narrow, because the learned judge evidently intended to lay down a wider rule. He did not confine his judgment to lies, but spoke only of wilfully doing an act which is calculated to and does cause physical harm; and this gives us the true *ratio*. It was immaterial that the particular form of mischief perpetrated by the defendant took the form of a verbal lie; it might have been some other act likely to cause harm, and the legal outcome would have been the same. This, indeed, is common sense. A person with Downton's juvenile sense of humour who dresses up as a ghost, or who puts fireworks under somebody else's chair, would doubtless be placed in the same legal category as Downton if injury were to ensue.

Again, the judge did not speak of fright when he formulated the principle of his decision. He spoke of causing physical harm, which is much wider. On this principle, an outrageous *threat* causing suffering is a tort. In a subsequent case[7] which approved *Wilkinson v Downton*, the defendant threatened to arrest and prosecute the plaintiff, a foreign maidservant, if she did not give certain information; the defendant knew that any charge he brought against the young woman would be quite unfounded, and the young woman became ill with distress. It was held that she had a good cause of action. Another application of the principle occurs where the harm operates directly on the plaintiff's body, not indirectly through the mind—as where the defendant blackens a towel which the plaintiff is about to use, or secretly adds poison to the plaintiff's drink. Although these situations have not been the subject of reported decisions, there is no doubt that they would fall under the principle of *Wilkinson v Downton*.

The reader may now be feeling rather puzzled to the meaning of *ratio decidendi*. We started off with a possible narrow *ratio decidendi* of the case, incorporating the fact of lying and the fact of fright. Then we passed to a wider *ratio*, which evidently accords with common sense as well as with the language of the judgment, in which the facts of lying and fright have disappeared. How can this be reconciled with our definition of *ratio decidendi* as the material facts plus the decision thereon? Were not the lie and the fright material facts in *Wilkinson v Downton*? If there had been no lie and no fright, and no equivalent facts in their place, the plaintiff would not have won. What exactly do we mean by a "material fact"?

The answer is that we have not been using this expression in a consistent way, and it is necessary to restate the position in more exact language. What is really involved in finding the *ratio decidendi* of a case is a process of abstraction. Abstraction is the mental operation of picking out certain qualities and relations from the facts of experience. Imagine a baby in whose household there is a terrier called Caesar. The baby will be probably learn to refer to the dog as "bow-wow", because "bow-wow" is easier to say than "Caesar". If the child sees another dog he will guess or be told that this other dog is to be called "bow-wow" as well. This is an example of one of the baby's earliest feats of abstraction. Abstraction comes through the perception of similarities between individual facts, and all language and all thinking depend upon it.

[7] *Janvier v Sweeney* [1919] 2 K.B. 316.

The next point to be noticed is that this process of abstraction may be carried to progressively higher flights. The individual dog Caesar is, at a low level of abstraction, a terrier; at a higher level he is a dog; higher still, a mammal and then an animal and a living thing. In the same way a man might say that he was born at the Fullerhope Maternity Hospital; in London; in England; in Europe. All these are "facts", but they are facts belonging to different levels of abstraction.

We are now in a better position to state the *ratio decidendi* of a case. The ascertainment of the *ratio decidendi* of a case depends upon a process of abstraction from the totality of facts that occurred in it. The higher the abstraction, the wider the *ratio decidendi*. Thus a rule that "it is a tort to tell a lie that is likely to and does cause fright and consequent physical harm" is a narrow rule, belonging to a low level of abstraction from the facts of the particular case in which it was laid down; leave out the reference to fright, and it becomes wider; replace "tell a lie" by "do any act with intent to affect the plaintiff in body or mind" and it becomes wider still. It is the last rule that is the *ratio decidendi* of *Wilkinson v Downton*. We carry on the process of abstraction until all the particular facts have been eliminated except the fact of the doing of an act that is intended to affect the plaintiff adversely and is likely to cause physical harm, and the fact of the occurrence of such harm.

How do we know when to stop with our abstraction? The answer is: primarily by reading what the judge says in the judgment, but partly also by our knowledge of the law in general, and by our common sense and our feeling for what the law ought to be. It so happens that in the case we have been considering the learned judge formulates the rule fairly clearly, but sometimes the rule stated in the judgment incorporates facts which as a matter of common sense are not essential, and sometimes it goes to the opposite extreme of being too sweeping—as can be demonstrated either by the use of common sense or by referring to other decided cases. The finding of the *ratio decidendi* is not an automatic process; it calls for lawyerly skill and knowledge.

Distinguishing

Certain general truths implicit in the foregoing discussion may now be stated more explicitly.

In the first place, a case may have not one but several *rationes deci-dendi*, of ascending degrees of generality. We have seen two or three possible *rationes* in *Wilkinson v Downton*. The third was accepted not only because it was stated by the judge but also because it accorded with common sense and with other authorities. Sometimes a judge will lay down a rule that is narrower than is required by common sense, and a later court may then say that the rule ought to be read more widely, by abandoning some limitation unnecessarily expressed in it.

Indeed, one such unnecessary limitation can be found in the judgment in *Wilkinson v Downton*. The rule stated by Wright J. refers to a person who has "wilfully" done an act calculated to cause physical harm, and the primary meaning of a "wilful" act is one that is done with the intention of bringing about a particular consequence.[8] Downton did not, perhaps, intend to cause Mrs Wilkinson a serious illness, but he did intend to frighten her, and that was sufficient. But, as a matter of common sense, the rule should be extended also to one who is merely *reckless*[9] as to the harm in question (and the word "wilful" is, indeed, capable of extending to recklessness). If Downton had made the lying statement to Mrs Wilkinson in order to persuade her to accompany him for some secret end of his own, realising that the statement would be likely to frighten her but not desiring (and therefore not intending) the fright itself, his liability should be just the same as for a tort of intention. This was the essential position in the case of the foreign servant referred to before: what the defendant intended in that case was to put pressure upon the young woman to make her talk; he must have foreseen the

---

[8] "Wilful act", or "doing an act wilfully", is a telescoped expression. In a sense, every act is wilful, or it is not an act but merely a spasm. In legal discussions, the notion of wilfulness or intention usually refers to the *consequences* of conduct; it is the consequence that is intended, or wilfully brought about, not the movement of the defendant's body that constitutes the act. Where mere movement is referred to, "intention" connotes knowledge of the circumstances.

[9] In *Secretary of State for the Home Department v Wainwright* [2001] EWCA Civ 2081; [2002] Q.B. 1334, the Court of Appeal indicated that the tort was indeed capable of commission by a "reckless" actor. The court does not elaborate upon what is meant by "recklessness" in this context. The House of Lords [2003] UKHL 53; [2004] 2 A.C. 406 agreed with the Court of Appeal that no damages were recoverable, since the facts of the case did not support a conclusion that the defendants had indeed acted "without caring" whether or not harm was caused.

possibility of causing her great distress, but his mind was directed towards making her do what he wanted, not towards distress. In analysis, the case is one of recklessness as to the plaintiff's fright, not one of intention as to the fright; but the legal liability should be, and is, the same.[10]

One may argue that there is another unnecessary limitation contained in the judgment in *Wilkinson v Downton*. The judge referred to the fact that the plaintiff had been in normal health, yet it is not only possible but probable that the decision would have been just the same even if her health had previously been poor—for the fact that the plaintiff is in poor health can be no excuse to a defendant who tells her a cruel lie that would be likely to cause her physical harm. The fact that the particular plaintiff had been in good health removed a complication that the judge might otherwise have had to consider, and for that reason the judge referred to it; but all the same a later court may, on mature consideration and when the question arises, decide that the limitation is unnecessary.

Conversely, it sometimes happens that a judge will lay down a rule that is unnecessarily wide for the decision of the case at hand; a later court may say that it is too wide, and needs to be cut down.

This point leads on to the second. The phrase "the *ratio decidendi* of a case" is slightly ambiguous. It may mean either (1) the rule that the judge who decided the case intended to lay down and apply to the facts, or (2) the rule that a later court concedes him to have had the power to lay down. The last sentence is rather clumsy, but what I mean is this. Courts do not accord to their predecessors an unlimited

---

[10] A word may here be added upon the meaning of the word "calculated", which Wright J. used in his judgment. Judges are fond of this word, but it is an unfortunate expression because it suggests a meaning which it is not intended to convey. Originally, "calculated to" bore its literal meaning of "intended to", but in time it came to mean merely "likely to", and it is in this sense that Wright J. uses it. What the learned judge means is that the defendant intended to give the plaintiff a fright (this was the "wilful act"), and what he did was likely ("calculated") to cause the injury it did, even though the defendant did not intend to cause the full degree of the injury that occurred. The judge's decision would not apply (1) if the defendant merely acted carelessly in passing on information which was not true (for then there would be no "wilful act"), or (2) if, although the defendant intentionally told a lie and intended to cause the plaintiff some slight perturbation, a reasonable man would not have foreseen that the plaintiff would be seriously upset (for then the lie would not be "calculated" to cause physical harm).

power of laying down wide rules. They are sometimes apt to say, in effect: "Oh yes, we know that in that case the learned judge purported to lay down such and such a rule; but that rule was unnecessarily wide for the decision of the case before him, because, you see, the rule makes no reference to fact A, which existed in the case, and which we regard as a material fact, and as a fact that ought to have been introduced into the *ratio decidendi*".[11] One circumstance that may induce a court to adopt this niggling attitude towards an earlier decision is the necessity of reconciling that decision with others. Or again, the court in the earlier case may have enunciated an unduly wide rule without considering all its possible consequences, some of which are unjust or inconvenient or otherwise objectionable. Yet another possibility is that the earlier decision is altogether unpalatable to the court in the later case, so that the latter court wishes to interpret it as narrowly as possible.

This process of cutting down the expressed *ratio decidendi* of a case is one kind of "distinguishing". It may be called "restrictive" distinguishing, to differentiate it from the other kind, genuine or non-restrictive distinguishing. Non-restrictive distinguishing occurs where a court accepts the expressed *ratio decidendi* of the earlier case, and does not seek to curtail it, but finds that the case before it does not fall within this *ratio decidendi* because of some material difference of fact. Restrictive distinguishing cuts down the expressed *ratio decidendi* of the earlier case by treating as material to the earlier decision some fact, present in the earlier case, which the earlier court regarded as immaterial,[12] or by introducing a qualification (exception) into the rule stated by the earlier court.

---

[11] A common form of statement is to say that the earlier judges "were speaking of, and their language must be understood by reference to, the particular facts which were brought before them in that case": 62 L.J.Ch. 126.

[12] Dr Goodhart in the article cited above, p.96, fn.4, says that (1) it is for the judge who decides the case, and for him alone, to determine what facts are material, and the judge may express his decision that facts are immaterial merely by leaving them out of the rule of law that he propounds. But on the other hand (2) the *ratio decidendi* of a case is not necessarily the rule of law stated by the judge, because that may be too wide. It seems to me that these two statements are contradictory, and the truth I take to be that the second is right and the first wrong. The rule stated by the judge may be "too wide" in the view of the later court, and that means that the judge does not have an unlimited discretion to jettison fact as being immaterial. For Dr Goodhart's reply to a controversy on this question, see (1959) 22 M.L.R. 117.

Wilkinson v Downton has not been cut down, because the wide principle has commended itself to later judges.[13] If, however, a case ever arises in which Wright J.'s wide rule is thought to carry the law too far, the decision can be restrictively distinguished.

This matter of distinguishing has been stressed because it plays a most important part in legal argument. Suppose that you are conducting a case in court, and that the other side cites a case against you. You then have only two alternatives (that is, if you are not prepared to throw your hand in altogether). One is to submit that the case cited is wrongly decided, and so should not be followed. This is possible only if the case is not binding on the court. The other is to "distinguish" it, by suggesting that it contains or lacks some vital fact that is absent or present in your client's case. Sometimes you may have the sympathy of the judge in your effort to distinguish it, even though the distinction you suggest involves tampering with the expressed *ratio decidendi* of the precedent case and even though you have no authority for the suggested distinction. Your judge may be gravely dissatisfied with the case and yet, owing to our excessively strict doctrine of precedent, it may be impossible to overrule it. In such circumstances it is simply human nature to distinguish it if possible. The judge may, in extreme and unusual circumstances, be apt to seize on almost any factual difference between this previous case and the case at hand in order to arrive at a different decision.[14] Some precedents are continually left on the shelf in this way; as a wag observed, they become very "distinguished". The limit of the process is reached when a judge says that the precedent is an authority only

---

[13] In *Khorasandjian v Bush* [1993] Q.B. 723, CA, an injunction was granted in reliance upon *Janvier v Sweeney* to prevent a person from making persistent harassing telephone calls, on the basis that it was feared that this might cause psychiatric injury. But in *Hunter v Canary Wharf* [1997] A.C. 655 the correctness of the decision was doubted by several members of the House of Lords, and the conduct complained of in that case is now the subject of legislation in the Protection from Harassment Act 1997. In *Wong v Parkside Health NHS Trust* [2001] ECWA Civ 1721, [2003] 3 All E.R. 932, the Court of Appeal confirmed that there was "nothing in *Hunter* that cast doubt upon . . . the principle in *Wilkinson v Downton*".

[14] Perhaps Pollock C.B. had restrictive distinguishing in mind when, in a letter to his grandson, "F.P.", in 1868, he made the following remark: "Even Parke, Lord Wensleydale (the greatest legal pedant that I believe ever existed) did not always follow even the House of Lords; he did not overrule—oh no! but he did not *act upon* cases which were nonsense (as many are)". Hanworth's *Lord Chief Baron Pollock* (1929), p.198.

"on its actual facts". For most practical purposes this is equivalent to announcing that it will never be followed. It is not suggested that this extreme form of distinguishing is a common occurrence, for generally judges defer to the decisions of their predecessors both in the letter and in the spirit, even though they dislike them. But restrictive distinguishing does happen, and the possibility of its happening makes it of great importance to the lawyer.

The modern significance of this line of case law has been tested recently in the Supreme Court in *O (A Child) v Rhodes*[15] in the context of an attempt to prevent the publication of a potentially damaging autobiography. A well-known concert pianist wished to publish a book which described his experiences of sexual abuse as a boy at school and its effects, and the healing effects of the music that had been his life subsequently. The language used in the book was extremely graphic, and the mother of the divorced couple's 11 year old son was worried that its publication might cause psychological and psychiatric harm to the boy, who had already been diagnosed as suffering from "Asperger's Syndrome, attention deficit hyperactivity disorder, dyspraxia and dysgraphia". It was alleged on the boy's behalf that this would constitute the tort of intentionally causing physical or psychological harm to the claimant. At first instance, the trial judge struck out the proceedings on the basis that the alleged tort did not extend beyond false or threatening words, but the Court of Appeal held that the claim should go to trial.

On the father's appeal, it was held (1) that there was no arguable case that the publication of the book would constitute the requisite conduct element of the tort and (2) that the required mental elements of the tort were not satisfied either, and the appeal was dismissed.

Analysing the earlier authorities relating to the first of these points, the Supreme Court held that the tort of intentionally causing physical or psychological harm (or wilfully infringing the right to personal safety) required words or conduct directed towards the claimant for which there was no justification or reasonable excuse. The book had been dedicated to the claimant's son, but it was also intended for a much wider audience, and the father had a right to tell his story to the world at large in the way in which he wanted to tell it. As to the second

[15] [2015] UKSC 32, [2016] A.C. 219.

point, the mental element. The tort required proof of an intention to cause physical harm or severe emotional and emotional distress, and mere recklessness would not suffice. There was no evidence that the father did so intend, and while in appropriate cases an intention could be inferred from the evidence, it was not to be imputed as a matter of law (as the Court of Appeal had held that it could be).

The decision clarifies and in certain respects restricts some of the wider rationes decidendi that have been discussed earlier. It is now clear that only intention will suffice, rather than recklessness, as had been suggested. The dimension to the decision that is missing from the earlier judgments lies in the fact that the father was exercising a right to freedom of expression, which the law is anxious to protect, especially where it is not suggested that the statements being made are untrue.

OBITER DICTUM

In contrast with the *ratio decidendi* is the *obiter dictum*. The latter is a mere saying "by the way", a chance remark, which is not binding upon future courts, though it may be respected according to the reputation of the judge, the eminence of the court, and the circumstances in which it came to be pronounced. An example would be a rule of law stated merely by way of analogy or illustration, or a suggested rule upon which the decision is not finally rested.[16] The reason for not regarding an *obiter dictum* as binding is that it was probably made without a full consideration of the cases on the point, and that, if very broad in its terms, it was probably made without a full consideration of all the consequences that may follow from it; alternatively the judge may not have expressed a concluded opinion.

---

[16] An example of this latter is to be found in the decision of the House of Lords in *R. v Howe* [1987] A.C. 417, in which the House of Lords contemplated altering the law of duress in murder to the effect that it might be treated as reducing murder to manslaughter when successfully pleaded by the person acting under duress. One possible disadvantage of that course was the decision of the Court of Appeal (Criminal Division) in *R. v Richards* [1974] Q.B. 776 holding that a secondary party to a criminal offence could not be made liable for an offence greater than that committed by the principal. The House cast doubt on *Richards* in such a way as effectively to overrule it, even though the eventual decision was that duress could never be a defence to a charge of murder. On any view of precedent, therefore, the observations could not be said to be any more than *obiter*. But in *R. (Pretty) v DPP* [2001] UKHL 61; [2002] 1 A.C. 800, at [111] it was said that *Richards* had indeed been overruled.

An example of an *obiter dictum* occurs in *Wilkinson v Downton* when the learned judge is considering the argument that the plaintiff is entitled to recover damages for the tort of deceit. At first sight this may seem a good argument, because the defendant could certainly be said in a popular sense to have deceived the plaintiff. But it is generally taken to be essential for the tort of deceit that the defendant should have intended the plaintiff to have acted on the statement, and that the plaintiff should have so acted to his detriment, for which detriment he now claims damages. Mrs Wilkinson recovered 1 shilling and 10 pence halfpenny as damages for deceit, because this was a sum of money that she had spent in reliance on the defendant's deceitful statement. But the fact that she became ill was not an act of reliance upon the statement. It was a spontaneous reaction to the statement. Consequently, the learned judge preferred not to rest his judgment upon this ground. He did not positively pronounce against it, but his words seem to indicate that he thought that as the law then stood, the claim could not properly be based on the tort of deceit. One may say, therefore, that there is a very tentative *dictum* against the plaintiff on this particular issue. But the point was not finally decided, and in any case was not made the ground of the decision, and so the observations made upon it were *obiter*.

There is another kind of *obiter dictum*, which perhaps is not, properly speaking, an *obiter dictum* at all, namely a *ratio decidendi* that in the view of a subsequent court is unnecessarily wide. It is not an *obiter dictum* in the primary meaning of that phrase, because it is constructed out of the facts of the case and the decision is rested upon it. But, as we have seen, later courts reserve the right to narrow it down, and in doing so they frequently attempt to justify themselves by declaring that the unnecessarily wide statement was *obiter*. The real justification for the practice of regarding what is really *ratio decidendi* as *obiter dictum*, that is to say for restrictive distinguishing, is the undesirability of hampering the growth of English law through the too extensive application of the doctrine of precedent. A court may restrictively distinguish its own decisions, or those of a court on the same level, but it will not generally dare to do this with the decisions of courts superior to it in the hierarchy, particularly the House of Lords or the Supreme Court.

It is frequently said that a ruling based upon hypothetical facts is *obiter*. This is often true. Thus if the judge says: "I decide for the defendant; but if the facts had been properly pleaded I should have found for the claimant", the latter part of the statement is *obiter*. But there is at least one exception. In the past, when the defendant pleaded an "objection in point of law" (a "demurrer"), legal argument might take place on this before the trial, and for the purpose of the argument and the decision it was assumed that all the facts stated in the plaintiff's pleadings were true. A decision pronounced on such assumed facts is not an *obiter dictum*.

If a decision would otherwise be a binding authority, it does not lose that status merely because the point was not argued by counsel (this will be important only as a way of attacking a decision that is of merely persuasive authority). But what is called a decision *sub silentio* is not binding: a subsequent court is not bound by a proposition of law assumed by an earlier court that was not the subject of argument before or consideration by that court.[17] This is so, at least, where the case is obvious, and where the precedent case is that of the same court. The Supreme Court would probably regard its own decision *sub silentio* as binding on the Court of Appeal.

HOW MUCH OF A CASE TO REMEMBER

A question that frequently vexes the beginner is: how many of the facts of a case should be remembered, for the purpose of learning the law and for the purpose of making a good showing in the exam? Ought the student to try to remember (1) all the facts stated in the report, or (2) a selection of those facts, or (3) only those facts that are incorporated in the statement of the *ratio decidendi*? Take again as an illustration the case of *Wilkinson v Downton*. The three possibilities just referred to are exemplified by (1) the passage from the judgment on pp.97–98, above, (2) the first attempt at condensation on pp.98–99, and (3) the statement of the *ratio decidendi* on p.101.

The answer to the question is that both (2) and (3) should be remembered. (1) is obviously ruled out; it would be a waste of effort to remember every minor circumstance that may be stated in the

---

[17] *R. v Brent Housing Board* [2001] Q.B. 955, applying *Barrs v Bethel* [1982] Ch. 294 and *Re Hetherington (dec'd)* [1990] Ch. 1.

report, such as the fact that Mr Wilkinson was alleged to be lying at The Elms at Leytonstone. On the other hand, (3) is as obviously included, for it is the pith and marrow of the law. About the necessity for remembering (2) the reader may be inclined to be argumentative. It could be contended that the student is learning to be a lawyer, not a chronicler of tragedies, and that if the rules of law are remembered, there is no need to burden the memory with the facts of cases that as a matter of history gave rise to those rules.

There are two answers to this objection, the first of interest to exam candidates only, and the second of wider interest.

The first answer is that examiners are suspicious creatures, and in particular they are suspicious of "footnote" knowledge. Suppose that in the exam your only reference to *Wilkinson v Downton* is as follows: "A person is liable in tort if he causes physical injury by an act intended to affect the plaintiff adversely and likely to cause injury: *Wilkinson v Downton*". The rule is correct and the name of the case is correct; and you may in fact have satisfied yourself that the rule is deducible from the case; but the examiner will not know it. For all the examiner knows, you saw the rule in your textbook and the name of the case in a footnote. To dispel that suspicion, you must give some statement of the concrete facts, however briefly.

The second answer is more important, but we need spend no further time over it because enough has really been said on it already. It is a mistake to suppose that every case has one and only one fixed and incontrovertible *ratio decidendi*. What exactly is the *ratio decidendi* of a case is often a matter for much argument. Also, the pick-lock art of distinguishing depends upon a critical examination of all the facts of the case that might by any possibility be regarded as material. If, therefore, there is any sort of doubt about the correctness of a decision, or about its limits, as many of the facts as can conceivably be looked upon as material should be remembered.

There are some cases, however, where nothing more than the simple *ratio decidendi* need be remembered, because apart from the facts stated in the *ratio decidendi* the case contains no facts except the trivialities of date, amount, etc. An illustration is *Byrne v Van Tienhoven*.[18] The facts of this case were as follows:

[18]   (1880) 5 C.P.D. 344.

October 1—The defendants in Cardiff by letter offered to sell to the plaintiffs 1,000 boxes of Hensol Tinplates.

October 11—The plaintiffs received this letter. The plaintiffs wired to defendants "Accept thousand Hensols". But,

October 8—The defendants posted a letter revoking their offer, ending "and we must consider our offer to be cancelled from this date".

October 20—The plaintiffs received second letter.

It was held that there was a good contract and that the defendants' revocation of their offer was ineffective.

The reason why the above facts are set out in a case book is to show the student how the legal question as to revocation of offers is likely to arise in practice. By digesting the facts and seeing how the problem arises out of them, the student is preparing to answer exam problems and to deal with cases in legal practice. But this does not mean that the student is expected to memorise any of the particular facts of *Byrne v van Tienhoven*. All the facts of this case are immaterial except the fact that the offerors attempted to revoke their offer by a letter that did not arrive until after the offerees had accepted; and the *ratio decidendi* is that such a revocation is ineffective. If this is grasped, all the rest of the facts can be forgotten.

DIVERGENT OPINIONS

The establishment of the *ratio decidendi* is more complicated when different members of a composite court express different opinions. The problem is particularly acute for the decisions of the House of Lords and the Supreme Court, where the members not uncommonly express separate opinions, which may show great diversity. As a result, their Lordships not infrequently make the law more uncertain than it was before the appeal. Conscious of this difficulty the Court of Appeal (particularly the Criminal Division) tends to deliver one judgment as being the judgment of the court.

Where the opinions of different judges differ so greatly that there is no majority for any single view, all that can be done, to ascertain the *ratio decidendi*, is to add up the facts regarded as material by any group of judges whose votes constitute a majority, and to base the *ratio* on those facts. The result is to confine the *ratio* to its narrowest form. For example, if Justices L and M hold that the material facts are A and B while Justices N and O hold that they are A, B and C, and Justice P dissents, the *ratio decidendi* must require the presence of A, B and C. It seems, however, that the confusion of opinion may be such that there cannot be said to be a *ratio decidendi*. This is so where, of the three majority Justices, Justice L holds that the material facts are A and B, Justice M holds that they are A and C, and Justice N holds that they are A and D, while Justices O and P dissent. It would be wholly artificial to say that *the ratio* requires the presence of A, B, C and D, since this is not the view of any one of the Justices.[19]

Further complications can arise. The minority Justices, O and P, may agree with Justice L in thinking that if the facts were A and B the conclusion would be X, but they may hold that there is insufficient evidence that fact B existed, and for this reason conclude that the answer in this case is not X. So on the abstract point of law there is a majority of the Court (L, O and P) in favour of L's view. Yet, strictly speaking, the expressions of opinion by O and P are *obiter*. All that can be said is that the joint opinion of L, O and P will carry great weight with lower courts, even though it is not binding.

THE HIERARCHY OF AUTHORITY

More important than the name of the case is the rank of the court in which it was decided. To mention the court that decided a case is a mark of awareness of the doctrine of precedent, with its hierarchy of authority. The rule is that every court binds lower courts[20] and

---

[19] See Sir Rupert Cross in "The *Ratio Decidendi* and a Plurality of Speeches in the House of Lords" (1977) 93 L.Q. R. 378. He took the view that the opinion of a majority of the majority can be controlling, even though it is a minority of the whole House (see p.381); *sed quaere*.

[20] *Broome v Cassell & Co Ltd* [1972] A.C. 1027. But it seems that, exceptionally, the decision of the Crown Court in the exercise of its appellate jurisdiction will not be a binding precedent for magistrates' courts in other cases: see (1976) 140 J.P.N. 242. It has been argued by A.J. Ashworth [1980] Crim. L.R. 402 that the absence of any systematic reporting system for Crown Court decisions means that the ordinary rules of precedent are inapplicable to decisions of that court. Although it is not absolutely clear whether a ruling on a point of law made by a judge sitting in the Crown Court with a jury is binding on magistrates' courts (for example), the better view would therefore seem to be that it is of persuasive force only.

that some courts bind even themselves. Whether a court is "lower" depends not only on whether an appeal lies from it to the other court but, additionally, on whether the latter court is inherently higher in rank. Thus a Divisional Court of the High Court exercising its appellate jurisdiction from magistrates regards itself as bound by decisions of the Court of Appeal even though the further appeal in these cases goes not to the Court of Appeal but direct to the Supreme Court.[21] When the appellate court reverses or overrules a case in the court below, the case so reversed or overruled loses all authority on the particular point of law upon which it is reversed. *Reversal* is when the same case is decided the other way on appeal; *overruling* is when a case in a lower court is considered in a different case taken on appeal, and held to be wrongly decided.

Precedent in the House of Lords and Supreme Court

In 1966 the House of Lords declared (departing from its previous practice) that it would not be bound by its own decisions where too rigid adherence to precedent may lead to injustice in a particular case and also unduly restrict the proper development of the law.[22] Their Lordships are still disinclined to exercise their freedom to treat earlier authorities as being no more than persuasive, taking the view that the mere fact that a later panel believes an earlier decision to have been "wrong" is not an adequate reason to depart from that earlier decision. In *R. v Kansal (No.2)*,[23] for example, the House declined by a majority of four to one to depart from a case decided some six months previously, even though they thought, by a three to two majority, that the previous decision was wrong ("plainly erroneous" as Lord Lloyd put it).

It is probably true to say that the grounds upon which the House of Lords (and the Supreme Court)[24] will act are constantly under

---

[21] See Sir Rupert Cross, *Precedent in English Law* (4th edn, 1991), p.121.

[22] *Practice Statement (Judicial Precedent)* [1966] 1 W.L.R. 1234. On the day after the declaration, Osbert Lancaster's cartoon in the *Daily Express* portrayed one Law Lord saying to another: "I say, Uptort, I can't get used to the fact that we can ever have been wrong".

[23] [2001] UKHL 62; [2002] 2 A.C. 69.

[24] In *Austin v Mayor and Burgesses of the London Borough of Southwark* [2010] UKSC 28, [2011] 1 A.C. 355, the Supreme Court noted that it had "not thought it necessary to

revision; the *Practice Statement* itself recognised "the danger of disturbing retrospectively the basis on which contracts, settlements of property and fiscal arrangements have been entered into and also the especial need for certainty in the criminal law". In *Kansal*, reference was made to the jurisprudence of the United States Supreme Court on the subject of departing from its own previous decisions. There it has been said that if the courts were to eye each issue afresh in every case, there was a danger that the judiciary will be seen as little different from the executive and the legislature, and this would be ultimately damaging to the rule of law. This possibility is even more acute in the House of Lords and Supreme Court, since appeal panels in the Supreme Court usually consist of a membership of five, whereas in the United States all members of the court sit in all cases. It would not be at all unlikely, therefore, that differences of view could arise from one case to the next merely because of a change in the composition of the court. Lord Hope in the minority in *Kansal* considered that not only was the previous decision wrong, but he took the view that the sooner error was expunged from the system the better.

The House does not need to refer to or rely upon the *Practice Statement* to depart from its previous decisions. A situation where the power might have been employed, but was not apparently considered by any of their Lordships, was in *Arthur J.S. Hall v Simons*,[25] where the House (consisting of a panel of seven) declined to follow *Rondel v Worsley*,[26] and held that advocates are no longer immune from suit for the negligent conduct of legal proceedings. This was done without reference to the *Practice Statement*, and the decision can be explained on the basis that the earlier decision was not wrong, but that the circumstances had changed since that decision to such an extent that it was no longer appropriate to follow it.

A rare example of the use of the power is to be found in *Murphy v Brentwood DC*,[27] where the House (of seven members) overruled the

re-issue the Practice Statement as a fresh statement of practice in the Court's own name. This is because it has as much effect in that Court as it did before the Appellate Committee in the House of Lords" at [24], *per* Lord Hope.

[25] [2002] 1 A.C. 615.
[26] [1969] 1 A.C. 191.
[27] [1991] 1 A.C. 398.

decision in *Anns v Merton*.[28] The latter decision was much criticised both by commentators and by members of the House itself in a series of decisions which did not, however, find it necessary to overrule the decision. In *R. v National Insurance Commissioner, ex p. Hudson*[29] their Lordships announced that they would not normally reconsider their own decisions on the construction of a statute. But in *Shivpuri*,[30] the House did precisely that, overruling its own decision in *Anderton v Ryan*[31] on the basis that the Law Commission Report preceding the Criminal Attempts Act 1981 had not been considered on the previous occasion. Similarly in the most celebrated recent use of the power in criminal cases is to be found in *G and R*,[32] in which the House over-ruled the decision in *Caldwell*[33] saying that the interpretation of the Criminal Damage Act 1971 there adopted had been shown to be a "misinterpretation". Their Lordships have proved to be less inhibited when sitting as the Privy Council, which is also not bound by its own previous decisions.[34]

Although the English courts will normally follow Strasbourg juris-prudence, the statutory obligation under the Human Rights Act 1998, s.2 is merely to take this "into account". The area is one of some political controversy, since the Human Rights Act is frequently criti-cised in the press as being the product of a European system that fails to appreciate the nuances of United Kingdom law. The Supreme Court has held that if a court is satisfied that the Strasbourg Court has misun-derstood English law or procedure, it can prefer the national authori-ties, and must prefer a decision of the Supreme Court itself to a decision of the European Court[35] Matters came to something of a head in *Al-Khawaja and Tahery v United Kingdom*,[36] where the Supreme Court had interpreted the relevant legislation in a manner that apparently conflicted with the Strasbourg jurisprudence. The Grand Chamber of the European Court of Human Rights held that in one of the two cases

---

[28] [1978] A.C. 398.
[29] [1972] A.C. 944.
[30] [1987] A.C. 1.
[31] [1985] A.C. 560.
[32] [2003] UKHL 50; [2004] 1 A.C. 1034.
[33] [1982] A.C. 341.
[34] See *Lewis v Att.-Gen. of Jamaica* [2001] 2 A.C. 50.
[35] See *R v Horncastle* [2010] UKSC 14, [2010] A.C. 373.
[36] 26766/05, (2012) 54 E.H.R.R. 107.

before it, there had been a violation of the defendant's rights, but it modified its position as to the scope of the applicable law as a result of the views expressed by the Supreme Court in *Horncastle*,[37] making the point that its jurisdiction was a supervisory one, the application of national laws being a matter for the local jurisdiction.[38]

Court of Appeal

The Court of Appeal generally binds itself, both on the civil and on the criminal sides. There has been a steady stream of criticism by writers of this "autolimitation" of the court, at any rate in civil cases, for when a decision of the Court of Appeal is plainly wrong, it seems absurd that the parties should be put to the expense of a further appeal to a superior court in order to get it set aside.[39] When an appellant perceives that there is no chance of success in the Court of Appeal because a precedent stands in the way, it will save money if leave can be obtained to use the "leapfrogging" procedure referred to earlier, and go direct to the Supreme Court.

In certain exceptional cases it is recognised that the Court of Appeal can refuse to follow one of its own previous decisions.[40] Although the precise scope of the exceptions is not fully agreed, it is generally thought that they are mainly as follows.

(1)   Where, by inadvertence or otherwise, the court arrives at inconsistent decisions, a later court must necessarily choose between them. It is not bound to follow either the earlier or the later.

(2)   The court is bound to refuse to follow its earlier decision that has been overruled by the House of Lords or Supreme Court,

---

[37] The position has been summarised in *R v Riat* [2012] EWCA Crim 1509, [2013] 1 Cr. App R. 2 which lays the particular issues to rest for the time being. But it may be expected that there will be disagreements between the two jurisdictions in the future as to the appropriate application of the relevant law.

[38] See generally M. Amos, "The Dialogue between United Kingdom courts and the European Court of Human Rights" (2012) I.C.L.Q. 557.

[39] The arguments for the autolimitation rule are ably demolished by C. Rickett, "Precedent in the Court of Appeal" (1980) 43 M.L.R. 136.

[40] *Young v Bristol Aeroplane Co Ltd* [1944] K.B. 718. Applied most recently in *Patel v Secretary of State for the Home Department* [2012] EWCA Civ 741.

or that cannot stand with a later decision of the House or Court (i.e. has been impliedly overruled).

(3) It need not follow its own decision given *per incuriam* (by oversight), as where a relevant statute was not considered, or was misconstrued because the court overlooked part of its provisions or arrived at a conclusion plainly contrary to the intention of the statute as a whole. In other words it must be clear that the earlier decision was mistaken and wrong—it is not enough merely that the later court would have decided the matter differently.[41] Presumably another example would be where a relevant decision of the Supreme Court or House of Lords was not considered.[42]

(4) It is also arguable that a special rule applies to the Criminal Division of the Court of Appeal. The court (in practice sitting as a "full court" of five judges instead of the usual three) can refuse to follow and in effect overrule its own prior decision rendered against the defendant in the precedent case (or the similar decision of the older courts that this court has superseded).[43] In practice, however, it almost never does so. The court is supposed to be bound by its own decisions rendered in favour of the defendant on a point of substantive law.

Involvement with the European jurisprudence has added a fifth, which is that

(5) Where the Court of Appeal considers that one of its own decisions is inconsistent with a subsequent decision of the European Court of Human Rights, it is free (but not obliged) to depart from that decision.[44]

---

[41] See Lord Donaldson M.R. in *Duke v Reliance Systems Ltd* [1988] 1 Q.B. 108 at 113.
[42] *Dixon v BBC* [1979] Q.B. 546. See generally on *per incuriam*, P. Wesley-Smith, "The Per Incuriam Doctrine" (1980) 15 J.S.P.T.L 58.
[43] *R. v Gould* [l968] 2 Q.B. 65. See G. Zellick, "Precedent in the Court of Appeal Criminal Division" [1974] Crim.L.R. 222, and R. Pattenden, "The Power of the Criminal Division of the Court of Appeal to Depart from Its Own Precedents" [1984] Crim. L.R. 592. In *R. v Spencer* [1985] Q.B. 771, the Criminal Division took the view that there was no difference between itself and the Civil Division, except that when the liberty of the subject was involved, it might decline to follow one of its own decisions.
[44] *R (RJM) v Secretary of State for Work and Pensions (Equality and Human Rights Commission intervening)* [2008] UKHL 63, [2009] 1 A.C. 311.

In addition to these four main exceptions, the court has shown a disposition to add to them whenever it feels a strong need to throw off the authority of its own precedent. So the court has held that it need not follow its own decision when it was inconsistent with a later pronouncement of the Privy Council,[45] or when it was the decision of a court of two relating to an interlocutory matter (a point of procedure arising before trial).[46] These pronouncements were not the result of any logical compulsion; they were merely ways of getting rid of particular precedents that now irked the court.

For several years Lord Denning M.R. (who was Master of the Rolls from 1962 until 1982) spoke in the Court of Appeal (Civil Division) in favour of a general freedom from the court's own past decisions when they subsequently appeared to be clearly wrong. These expressions of opinion culminated in *Davis v Johnson*,[47] where the court had to consider two of its own previous decisions restrictively interpreting a recent statute passed for the purpose of protecting a woman who was attacked by the man with whom she was living, whether or not she was married to him. The restrictive interpretations had been severely criticised in the press, and the Court of Appeal, sitting as a court of five, was evidently anxious to disembarrass itself of them. A bare majority of the court decided that it was free to do so. Lord Denning gave his accustomed reason that the court was not bound by its own decisions. Sir George Baker, President of the Family Division, concurred in the result but assigned a narrower reason:

"The court is not bound to follow a previous decision of its own if satisfied that that decision was clearly wrong and cannot stand in the face of the will and intention of Parliament expressed in simple language in a recent statute passed to remedy a serious mischief or abuse, and further adherence to the previous decision must lead

---

[45] Sir Rupert Cross, *Precedent in English Law* (4th edn, 1991), p.102, fn.2. Indeed in *James* [2006] EWCA Crim 14, [2006] Q.B. 558 the five judges of the Court of Appeal declined to follow a decision of the House of Lords in *Smith (Morgan)* [2001] 1 A.C. 146 in favour of a decision of the Privy Council in *Att.-Gen. for Jersey v Holley* [2005] UKPC 23; [2005] 2 A.C. 580, on the grounds that in that case nine current members of the House of Lords had agreed that their decision in the Privy Council case clarified definitively the state of English law on the particular issue in question.

[46] *Boys v Chaplin* [1968] 2 Q.B. 1.

[47] [1979] A.C. 264.

to injustice in the particular case and unduly restrict the proper development of the law with injustice to others."

Judges who make up exceptions in this way are in effect throwing off the compulsive force of precedent, and it would be more convenient to say so. In form, however, the decision of the Court of Appeal merely adds one more exception to the general rule, though there was no agreement on its wording. On further appeal, all the Law Lords expressed the decided opinion that the Court of Appeal was (exceptions apart) bound by its own decisions. The practical effect of denying the Court of Appeal the power to correct its own errors is to force a further appeal to the Supreme Court, with its attendant delay and expense.

When it appears that counsel may wish to ask the Court of Appeal not to follow its own previous decision on one of these grounds, the court may be arranged to sit with five or more members (the so-called "full court") instead of the usual three,[48] though it must be said that this practice is extremely rare.

The exceptional rules freeing the Court of Appeal from the authority of its own previous decisions do not operate to free it from the authority of the House of Lords or the Supreme Court. Their Lordships (members of the Supreme Court) are likely to take it amiss if the Court of Appeal announces that a decision of the higher court was *per incuriam*. On one occasion when the Court of Appeal did this and a further appeal was taken to the House of Lords, their Lordships expressed strong disapproval. They regarded the action of the lower court, in the words of Lord Denning (speaking subsequently in the Court of Appeal), "as a piece of *lèse-majesté*. The House of Lords never does anything *per incuriam*."[49] For a time thereafter, the position was that if the House decided a case in ignorance of a previous decision of its own going the other way, the Court of Appeal would nevertheless regard itself as bound to follow the later of the two

---

[48] But this is not essential. For example, *R. v Gould* [1968] 2 Q.B. 65 was decided by a court of three, which declined to follow an earlier decision of the Court of Criminal Appeal rendered against the defendant. In *Simpson* [2003] EWCA Crim 1499; [2004] Q.B. 118, the Court of Appeal said that the constitution of the court was relevant to the exercise of the discretion of the court not to follow an earlier decision.

[49] *Fellowes & Son v Fisher* [1976] Q.B. 132 E.

decisions.[50] So the law will remain uncertain until a litigant who has ample private means or who can call on the legal aid fund takes the point to the Supreme Court for reconsideration.

Attitudes may have softened subsequently; in *I.M. Properties v Cape & Dalgleish*,[51] the Court of Appeal refused to follow the House of Lords in *Westdeutsche Llandesbank Girozenstrale v Islington LBC*[52] on the grounds that an earlier and contradictory decision of the House[53] had not been considered and was therefore on the central point *per incuriam*. On this occasion, not only did the House not take exception—it refused leave to appeal. Some years after this, it explicitly decided not to follow the earlier decision.[54] It appears, therefore, that when there are conflicting decisions of the House of Lords or the Supreme Court, and the later judgment has been delivered without any reference to the former, the Court of Appeal is at liberty to say that it prefers the earlier reasoning.

Divisional Court

Turning to the Divisional Court; its decisions are binding precedents for magistrates' courts in other cases. The Divisional Court used formerly to be regarded as binding itself.[55] In *R. v Greater Manchester Coroner, ex p. Tal*,[56] however, it was decided that (as is the case with the High Court) it was not bound, but would follow the decision of another judge unless convinced that this was wrong, except that it will presumably exercise the same freedom in criminal cases as the Court of Appeal. Presumably the Divisional Court binds judges and recorders when the latter hear appeals from magistrates' courts, because the Divisional Court is superior in the hierarchy—as was said before, a further appeal can be brought from the Crown Court to the Divisional Court.

---

[50] *Fellowes & Son v Fisher* [1976] Q.B. 132 E; *Miliangos v Frank (Textiles) Ltd* [1976] A.C. 443 at 476–479. See also *Moodie v Inland Revenue Commissioners* [1993] 1 W.L.R. 266.

[51] [1999] Q.B. 297.

[52] [1996] A.C. 669.

[53] *President of India v La Pintada Compania Navigacion SA* [1985] A.C. 104.

[54] *Sempra Metals Ltd v Inland Revenue Commissioners* [2008] 1 A.C. 561.

[55] *Huddersfield Police Authority v Watson* [1947] K.B. 842.

[56] [1985] Q.B. 67.

However, the Divisional Court does not bind Crown Court judges who try cases with juries.[57] The Crown Court is a branch of the Senior Court having equal status with the High Court,[58] and therefore with a Divisional Court of the High Court. It makes no difference that only one judge sits in the Crown Court while two or more sit in the Divisional Court.[59]

Single judges of the High Court trying civil cases bind inferior courts (county courts, and magistrates' courts in their civil jurisdiction), but they do not absolutely bind other High Court judges.[60] One such judge may refuse to follow another judge, and the result will be a conflict of authority that will one day have to be settled by the Court of Appeal. In other words, a High Court judge cannot overrule a judicial colleague, but can only "disapprove" the decision and "not follow" it. Refusal to follow is, however, rare.

Decisions of courts inferior to the High Court do not bind anybody, not even themselves. In legal theory decisions of the Judicial Committee of the Privy Council do not bind English courts, nor even the Judicial Committee itself. But they have great "persuasive" authority.[61]

My suggestion is that the student should try to remember when a case belongs to the Supreme Court, the House of Lords, the Court of Appeal (or in very rare cases its predecessors the Court of Exchequer Chamber, the Court of Appeal in Chancery, the Court for Crown Cases Reserved, and the Court of Criminal Appeal), or the Privy Council. Since the student cannot be expected to remember everything, it is usually permissible to forget the exact court that decided cases of authority inferior to these. Nothing is gained by trying to distinguish between the three common law courts (King's Bench, Common Pleas,

---

[57] *R. v Colyer* [1974] Crim.L.R. 243.

[58] Supreme Court Act 1981, s.1. Until 2009, the higher courts were known collectively as members of the Supreme Court, but with the creation of a new Supreme Court, a change of nomenclature was required, and the expression "senior court" was chosen in the Constitutional Reform Act 2005.

[59] For other problems relating to the Crown Court, see A.J. Ashworth [1980] Crim. L.R. 402.

[60] Including Deputy High Court judges: *Howard de Walden Estates v Aggio* [2008] Ch 26.

[61] The Privy Council is not itself bound by English cases, and it has made it clear that the jurisdictions from which it hears appeals are free to develop the common law along different lines from English law; see *Invercargill City Council v Hamlin* [1996] A.C. 624.

Exchequer) before 1875, or the various branches of the High Court today. Also, it should be noted that a particular decision was simply that of a judge given by way of direction to a jury. Such decisions are of inferior authority, largely because in a jury trial questions of law are unlikely to have been fully debated. It is very rare to report these directions to a jury, though, as Pollock says, "many of the older ones have become good authority by subsequent approval, and some of them are the only definite reported authority for points of law now received as not only settled but elementary".[62] It may be added that directions to a jury have been more important in criminal than in civil law, because there used to be no appeal from a jury verdict of not guilty, and thus if on a particular point of law judges were in the habit of directing the jury in the defendant's favour the appeal court may have had no opportunity to pronounce upon it. Since 1972 the Attorney-General may refer an acquittal for the opinion of the appellate courts to clarify the law which is regarded as unsatisfactory, but this does not affect the particular defendant.[63]

A word may be said about international law. In studying this subject the student will be expected to know the more important decisions of international and municipal (i.e. national) tribunals. Always distinguish between the two, for the pronouncement of an international court is generally more authoritative for other international tribunals on a matter of international law than that of a merely national body. (But the decision of a municipal court may be more authoritative for other courts of the same state).

CIRCUMSTANCES AFFECTING THE WEIGHT OF A DECISION

The good lawyer will often make a mental note of some circumstances that go to increase or diminish the authority of a case.

Among the circumstances adding to its authority are: the eminence of the particular judge or judges who decided it; the large number of judges who took part in it; and the fact that the judgment was a

---

[62] *First Book of Jurisprudence* (6th edn, 1929), p.348. The old *nisi prius* cases are reprinted in Vols 170–176 of the *English Reports*.

[63] Criminal Justice Act 1972, s.36.

"reserved" one, i.e. not delivered on the spur of the moment. (This last is indicated in the report, at the end of the arguments of counsel, by the letters C.A.V., or words *Curia advisari vult.*—the court wishes to be advised.) Naturally, a case is reinforced if it has been frequently followed, or has created expectations in commercial or proprietary matters. Some say that any decision of long standing is unlikely to be disturbed[64]; on the other hand, it may be hard to persuade a court to depart from its own precedent established only a few years before, for that would look like vacillation.[65] So this can be "Catch 22" for a party seeking to challenge a decision.

Among the circumstances detracting from the authority of a case are: the presence of strong dissenting judgments; the fact that the majority do not agree in their reasoning but only in the result; the failure of counsel to cite an inconsistent case in argument; the disapproval of the profession including academic writings; and the fact that the case was taken on appeal and that the appeal went off on another point.

These circumstances have no importance if the case is absolutely binding on the court before which it is cited and if it is incapable of being distinguished. But they are of great importance if the case is not absolutely binding, or if on the facts of the later case it is capable of being distinguished or extended at the pleasure of the court.

JUDICIAL LAW-MAKING

Rules of precedent instruct judges that they are or are not bound to decide the case before them in a particular way. The rules do not tell the judge what principles to act upon when the situation is unconstrained by authority, for example when faced by a precedent in a lower court which is not binding. The judge then has to choose between notions of justice, convenience, public policy, morality, analogy, and so on, perhaps taking into account the opinions of other judges (in American, Canadian, Australian and Scottish cases, for instance) or of writers. The various considerations may not point in the same direction, but conflict with each other.

---

[64] *per* Lord Simon in *Farrell v Alexander* [1977] A.C. 59 at 90G.
[65] *cf. DPP v Nock* [1978] A.C. 979 at 997E. This was the problem for the appellant in *Kansal*, discussed at p.113 above.

Judges do not generally dwell upon the fact that they make law; but they no longer hide behind the "fairy tale" (as Lord Reid once termed it) that the common law is a miraculous something existing from eternity and not made by anyone. They would much prefer to put it in terms of the so-called "declaratory theory" which recognises that it may be necessary for the law to change. As Lord Hobhouse put it[66]:

"The common law develops as circumstances change and the balance of legal, social, and economic needs changes. New concepts come into play; new statutes influence the non-statutory law. The strength of the common law is its ability to develop and evolve. All this carries with it the inevitable need to recognise that decisions may change. What was previously thought to be the law is open to challenge and review; if the challenge is successful, a new statement of the law will take the place of the old statement."

With increasing frequency, judges do consider (and are constrained by) such matters as the rights articulated in the Human Rights Act 1998 or the ideals to be found in international conventions and treaties. One consequence is that the modern judges more readily consider the principles on which they should act in deciding whether or not to introduce a change. But there are clearly permissible limits to their law-making powers—at the end of the day, they are judges and not legislators. In the criminal law sphere, for example, the House of Lords has offered the following guidance to the judges[67]:

"(1) if the solution is doubtful, the judges should beware of imposing their own remedy; (2) caution should prevail if Parliament has rejected opportunities of clearing up a known difficulty or has legislated while leaving the difficulty untouched; (3) disputed matters of social policy are less suitable areas for judicial intervention than purely legal problems; (4) fundamental legal doctrines should not lightly be set aside; (5) judges should not make change unless they can achieve finality and certainty."

---

[66] *R. v Governor of Brockhill Prison, ex p. Evans (No.2)* [2001] 2 A.C. 19 at 48.
[67] *C v DPP* [1996] 1 A.C. 1 at 28.

One generalisation can be made. The judge has to balance two opposing needs in the law: the need for stability and certainty and the need for change. It would obviously be going too far to say that a judge can scrap or alter any established rule whenever the rule appears objectionable. The judge, even when free from binding authority, must take account of people's understanding of what the law is—as when they make contracts, or insure against liability. But not all judicial legislation defeats expectations. For example, a judgment restricting the area of liability does not do so (except to the extent that it defeats the claimant/prosecutor's expectation of succeeding in the particular proceedings). Again, the law of procedure and evidence does not create expectations in the ordinary citizen, and the judges are for this reason more prepared to exercise their creative powers more readily in this sphere.

Lawyers are rather prone to assume that what has been decided cannot be upset. It often happens that a plainly wrong decision is given at first instance or even by the Court of Appeal, which is followed unquestioningly for many years because counsel do not advise their clients to take the point further on appeal. When, eventually, some counsel is found who has the courage and acumen to take the point, the precedent is reversed. As the House of Lords has decided that it can question its own previous decisions, there is hardly any decided point that cannot be reopened if the arguments against it are strong enough.[68]

FURTHER READING

On precedent and the judicial function, Michael Zander's *The Law-Making Process* (7th edn, 2015), Chapters 4, 6 and 7 may be warmly recommended. See also Manchester, Salter, *Exploring the Law: The Dynamics of Precedent and Statutory Interpretation* (4th edn, 2011) and J.A. Holland and J.S. Webb, *Learning Legal Rules* (9th edn, 2016).

---

[68] e.g. *R. v Gould* [1968] 2 Q.B. 65. In *R. v Taylor* [1950] 2 K.B. 368 counsel had allowed his client to plead guilty on the strength of a decision in an earlier case notwithstanding that it was plainly erroneous. An appeal was taken against the sentence only, but, on being informed of the facts and of the earlier decision, the Court of Criminal Appeal was so surprised that it allowed the appeal to be converted into an appeal against conviction; it then allowed the appeal and overruled the precedent.

7 THE INTERPRETATION OF STATUTES

> "The golden rule is that there are no golden rules."[1]
>
> —G.B. Shaw, *Man and Superman.*

Modern pressures upon the syllabus are such that the subject of the legislative process and statutory interpretation is rarely taught in law schools other than as a small part of an English Legal System or similar course. Yet statutes, Acts of Parliament and secondary legislation are unquestionably the most important source of the law, and I hope that even that degree of exposure will persuade you of the importance of this facet of the law. A practitioner with any pretension to legal learning should certainly know the lines of argument that may be open on the reading of a statute; as Lord Steyn observed, "the preponderance of enacted law over common law is increasing year by year, . . . and the subject of interpretation has moved to the centre of the legal stage" [2] and most cases in the law reports turn on disputed points of statutory interpretation.

What follows is intended largely to show how the complex business of extracting precise meanings from an apparently simple set of words is assisted by certain practices and understandings. It will be seen that there are certain principles at work, and various presumptions that have a bearing on the task. Parliament has recently affected

---

[1] Shaw's aphorism has been elaborated upon in the context of statutory interpretation by Francis Bennion: "Alas, . . . there is no golden rule. Nor is there a mischief rule, or a literal rule or any other cure-all rule of thumb. Instead, there are a thousand and one interpretative *criteria*" (1997) 147 New L.J. 684. Bennion refers the reader to his own excellent monograph, *Statutory Interpretation* (now *Bennion on Statutory Interpretation* (6th edn, 2013) plus supplements, for an elaboration of the point. Whilst I do not dissent from Mr Bennion's stance, I take the view that the student might nevertheless benefit from considering the difficulties inherent in the apparently straightforward tasks of interpretation and that the three "rules" (discussed below) afford a framework for discussion, not a "cure-all" for decision-making.

[2] *"Pepper v Hart*; a Re-examination" (2001) 21 O.J.L.S. 59.

the process by enacting s.3 of the Human Rights Act 1988, which considerably alters the traditional role of the courts in this respect.[3]

THE STRUCTURE OF A STATUTE

A few words first about the structure of a statute. An Act of Parliament consists of a number of parts; there is the short title, the long title, the date of Royal assent, the enacting formula, the sections and subsections, marginal notes, the citation, the extent (territorial) and the commencement. In addition you will normally find definition sections, savings and repeals and (at the end of the Act), the schedules. Not all of these are of equal significance as indicators of the meaning of the statute. There is a good deal of ancient learning about the matter, but the essential distinction is that some of these features are the enacting parts of the statutes (which can be considered and amended by Parliament), whereas the others (the cross-headings, the side-notes or marginal notes and the punctuation) are regarded as being of less significance since they do not enact anything.[4] It seems likely, however, that a court post *Pepper v Hart*[5] would permit some use to be made of them if they shed light on the meaning of the Act. Indeed, in *Calley v Gray*,[6] the Court of Appeal acknowledged that it had derived considerable assistance from the explanatory notes by which the statute under construction was accompanied when it was first introduced into Parliament, notwithstanding that the notes specifically state that "they do not form part of the Bill and have not been endorsed by Parliament".

THE IMPORTANCE OF CONTEXT

When Parliament has passed an Act the words of the Act are authoritative as words. In ordinary life, if someone says something that you

---

[3] Further discussed below, p.146.

[4] Affirmed by the House of Lords in *Montila* [2004] UKHL 50; [2004] 1 W.L.R. 3141.

[5] [1993] A.C. 593. The significance of the point will become apparent when readers have considered the section dealing with that case at p.138 below.

[6] [2001] 1 W.L.R. 2124. See also Lord Hope in *R. v A (No.2)* [2001] UKHL 25 at [82]; [2001] 1 A.C. 45 who took the view that such recourse was permissible. On the use of "explanatory notes" see R. Munday [2005] Crim. L.R. 337.

do not understand, you ask for a fuller explanation. This is impossible with the interpretation of statutes, because only the words of the statute have passed through the legal machinery of law-making, and individual Members of Parliament cannot be put into the witness-box to supplement or interpret what has been formally enacted. Hence the words of an Act carry a sort of disembodied or dehumanised meaning: not necessarily the meaning intended by any actual person in particular, but the meaning that is conventionally attached to such words. The point must not be pressed too far, since the statute obviously has a broad purpose (or, to speak more precisely, those who collaborated in framing and passing the statute had a broad purpose) which is expressed in the words.

The most important rules[7] for the interpretation (otherwise called construction) of statutes are those suggested by common sense. The judge may look up the meaning of a word in a dictionary or technical work; but this ordinary meaning may be controlled by the particular context. As everyone knows who has translated from a foreign language, it is no excuse for a bad translation that the meaning chosen was found in the dictionary; for the document may be its own dictionary, showing an intention to use words in some special shade of meaning. This rule, requiring regard to be had to the context, is sometimes expressed in the Latin maxim *noscitur a sociis*, which Henry Fielding translated: a word may be known by the company it keeps. One may look not only at the rest of the section in which the word appears but at the statute as a whole, and even at earlier legislation dealing with the same subject-matter—for it is assumed that when Parliament passed an Act, it probably had the earlier legislation in mind, and probably intended to use words with the same meaning as before.[8] However, words need not always have a consistent meaning attributed to them: the context may show that the same word bears two different senses even when it is repeated in the same section.[9]

---

[7] The word "principles" would capture the function of these guides to interpretation more accurately than the term "rules", since principles (unlike rules) are not determinative of the particular issue to which they are applied—they act as guides.

[8] Maxwell, *Interpretation of Statutes* (12th edn, 1969), pp.64 *et seq.*

[9] *R. v Allen* (1872) 1 C.C.R. at 374; *West Midlands Joint Electricity Authority v Pitt* [1932] 2 K.B. 1 at 46.

Formerly, the rule permitting recourse to earlier statutes was taken to allow the court to compare the wording of a consolidation Act with the Acts that it superseded, and to conclude that variation of wording indicated a change of meaning. But this tended to defeat the object of consolidation, which was to supersede a jumble of Acts of various dates by a single statute. Consolidation would be little help if one still had to look at the old repealed Acts in order to interpret the new one. Consequently, the rule laid down by the House of Lords is that where in construing a consolidation Act:

> "the actual words are clear and unambiguous it is not permissible to have recourse to the corresponding provisions in the earlier statute repealed by the consolidation Act and to treat any difference in their wording as capable of casting doubt upon what is clear and unambiguous language in the consolidation Act itself."[10]

DEFINITION SECTIONS

In reading a statute, always look for a definition section, assigning special meanings to some of the words in the statute. Parliamentary counsel adopt the inconsiderate practice of not telling you (for example, in a footnote or marginal note) that a particular word in the section is defined somewhere else in the statute; you have to ferret out the information for yourself. In addition to the interpretation section in the statute, the Interpretation Act 1978 operates as a standing legal dictionary of some of the most important words used in legislation. This Act declares, among other things, that the plural includes the singular, and the singular the plural, unless a contrary intention appears. Also, by virtue of the Act, if not independently of it, "words importing the feminine gender include the masculine", and *vice versa*. These special meanings are duly noticed in the various annotations of statutes, such as *Halsbury's Statutes* and *Current Law Statutes*, but not in the official versions of the statutes.

---

[10] *per* Lord Diplock in *Commissioner of Police of the Metropolis v Curran* [1976] 1 W.L.R. 87 at 90H–91A; [1976] 1 All E.R. 162 at 165b, reaffirmed by a majority of the Lords in *Farrell v Alexander* [1977] A.C. 59; see the reservations by Lord Simon at 84.

INTERPRETATION IN THE LIGHT OF POLICY: FRINGE MEANING

When interpreting statutes the courts often announce that they are trying to discover "the intention of the legislature".[11] In actual fact, if a court finds it hard to know whether a particular situation comes within the words of a statute or not, the probability is the situation was not foreseen by the legislature, so that the Lords and Members of Parliament would be just as puzzled by it as the judges are. Here, the "intention of the legislature" is a fiction.

Because of this difficulty, some deny that the courts are really concerned with the intention of Parliament.

"In the construction of written documents including statutes, what the court is concerned to ascertain is, not what the promulgators of the instruments meant to say, but the meaning of what they have said."[12]

Others, however, think it proper to speak of the intention of Parliament, in the sense of "the meaning which Parliament must have intended the words to convey".[13] In case of doubt the court has to guess what meaning Parliament would have picked on if it had thought of the point. The intention is not actual but hypothetical.[14] There is, of course, a limit to what a court can do by way of filling out a statute, but to some extent this is possible.

An illustration is the familiar legal problem of "fringe meaning". The words we use, though they have a central core of meaning that

---

[11] Lord Steyn in the House of Lords in *R. v K.* [2001] UKHL 41; [2002] 1 A.C. 462 at [30] cites with approval the remarks of Lord Reid in *Black-Clawson International Ltd v Papierwerke Waldhof-Aschaffenburg AG* [1975] A.C. 591 at 613–615: "We often say that we are looking for the intention of Parliament, but that is not quite accurate. We are seeking the meaning of the words which Parliament used." "The contextual meaning of the enacted text" added Lord Steyn, "is controlling". Incidentally, the citation may look incorrect, but it is not. The first number, it will be recalled, is the number officially allotted to the judgment itself. The second is a reference to the paragraph number in the judgment.

[12] *per* Lord Simon in *Farrell v Alexander* [1977] A.C. 59 at 81G.

[13] *per* Lord Edmund-Davies, *Farrell v Alexander* [1977] A.C. 59 at 95B.

[14] Fresh controversy as to the utility and scope of legislative intent functioning as a guide to statutory interpretation has been aroused by Richard Ekins in his book, *The Nature of Legislative Intent* (2012).

is relatively fixed, have a fringe of uncertainty when applied to the infinitely variable facts of experience. For example, the general notion of a "building" is clear, but a judge may not find it easy to decide whether a temporary wooden hut, or a telephone kiosk, or a wall, or a tent, is a "building". In problems like this, the process of interpretation is indistinguishable from legislation: the judge is, like it or not, a legislator. For, if the conclusion is that the wooden hut is a building, this is in effect adding an interpretation clause to the statute which gives "building" an extended application; whereas to decide that the hut is not a building, effectively adds a clause to the statute and gives it a narrower meaning. The words of the statute, as they stand, do not give an answer to the question before the judge; and the question is therefore legislative rather than interpretative. This simple truth is rarely perceived or admitted: almost always the judge pretends to get the solution out of the words of the Act, though confessing in so doing to be guided by its general policy. The rational approach would be to say candidly that the question, being legislative, must be settled with the help of the policy implicit in the Act, or by reference to convenience or social requirements or generally accepted principles of fairness.

This kind of "interpretation" may be legally and socially sound although it reaches results that would surprise the lexicographer. Thus it has actually been held that murder can be an "accident".[15] The word "accident" was being interpreted in the context of the Workmen's Compensation Act 1906, and the result of the decision was that the widow of the deceased workman was entitled to compensation from

---

[15] *Nisbet v Rayne & Burn* [1910] 2 K.B. 689. See *Morris v K.L.M. Royal Dutch Airlines* [2002] UKHL 7; [2002] 2 A.C. 628, where the claimant was seeking damages when she suffered clinical depression following an assault on her by a fellow passenger. Although the incident was treated by the court as being clearly an "accident", she nevertheless was unable to recover since (so it was held) "bodily injury" did not include mental injury, on the grounds that this could not have been present to the minds of those drafting the relevant international Convention in 1929. Yet in *R. v Ireland* [1998] A.C. 147, it was held that psychiatric illness fell within the scope of an offence under the Offences Against the Person Act 1861, and by causing it the appellant had been guilty of a serious criminal offence, notwithstanding that the "Victorian legislator . . . would not have had in mind psychiatric illness . . . ". "It is a matter of interpretation whether a court must search for the historical or original meaning of a statute or whether it is free to apply the current meaning of the statute to present day conditions": *per* Lord Steyn at 158. This looks, it must be said, suspiciously like judicial legislation.

the employer, because the murder in question arose out of and in the course of the employment. The court admitted that it was giving an unusual meaning to the word, for "an historian who described the end of Rizzio by saying that he met with a fatal accident in Holyrood Palace would . . . fairly be charged with a misleading statement of fact". Similarly, Farwell L.J. remarked that one would not in ordinary parlance say that Desdemona died by accident, because "the horror of the crime dominates the imagination and compels the expression of the situation in terms related to the crime and the criminal alone." Yet, if one looks at the situation from the point of view of the victim, it is an accident, in the sense that it was not expected or intended by the victim himself. In preferring this wider meaning of the term "accident" the court looked to the general purpose of the Act.

THE LITERAL RULE

Granted that words have a certain elasticity of meaning, the general rule remains that the judges regard themselves as bound by the words of a statute when these words clearly govern the situation before the court. The words must be applied with nothing added and nothing taken away. More precisely, the general principle is that the court can neither extend the statute to a case not within its terms though perhaps within its purpose nor curtail it by leaving out a case that the statute literally includes, though it should not have. Lord Diplock expressed the argument in favour of judicial self-restraint as follows:

"At a time when more and more cases involve the application of legislation which gives effect to policies that are the subject of bitter public and parliamentary controversy, it cannot be too strongly emphasised that the British constitution, though largely unwritten, is firmly based upon the separation of powers; Parliament makes the laws, the judiciary interpret them. When Parliament legislates to remedy what the majority of its members at the time perceive to be a defect or a lacuna in the existing law (whether it be the written law enacted by existing statutes or the unwritten common law as it has been expounded by the judges in decided cases), the role of the judiciary is confined to ascertaining from the words that Parliament has approved as expressing its intention what that intention was, and to giving effect to it. Where the meaning of the statutory words is plain and unambiguous it is not for the judges to invent fancied ambiguities as an excuse for failing to give effect to its plain meaning because they themselves consider that the consequences of doing so would be inexpedient, or even unjust or immoral. In controversial matters such as are involved in industrial relations there is room for differences of opinion as to what is expedient, what is just and what is morally justifiable. Under our constitution it is Parliament's opinion on these matters that is paramount."[16]

Lord Diplock went on to say that the principle applies even though there is reason to think that if Parliament had foreseen the situation before the court it would have modified the words it used: "If this be the case it is for Parliament, not for the judiciary, to decide whether any changes should be made to the law as stated in the Acts."

According to this, courts should not use the alternative principles of construction[17] when the statute is "plain and unambiguous". They can decline to apply the literal rule if the statute is ambiguous, but must not "invent fancied ambiguities" in order to do so.

It is, nevertheless, difficult to reconcile the literal rule with the "context" rule. We understand the meaning of words from their context, and in ordinary life the context includes not only other words used at the same time but the whole human or social situation in which the words are used. Professor Zander gives the example of parents asking a childminder to keep the children amused by teaching them a card game. In the parents' absence the childminder teaches the children to play strip poker. There is no doubt that strip poker is a card game, but equally no doubt that it was not the sort of card game intended by the instructions given. One knows this not from anything the parents have said but from customary ideas as to the proper behaviour and upbringing of children. On its face, the literal rule seems to forbid this common-sense approach to statutory interpretation.

The literal rule has often been criticised by writers. Blindly applied, it is a rule against using intelligence in understanding language.

---

[16] *Duport Steels Ltd v Sirs* [1980] 1 W.L.R. 142 at 157; 1 All E.R. 529. For earlier pronouncements to the same effect see *Magor and St Mellons v Newport Corpn* [1952] A.C. 189; *Stock v Frank Jones (Tipton) Ltd* [1978] 1 W.L.R. 231; 1 All E.R. 948.

[17] Such as the mischief rule discussed further below, p. 137

Anyone who in ordinary life interpreted words literally, being indifferent to what the speaker or writer meant, would be regarded as a pedant, a mischief-maker or an eccentric.

Applying the rule also occasions difficulty. What is a real ambiguity, and what is a fancied ambiguity? Consider the following case decided by the House of Lords on the construction of the Factories Act. This Act[18] required dangerous parts of machines to be constantly fenced while they were in motion. A workman repairing a machine removed the fence and turned the machine by hand in order to do the job. Unfortunately he crushed his finger. Whether the employers were in breach of the statute and liable in damages for breach of statutory duty depended on whether the machine was "in motion" at the time of the accident. In the primary or literal sense of the words it was; but since the machine was not working under power and was only in temporary motion for necessary adjustment, the House of Lords chose to give the words the secondary meaning of "mechanical propulsion".[19] Since the machine was not being mechanically propelled it was not in motion, and the employers were not liable.

This was a decision of the House of Lords 25 years before the pronouncement of Lord Diplock previously quoted, and no doubt has been cast upon it. Is the provision in the Factories Act ambiguous or not? "Motion" primarily means movement; the machine was in movement, and therefore, in the ordinary meaning of the phrase, was in motion. The reason why the House of Lords cut down the meaning of the phrase must have been because the House did not believe that Parliament intended to cover the particular situation. According to Lord Diplock it is improper to do this if the meaning of the statute is plain. So the decision in the Factories Act case was justifiable only if the Act was regarded as not plain. But in what way was it not plain? "In motion" is on its face a perfectly plain phrase.

Was not the reason why the House thought it not plain that their Lordships believed that Parliament did not have this situation in mind and would have cut down the wording if it had? Yet it seems that according to Lord Diplock such reasoning is merely the invention of a

---

[18] A predecessor of the Health and Safety at Work Act 1974.
[19] *Richard Thomas & Baldwins Ltd v Cummings* [1955] A.C. 321. For a fuller discussion see J. Bell and G. Engle, *Cross, Statutory Interpretation* (3rd edn, 1995), pp.88–90.

fancied ambiguity, which is no reason for denying the "plain" meaning of a statute.

One practical reason for the literal rule is that judges have no wish to be accused of making political judgments at variance with the purpose of Parliament when it passed the Act. This fear is sometimes understandable, but not all statutes divide Parliament on party lines.

Other reasons advanced for the literal rule may be briefly answered.[20] "Many statutes are passed by political bargaining and snap judgments of expediency; the courts can rarely be sure that Parliament would have altered the wording if it had foreseen the situation." This may be true, but is it any reason why the courts should not do justice as best they can, leaving it to Parliament to intervene again if the decision does not meet with Parliament's approval? "If courts habitually rewrote statutes in order to effect supposed improvements, this might cause statutes to become more complex in order to exclude judicial rewriting in a way that was politically unacceptable." This supposes that the court misjudges what Parliament would wish it to do, whereas in fact the decision may win general approval. A court that tries to decide as Parliament would have wished is more likely to be right than a court that follows the words believing it was not what Parliament intended. "People are entitled to follow statutes as they are; they should not have to speculate as to Parliament's intention." This is a strong reason against the extensive construction of prohibitory (criminal) legislation, but is less persuasive in other cases. "If the courts undertook to rewrite statutes this would tend to foment litigation, because it would encourage people who objected to the legislation to try their luck with the courts." To suggest that the courts will ever completely rewrite a statute is a great exaggeration; and even judges who accept the literal rule in words will depart from it when the circumstances press them hard enough.

Lord Diplock says that there may be differences of opinion as to what is expedient, just and moral, and that Parliament's opinion on these questions is paramount. This is obviously true, once Parliament's opinion is established. It is also true that Parliament's opinion is ascertained primarily from the words it has used.

---

[20] Some of these reasons are given by Lord Simon in *Stock v Frank Jones (Tipton) Ltd* [1978] 1 W.L.R. 231 at 236–237; 1 All E.R. 948 at 953–954.

Nevertheless, the facts of the case may be such as to raise serious doubts whether Parliament intended its words to apply. The decision by a court that a particular situation was not intended to come within the ambit of a statute, though within its words in what may be their most obvious meaning, does not deny the supremacy of Parliament, for if Parliament disagrees with the decision it can pass another Act dealing specifically with the type of case. However, the hard truth is that Parliament generally pays little attention to the working of the law. It is not merely that Parliament fails to keep old law under continuous revision; it loses interest in its new creations as soon as they are on the statute book.

A "PURPOSIVE" APPROACH: THE MISCHIEF RULE

As can be seen from the illustration just given, the task of interpreting statutes gives judges the chance of expressing their own opinions as to social policy; and, inevitably, their opinions do not always command universal assent. However, the judges are on fairly safe ground if they apply the "mischief" rule, otherwise known as the rule in *Heydon's Case*.[21] This bids them to look at the common law (i.e. the legal position) before the Act, and the mischief that the statute was intended to remedy; the Act is then to be construed in such a way as to suppress the mischief and advance the remedy. This approach to the reading of statutes is an early example of what is now commonly referred to as a "purposive" approach,[22] which goes rather wider than merely ascertaining the mischief. Lord Nicholls explains:

"Nowadays, the courts look at external aids for more than merely identifying the mischief the statute is intended to cure. In adopting a purposive approach to the interpretation of statutory language, courts seek to identify and give effect to the purpose of the legislation. To the extent that extraneous material assists in identifying the purpose of the legislation, it is a useful tool."[23]

---

[21] (1584) 3 Co.Rep. at 7b; 76 E.R. at 638.

[22] See, e.g. Lord Griffiths in *Pepper v Hart* [1993] A.C. 593 at 617; Lord Nicholls in *Associated Dairies Ltd v Baines* [1997] A.C. 524 at 532.

[23] *R. v Secretary of State for the Environment, Transport and the Regions, ex p. Spath Holme* [2001] 2 A.C. 349 at 397E, HL.

So stated, the purposive approach is rather wider than the mischief rule, since it does not suppose (as the older rule does) that all statutes are passed for the purpose of remedying a mischief, as opposed to promoting some social good or purpose. In recent years, the purposive approach has supplanted both the literal rule and the mischief rule as the proper approach to the ascertainment of Parliament's will.[24]

Pepper v Hart

The practical utility of the mischief rule depends to some extent upon the means that the courts are entitled to employ in order to ascertain what mischief the Act was intended to remedy. A true historical investigation would take account of press agitation, party conferences, government pronouncements, and debates in Parliament. Until comparatively recently, all of these were ignored as the result of a rule excluding evidence of the political history of a statute. The exclusionary rule was justified by the burden that would otherwise be placed upon legal advisers (and the resulting costs to their clients) and the uncertainty that would be introduced into the law if such historical materials had to be consulted.[25] In practice, therefore, the judge generally gathered the object of a statute merely from perusal of its language, in the light of his knowledge of the previous law and general

---

[24] It is at least plausible that membership of the European Union has involved the adoption of fresh approaches to interpretation; a fuller discussion of the point is beyond my scope, but see J. Bell in ed A. Burrows, *English Private Law* (3rd edn, 2013), p.17 for a discussion of "European teleological approaches". He concludes: "the role assigned to the court as interpreter by the European teleological approach is more active than would be acceptable in domestic law. In domestic law, the sources of information about the purpose of the legislation are more focused and public . . . ".

[25] Where a statute is passed to give effect to an international treaty (convention), the courts will apply the continental rule that the discussions leading to the treaty may be looked at: *Fothergill v Monarch Airlines Ltd* [1981] A.C. 251. But the consensus is that such *travaux préparatoires* should be used only where the text is ambiguous or where a literal construction appears to conflict with the purpose of the treaty. It is important that the interpretation adopted in the United Kingdom should be the same as that adopted in other states. Thus in *Morris v K.L.M. Royal Dutch Airlines* [2002] Q.B. 100, the Court of Appeal relied upon a decision of the United States Court of Appeal, Second Circuit on the meaning of "accident" (holding that it might encompass an intentional assault on an air passenger). Such decisions are not binding, but: "respect falls to be paid to relevant decisions of courts of other signatories . . . " [12].

knowledge of social conditions.[26] However, in *Pepper (Inspector of Taxes) v Hart*,[27] it was held that in certain limited situations and for certain limited purposes, *Hansard* (i.e. the Parliamentary record) can be consulted for the purposes of ascertaining the intention of the legislature. The precise limits is which this may be done are somewhat unclear, and remain hotly contested.[28] According to Lord Oliver, this is permissible

"only . . . where the expression of the legislative intention is genuinely ambiguous or obscure or where a literal or prima facie construction leads to a manifest absurdity and where the difficulty can be resolved by a clear statement to the matter in issue".[29]

The conditions for consulting legislative history were summarised in the headnote as follows:

(a)   legislation is ambiguous or obscure or leads to an absurdity;

(b)   the material relied upon consists of one or more statements by a Minister or other promoter of the Bill together . . . with such other Parliamentary material as is necessary to understand such statements and their effect;

(c)   the statements relied upon are clear.

Exactly how these conditions should apply in any particular case is, however, still a matter of some controversy. In *R. v Secretary of State for the Environment, Transport and the Regions, ex p. Spath Holme Ltd*,[30] two members of the House (Lords Nicholls[31] and

---

[26] See, e.g. *Davis v Johnson* [1979] A.C. 264 at 338F.

[27] [1993] A.C. 593.

[28] One of the most hostile and vocal critics of the decision is Lord Steyn. See his article, cited above, p.127, fn.2. See also A. Kavanagh, "*Pepper v Hart* and Matters of Constitutional Principle" (2005) 121 L.Q.R. 98.

[29] [1993] A.C. 593 at 620. Applied in *Craftrule Ltd v 41–60 Albert Mansion Palace Mansions Ltd*; [2011] 1 W.L.R. 2425; [2011] EWCA Civ 185 at [25] where it was held that the conditions were not satisfied, and *Hansard* was accordingly ignored.

[30] [2001] 2 A.C. 349.

[31] In *R. (Jackson) v Att.-Gen.*; [2005] UKHL 56; [2006] 1 A.C. 262 at [65] Lord Nicholls acknowledged that the practice of referring to Hansard is "currently under something of a judicial cloud".

Cooke) dissented on the use to which *Hansard* might be put. Section 31 of the Landlord and Tenant Act 1985 gave the Minister a power to make rent restriction orders. The grounds upon which the Minister could rely in making such an order were unclear, but might have included either or both (i) the desirability of reflecting equities between landlords and tenants and/or (ii) the need to control inflation. The majority (Lords Bingham, Hope and Hutton) took the view that two of the thresholds set by Lord Browne-Wilkinson in *Pepper v Hart*, namely paragraphs (a) and (b) had not been met and that reference to *Hansard* was therefore impermissible to resolve the dilemma. The minority took the view that they could consult various parliamentary statements, but decided that they were inconclusive of the issue and concluded (with the majority) that the Minister was free to use both criteria.

Under the purposive approach, it is still necessary to answer the question: when is a provision ambiguous? Lord Cooke in his speech said that "a provision is ambiguous if reasonably open on orthodox rules of construction to more than one meaning", and concluded that the section under consideration fell within that ambit. He took the view that there are cases in which the court can in the end derive real help from *Hansard*, even if it is not necessarily decisive help. If the answer is not "decisive" one way or the other as to Parliament's meaning, it shows that the court has a real choice to make.

Another difficulty is that the statements to be relied upon must be "clear". But the question arises: how do you know whether they are clear until you have looked at them? Lord Mackay dissented in *Pepper v Hart*. His objections were the practical and pragmatic ones, concerned as they were with the availability (or rather the unavailability) of the background materials, and the costs of undertaking research into them. In other words, it is still necessary for legal advisers to undertake all the research work the avoidance of which is behind the majority approach in the *Spath Holme* decision even in order to know whether or not what has been said is "clear".

More recently still, a far more restrictive approach to the use of legislative history has been suggested. It has been argued that the only purpose for which such material should be consulted would be to prevent a government or minister from denying before the courts what he or she had asserted before Parliament.[32] Whilst it is true that this was what happened in *Pepper v Hart* itself, Lord Hope's view is a minority one.

Many statutes are the result of recommendations made by the Royal Commissions and departmental committees. Can the reports of these commissions and committees be looked at as an aid to construction? The short answer is that they can be consulted for the same purposes and to the same extent as *Hansard* itself. And they can still be consulted to show the mischief against which the Act was directed. A nice example of the use of such a report for these purposes is to be found in the prosecution for "making off without payment", *Allen*.[33] The question was whether a person who left without paying a bill could be convicted in the absence of proof that he or she intended never to pay. The Theft Act 1978 was silent on the point, but the Thirteenth Report of the Criminal Law Revision Committee made it clear that such an intention must be proved. The Court of Appeal refused to consult the Report, taking the view that it was not permitted to consult, but arrived at the "correct" conclusion unaided. The House of Lords did look at the Report and reinforced its own conclusions about the mischief at which the section was aimed. It may be expected that the practice of referring to these reports will extend itself in the future, because they often supply the best commentary upon the wording of an Act.[34]

INTERPRETATIONS TO AVOID ABSURDITY: THE GOLDEN RULE

As the Factories Act case discussed earlier illustrates, the courts sometimes allow themselves to construe a statute in such a way as to produce a reasonable result, even though this involves departing from the prima facie meaning of the words. The rule that a statute may be construed to avoid absurdity is conveniently called the

---

[32] See in particular Lord Hope in *Spath Holme* [2001] 2 A.C. 349 at 407–408. Lord Steyn in *R. (Jackson v Attorney General* [2005] UKHL 56; [2006] 1 A.C. 262 at [97] lent support to the views of Lord Hope.

[33] [1985] A.C. 1029.

[34] See also *I v DPP* [2001] UKHL 10; [2002] 1 A.C. 285 (affray).

"golden rule".[35] It is by no means unlimited, and seems to apply only in three types of case.

The golden rule allows the court to prefer a sensible meaning to an absurd meaning, where both are linguistically possible. It does not matter that the absurd meaning is the more natural and obvious meaning of the words. Lord Reid:

"Where a statutory provision on one interpretation brings about a startling and inequitable result, this may lead the court to seek another possible interpretation which will do better justice."[36]

On another occasion Lord Reid put the point more strongly.

"It is only where the words are absolutely incapable of a construction which will accord with the apparent intention of the provision and will avoid a wholly unreasonable result that the words of the enactment must prevail."[37]

This application of the golden rule does not contradict the literal rule, *provided* that the absurdity of the particular proposed application of the statute is conceded to be a reason for finding an ambiguity in it. If one accepts the golden rule, this involves rejecting Lord Diplock's opinion that the inexpediency, injustice or immorality of the proposed application of the statute cannot in itself be a reason for finding an ambiguity in the statute. According to the golden rule it can be a powerful motivating force leading the court to detect such an ambiguity.

---

[35] *Mattison v Hart* (1854) 14 C.B. at 385, 139 E.R. at 159. The general statement of the golden rule is that the literal (primary) meaning must be adopted unless this results in absurdity. It must be admitted, however, that it is now rare to find the judges using the expression in that sense. In *Cotgrave v Cotgrave* [1992] Fam. 33, Butler-Sloss L.J. reacted to a suggestion that legislation produced a result that was "illogical, unreasonable and unfair" by saying that "that is how Parliament has enacted . . . " the relevant legislation. Since the avoidance of "absurdity" will be encompassed within the purposive approach and permit parliamentary materials to be consulted for the purpose, it must be acknowledged that the "golden rule" might have been in effect supplanted. It would be most unusual to find, surely, that Parliament had deliberately legislated for a result that is later condemned as "absurd".

[36] *Coutts & Co v Inland Revenue Commissioners* [1953] A.C. 267 at 281.

[37] *Luke v Inland Revenue Commissioners* [1963] A.C. 557 at 577.

It is frequently said that the question of absurdity cannot influence a decision in any type of case except the one just stated. Nevertheless, the courts sometimes act on a second principle, stated by Cross as follows:

"The judge may read in words which he considers to be necessarily implied by words which are already in the statute, and he has a limited power to add to, alter or ignore statutory words in order to prevent a provision from being unintelligible or absurd or totally unreasonable, unworkable or totally irreconcilable with the rest of the Statute."[38]

Acting on this principle judges have occasionally corrected a statute that foolishly said "and" when it meant "or", or that foolishly said "or" when it meant "and". However, the argument must be very strong to induce the court to meddle with a statute.[39] Instances occur where the courts feel obliged to construe a statute in a way that they themselves acknowledge creates outrageous injustice.

PRESUMPTIONS

In interpreting statutes, various presumptions may be applied, most of which are of a negative or restrictive character. They are the background of legal principles against which the Act is viewed, and in the light of which Parliament is assumed to have legislated, without being expected to express them. Some embody traditional notions of justice, such as the rule that a statute is presumed not to be retrospective (except in procedural matters). Others reflect what was almost certainly the intention of Parliament, as that an Act applies only to the United Kingdom unless the contrary is expressed. The most controversial presumptions are those enshrining the values of a

---

[38] *Cross, Statutory Interpretation* (3rd edn, 1995). p.93. For the power of the courts to rewrite legislation in cases where the draftsman has clearly made a drafting mistake, see *Inco Europe v First Choice Distribution* [2000] 1 W.L.R. 586; [2000] 2 All E.R. 109.

[39] In the Public Order Act 1986, a power of arrest was conferred to restrain a person engaging in disorderly conduct. But the power was conferred only upon "the" policeman who had first required the person at risk of arrest to desist from the objectionable conduct, and the court in *DPP v Hancock and Tuttle* [1995] Crim. L.R.139 declined to read this to cover "any" or "a" policeman. Parliament put the matter right in the Public Order (Amendment) Act 1996.

capitalist society—the presumption against interference with vested rights, the presumption against the taking of property without compensation, and the presumption against interference with contract. The last of these now has few followers, but the first two still retain vitality. Even so, the judges are hampered by the thought that they must not run counter to political trends, for example by implying a right to full compensation for the appropriation of property when a legislature (acting for reasons of wealth redistribution) did not in terms provide for such compensation. The traditional presumption upon which a clear consensus still exists is that against interference with personal liberty.

Presumptions may be regarded as instances of the proposition that the duty of judges goes beyond the automatic enforcement of the dictates of Parliament. The judges' function is also to do justice in accordance with certain settled principles of law in a free society; and they are entitled to assume that Parliament does not intend to subvert these principles, unless there is a clear statement that it does. For this reason, the courts apply the rule that when Parliament has conferred a judicial or quasi-judicial power upon a person, that power must be exercised in accordance with the rules of natural justice. When Parliament creates a new crime, this is presumed to be subject to certain defences at common law, such as self-defence and duress, and also (very frequently) to the requirement of a state of mind (intention, knowledge or recklessness).[40] These are judge-made principles required by our ideas of justice and grafted on the statute by "implication" although there may be no words in the statute to suggest them.

The common law provides quite an armoury of such principles, and new applications can be found for them by a bold judge. A striking example is *Re Sigsworth*.[41] Under legislation (in force then and now) a child has certain rights of succession on the death of the parent intestate. For the purpose of his decision in *Re Sigsworth*, the trial judge assumed it to have been proved that the deceased, Mary Ann Sigsworth, had been murdered by her son; and the question was whether the son was entitled to her estate as "issue" under the Act.

---

[40] *B (a Minor) v DPP* [2000] 2 A.C. 428; *R. v K* [2001] UKHL 41; [2002] 1 A.C. 462.
[41] [1935] Ch. 89.

The learned judge held not, for the reason that no one is entitled to profit from his own wrong. The decision was rendered somewhat easier by the fact that a similar conclusion had already been arrived at in the law of wills: a murderer cannot take under the victim's will. Long before that— at least as early as 1775—the courts had laid down the general principle of law that a person cannot bring an action based on his own wrong (*ex turpi causa non oritur actio*).[42] In *Re Sigsworth*, the judge applied this principle to the interpretation of the intestacy statute which made no mention of it. Even statutes may be read as subject to certain fundamental principles of justice which are to be discovered in the common law.

Incidentally, *Re Sigsworth* is enough to disprove the oft-repeated assertion that "where the words of an Act of Parliament are clear, there is no room for applying any principles of interpretation".[43] This proposition may have a useful application in limiting some of the more pedantic canons of interpretation, but it does not exclude the application of a presumption or certain common-sense principles. Although *Re Sigsworth* was only the decision of a judge at first instance, it has been approved by the Court of Appeal and extended to other statutes raising a similar question.[44] One can therefore say that the courts retain the power to read statutes in the light of general principles, the only question being whether the particular court will be able to find or invent a general principle that will enable it to give a sensible effect to the statute. Much will depend on the legal knowledge and ingenuity of counsel and the court, as well as on the readiness of the court to take a liberal view.

A liberal interpretation to prevent the statute operating upon an accidental inclusion may sometimes be comparatively easy, as it was in *Re Sigsworth*. Although the courts have not expressly said so, it may be more difficult to do anything in the situation where Parliament has left out something germane. To extend a statute to a regrettably omitted case looks too much like legislation. Even so, it is possible for a court to interpret a statute as covering what looks at first sight as

---

[42] See *Broom's Legal Maxims* (10th edn, 1937), p.497.
[43] *per* Scott L.J. in *Croxford v Universal Insurance Co* [1936] 2 K.B. 253 at 280.
[44] *R. v Chief National Insurance Commissioners, ex p. O'Connor* [1981] Q.B. 758; *R. v Secretary of State for the Home Department, ex p. Puttick* [1981] Q.B. 767; *Whiston v Whiston* [1995] Fam. 198; *Re DWS (decd)* [2001] Ch. 568.

an omission if it can find or invent some plausible general principle of interpretation, an exercise that may call for a little ingenuity.

Consider, for example, *Adler v George*.[45] The Official Secrets Act 1920, s.3, prohibits persons "in the vicinity of" any prohibited place from impeding sentries. The defendant impeded a sentry when he was inside a prohibited place. The argument for the defence was that the defendant, being inside, was not "in the vicinity of" the place, which meant outside. The court rejected the argument, holding that the statute was to be read as if it were "in or in the vicinity of". Obviously, the case was stronger than the one actually provided for, so it could be regarded as *a fortiori*.[46] Just as the greater includes the less, so a provision for the marginal case must include the central case. *Adler v George* shows that statutes may be read not only against the background of notions of justice and settled legal principle (which tend to limit their operation) but also against the background of notions of ordinary common sense (which may extend their operation).

There is a long-standing presumption that Acts of Parliament are not intended to derogate from the requirements of international law. When interpreting legislation, therefore, the courts presume that Parliament must have intended to act in accordance with international obligations. For many years, the European Convention on Human Rights was treated as no more than an aid to construction of this kind, although one that assumed increasing significance after a right of individual petition to the European Court of Human Rights was accorded in 1966. Technically, the International Covenant on Civil and Political Rights is a treaty of the same status as the European Convention before incorporation. But its provisions are only rarely noted, even though binding on us as a matter of international law.

HUMAN RIGHTS ACT 1998, S.3

Section 3 of the Human Rights Act 1998 warrants separate consideration because it introduces special considerations in cases where the protection of certain human rights is involved. The section provides

[45] [1964] 2 Q.B 7.
[46] "With stronger reason"—generally anglicised as "ay forsheeory".

that, "So far as it is possible to do so, primary legislation and sub-ordinate legislation must be read and given effect in a way which is compatible with Convention rights". If the court is unable to achieve a reading of the statute in conformity with the Convention rights, it may then grant a "declaration of incompatibility" whose effect is that the law must be changed subsequently in order to make it consistent with Convention rights. It will be clear that, at a stroke, Parliament has thereby rendered relevant to the interpretation process many con-siderations that would otherwise have been irrelevant, or of doubt-ful standing, and at the same time introduced a fundamentally new approach to the task of interpretation.

The section has been already been considered on hundreds of occa-sions since it came into force on 2 October 2000. Its potential to make a difference to the outcome of a dispute is illustrated by the decision of the House of Lords in *R. v A (No.2)*[47] where the protection afforded to rape victims in court was the subject of consideration. Parliament had enacted legislation (s.41 of the Youth Justice and Criminal Evidence Act 1999) setting out with some precision the circumstances in which a judge might give leave to permit the questioning of a rape victim. The ban apparently prevented the defendant from adducing evidence or asking questions as to his own previous relationship with the complainant, even in a case where the defence was that the com-plainant had consented. Four members of the House agreed that, according to the ordinary canons of construction, the statute would indeed have that result which meant that a court would be unable to hear evidence that might be highly relevant to the defence. The majority in the House were clear that s.3 permitted (or even required) the court to take into account Article 6 of the European Convention guaranteeing a fair trial whatever violence this might do to the lan-guage of s.41. Lord Hope was in a minority. He disagreed about the potential relevance of the evidence (the mere fact that the complain-ant might have consented on previous occasions is no evidence that she consented on the occasion giving rise to the charge), and took the line that Parliament did indeed intend that a defendant should not have been permitted to ask the disputed questions. Section 3 "does not entitle the judges to act as legislators". The courts have said on

[47] [2002] 1 A.C. 45.

a number of occasions that they must respect the distinction between interpreting and legislating, but as critics point out,[48] the line is a difficult one to draw.

It is at least arguable that the line between interpretation and legislation was overstepped by a majority of the House of Lords in *Ghaidan v Godin-Mendoza*,[49] where the decision in *R v A* was affirmed. There the House of Lords held that legislation (which traced its origins back to 1977) protecting the inheritance rights of a deceased's "spouse" could be extended to protect a same sex partner even though this could not have been in the contemplation of the legislature when the provision was first enacted. The House was unanimous in deciding that the legislation did violate the anti-discrimination provisions of s. 14 of the Human Rights Act, but divided as to the question whether it was legitimate to interpret the word "spouse" in a way that was never intended by Parliament in the first place. To the puzzlement of the critics,[50] a majority decided that it was possible to find the rights compliant "meaning" through the use of section 3.

This involves a reading of the legislation to produce a result that the legislature did not intend, and there can be little doubt that the implementation of the Human Rights Act involving decisions such as these has materially contributed to the tensions that have developed between the executive and the judiciary, a tension frequently inflamed by sensational press coverage of particular decisions.[51]

Section 3 therefore creates tension between judges as interpreters and judges as quasi-legislators. In the first place, s.3 obliges the judges to find a compatible interpretation "so far as it is possible to do so". The meaning of the words that Parliament has used must set some limits to what is "possible" in any particular case. The approach of the majority in *A* enables the courts to nullify the effect of statutory

[48] See A. Kavanagh (above 000) at 29ff.

[49] [2004] UKHL 30, [2004] 2 AC 557. There is excellent treatment of the issues arising from this decision in A. Kavanagh, *Constitutional Review under the Human Rights Act* (2009), especially chapters 2–5.

[50] The Supreme Court of Victoria in *R v Momcilovic* [2010] VCSA 5, [69]-[110] declined to follow the approach of the House of Lords, taking the view that it was not entitled to interpret legislation in a way that was clearly at variance with what the legislature must have intended. But the equivalent interpretation section there is differently worded.

[51] This was the stated view of the House of Lord's Committee on the Constitution, "Relations between the executive, the judiciary and Parliament", 6th report of Session 2006–7, discussed by A.W. Bradley [2008] P.L. 470.

provisions and it may be doubted whether that is the purpose of s.3. Rather, if the courts are forced to a conclusion that it is simply not possible to find an interpretation that protects one of the enshrined rights, then it has the power to make (under s.4 of the Human Rights Act 1998) a "declaration of incompatibility" leaving Parliament to set the matter right.

It is hoped that these few words are sufficient to enable the student to understand something of the complexities that are involved in the interpretation of statutes.

FURTHER READING

For an enlargement upon the theme of interpretation, see Michael Zander, *The Law-Making Process* (7th edn, 2015), Ch.3. A fuller account of the technical rules will be found in J. Bell and G. Engle eds, *Cross, Statutory Interpretation* (3rd edn, 1995). The practitioner's work is F.A.R. Bennion, *Statutory Interpretation* (6th edn, 2013). A new edition is expected imminently. The same author has written *Understanding Common Law Legislation* (2009). See also J. Bell, "Sources of Law" in A. Burrows ed., *English Private Law* (2nd edn, 2007), Ch.1; Manchester and Salter, *Exploring the Law: The Dynamics of Precedent and Statutory Interpretation* (4th edn, 2011).

8 WORKING OUT PROBLEMS

"I scarce think it is harder to resolve very difficult cases in law, than it is to direct a young gentleman what course he should take to enable himself so to do."

—Sir Roger North, *On the Study of the Laws*.[1]

[Since much of the value of this chapter must depend upon the concrete illustrations it gives, I have been forced to assume the reader's knowledge of a certain amount of elementary law. You should postpone reading it until you have made a start with the study of a case-law subject like constitutional and administrative law, criminal law, contract or tort.]

It is not easy even for an intelligent candidate in the heat of the examination to show the calm judgment that answering a problem question requires. It is, therefore, most important to train oneself in problem answering well in advance. In doing this, the student will not merely be preparing in the best possible way for the examination: this practice will also be developing the mind as a working instrument and preparation for later legal life. The technique of solving academic problems is almost the same as the technique of writing a legal opinion upon a practical point. The chief difference is that in practical problems the material facts often lie buried in a much larger mass of immaterial detail, while the examination problem should contain comparatively little beyond the material facts.

If the student is studying under a tutor or supervisor, an adequate number of problems should be supplied in the course of study, often

---

[1] Sir Roger North was quite a polymath. A successful barrister (which might have owed something to the fact that his brother was the Lord Chancellor), he "found time to study optics and mathematics, to listen to and to theorise about music, to collect pictures, to plant and to build"; H. Colvin, *A Biographical Dictionary of British Architects 1600–1840* (3rd edn, 1995), p.709. That work records that it was North and not, as was commonly supposed, his good friend Sir Christopher Wren, who designed the Great Gateway to the Temple in Fleet Street.

taken from previous examination papers. It is also necessary to consult the syllabus of the course being studied, because that will set the parameters within which the examiners should be setting the examination. This should tell you both what is examinable—sometimes in fairly general terms—and more importantly what is not to be expected. The syllabus may well say, for example, that you are not expected in criminal law to have a detailed knowledge of particular offences (some specified offences excepted) other than are necessary to illustrate the application of general principles, and in the law of tort that wrongs such as passing-off and other forms of unfair competition, interference with goods, abuse of legal process and so forth are not required to be considered.

Perhaps the most important piece of advice with problems, as with all examination questions, is to *read every word of the problem*. Almost every word has been put in for a purpose and needs to be commented upon. In a land law question, for instance, the word "orally" or "verbally" or "on the telephone", in describing the formation of a contract for the sale of land, will invite discussion of s.40 of the Law of Property Act 1925, and quite probably s.2 of the Law of Property (Miscellaneous Provisions) Act 1989. Even if you are of the opinion that a fact stated in the problem is immaterial,[2] you should not (in general) pass it by in silence but should express your opinion that it is immaterial, and, if possible, give reasons. However, there is no need to deal in this way with an argument that, if raised, would not receive a moment's serious consideration.

FACTS STATED IN THE PROBLEM ARE CONCLUSIVE

A common query on the part of the novice upon reading an examination problem is: how could such facts ever be proved? The teacher's answer is that the student must assume this proof. (Actually, it is surprising how facts often can be proved in practice that at first sight seem to be unprovable if the defendant is prepared to contradict them. But in any case the student is not concerned with this question.)

The student should not assume facts contrary to those stated in the problem for the purpose of giving the examiner a piece of information for which the question did not ask. Also, there is generally no need

---

[2] It would be poor examination practice on the part of an examiner to include an immaterial fact; but even examiners are not perfect.

to assume facts that go clean beyond those given in the problem: had the examiner wanted a discussion of such facts these would have been inserted. Here is an example of a problem in criminal law where the examiner clearly wanted to confine the facts to a narrow compass.

> X and Y, discovering that Z intended to commit a burglary in A's house, arranged together to persuade him to steal therefrom certain articles for them. Have X, Y or Z committed an offence?

The fact that the question is thrown into the past tense shows beyond doubt that no other facts than those stated in the first sentence are to be assumed. The question is: have they on those facts alone committed an offence? An answer that assumes that X and Y have persuaded Z to steal, or that Z has stolen, will therefore miss the mark. The correct answer to the question is that X and Y are guilty of conspiring to incite (or, indeed, of conspiring to commit) burglary or theft. (There are technical points relating to the charge that need not be considered here.)

OMITTED FACTS

Although supplementary facts should not, in general, be added to a problem, the case is different with what may be called omitted facts. One of the marks of a competent lawyer is the ability to know what gaps there are in the facts of a case. The solicitor, for example, when interviewing a client has to draw out by questions many legally relevant facts that the client has not thought of disclosing. The barrister, too, may find that such facts are missing from the brief, and have to extract them from the instructing solicitor. In order to test the candidate's perspicacity a problem may deliberately omit something that is important. Always look for such omissions and state how your answer will be affected by the presence or absence of the fact in question. Here is a simple illustration from the law of tort.

> B is A's employee. Discuss A's liability for an accident caused by B's negligence in the following cases:
>
> (i) B when driving A's van, picks up his friend C and gives her a lift to the station. An accident happens by B's negligence.
>
> (ii) [etc.]

Three vital facts are omitted from this casually stated problem. First, we are not told who, if anyone, was injured. We are to understand that owing to B's negligence an injury was sustained either by C or by some other user of the highway. But the answer may differ according to whether the person injured was C or some other user of the highway. This distinction should therefore be taken, and each of the two possibilities discussed separately.

Secondly, we are not told whether the station lay on or near B's proper route, or whether it was so much off the route that every yard travelled was a yard away from the employment and not towards it. This distinction, coupled with the previous one, yields four possible combinations of fact, each needing discussion.

Thirdly, we are not told whether A had instructed B not to pick up passengers which, again, may have a bearing on the solution to this problem.

Another example of an economically worded problem, this time taken from criminal law:

A killed her baby thinking that it was a rabbit. Discuss A's criminal responsibility.

Here A's mistake is so extraordinary that we are justified in wondering whether she was insane at the time of the deed, the insanity being an omitted fact. On the other hand we are not positively told that she was insane, and so we must also consider the unlikely hypothesis that the mistake was merely an act of great carelessness. Or there is the possibility that A killed her baby in the course of a dream.[3] The answer, then, again falls into two parts: (i) on the assumption that A was sane, (ii) on the assumption that she was insane. However, it is not justifiable to discuss a problem from the angle of insanity if there is no indication of insanity in the facts of the problem.

One more example, again from criminal law:

A, a mountaineer roped to his fellows, cut the rope in order to prevent them from dragging the leader of the party to death. Discuss.

Presumably A is being prosecuted for murder; but the question does not actually say that A's fellows were killed as a result of what he

---

[3] As in *H.M. Advocate v Fraser* (1878) 4 Couper 70.

did. We must assume that they were killed, or at least injured, in order to create a legal problem. Presumably, too, A sets up the defence of necessity; we are not expressly told that there was (or that A thought there was) no other way of saving the leader's life, but this is a fair inference from the question. Finally, the question tells us that A's object was to save the leader; it does not tell us whether his object was also to save himself. In other words it does not tell us whether he cut the rope above or below himself. If he cut it below himself his object was presumably to save himself as well as his leader. If he cut it above himself he presumably fell, and in that case his life was evidently saved by something approaching a miracle—at any rate, we know that he was saved because otherwise he would be beyond the jurisdiction and the question would have no legal interest. Perhaps this last doubt is irrelevant; it may not matter whether A's object was entirely altruistic or partially self-interested. But on the other hand it may, and so the point ought to be taken. Having thus discussed the interpretation of this problem, you would, of course, go on to consider the law relating to it.

If, as in the last illustration, you decide that a fact can be inferred from what is given, though not explicitly stated, it is wise to guard yourself by stating expressly that you assume the fact to exist. For the examiner may not agree that the fact is implied in the question; but will not mind about this if it is clear that your assumption is not the result of carelessness but is your considered interpretation of the question. If you are in any doubt whether a fact is implied, you should "play safe" and take the problem each way, that is, first on the assumption that the fact exists and then on the assumption that it does not exist.

Even if all the relevant facts are stated, what is legally called a "question of fact" may still arise on the problem, for example, a question whether the defendant has, on the facts, been negligent, or whether use of a particular degree of force is "reasonable". In a real case these would be questions for the jury (if the case were tried with a jury). On such a problem, although you may venture an opinion as to the proper verdict on the point, and argue your opinion to the best of your ability, you should not categorically assert that this or that is the "right" answer on such a question of fact. The most you should say is that on these facts there is evidence of negligence (or unreasonableness), and that a finding to that effect would clearly be right (or conversely). If the point is at all doubtful, take the facts each way and state the legal result following on each possible finding.

The following problem in the law of contract illustrates the importance of this.

> A emailed an offer to sell his library to B for £30,000. B emailed in reply: "I will give £25,000." A day elapsed in which nothing further occurred. Then at 9 a.m. A sent a further email to B: "You can have the library for £25,000. A." At almost exactly the same moment B sent a further email to A: "Cancel my first email. I will take the library for £30,000. B." A received B's email at 9.30 a.m. B. received A's email at 9.40 a.m. What contract, if any, exists?

Apart from the interesting (and, as yet, not fully resolved) question whether the acceptance of an offer (or, in this case, B's counter-offer) sent by email takes effect at the moment when it is sent or at some later time, much in this problem turns on the unobtrusive sentence: "A day elapsed. . .". The question is whether this was an unreasonable delay on the part of A in replying to B's counter-offer of £25,000. If it was unreasonable, the offer (i.e. B's counter-offer) has lapsed and there is no contract. If it was not unreasonable, the offer was still alive when A's email was sent and it was still possible for a completed contract to be concluded.[4] Now it is not possible to give a confident answer to the question whether the delay was unreasonable. The only rule of law is that an offer by express method such as an email raises a presumption that a speedy reply is expected (*Quenerduaine v Cole*[5]), and therefore the lapse of a whole day would normally be too long.

Since, on facts such as these, there is not a completely arguable case one way or the other, because it is not obvious whether a court would rule that a delay of a day was unreasonable, you would be justified in taking the problem each way. However, since on the one alternative assumption (i.e. that the delay was unreasonable) you would have very little more to say, it would be wise, having made this point, to pursue the other alternative. This would give you the opportunity to examine the present state of the law relating to emailed acceptances, which is also raised by the problem.

---

[4] *Cowan v O'Connor* (1888) 20 Q.B.D. 640. Distinguish the Telex case, *Entores Ltd v Miles Far East Corporation* [1955] 2 Q.B. 327.

[5] (1883) 32 W.R. 185.

TWO POINTS OF TECHNIQUE

Some examiners conclude the statement of facts in a problem with the direction to discuss it: others adopt the mannerism of requesting you to advise one of the parties. This second form of question does not mean that you are expected to bias your answer in favour of the particular party; the legal advice you give in your answer will generally be the same whichever party you are supposed to be advising. However, there may be some practical advice to be given to the party you are supposed to be advising, and you should certainly comply with the examiner's direction as far as you are able. By the way, do not use the second person in your answer—make the answer impersonal, thus you should say "X is liable", not "You are liable".

RULES AND AUTHORITIES

Next, a few remarks upon the giving of reasons and authorities for an opinion. A bald answer to a problem, even though correct, will not earn many (perhaps not any) marks, because the examiner cannot tell whether the student has knowledge or is just guessing. Reasons and authorities should, therefore, always be given. Pretend to yourself that the examiner may disagree with your point of view, and set yourself to persuade by argument.

One of the most important of a lawyer's accomplishments is the ability to resolve facts into their legal categories. The student should therefore take pains to argue in terms of legal rules and concepts. It is a not uncommon fault, particularly in criminal law, to give the impression that the answer is based wholly upon common sense and a few gleanings from the Sunday newspapers.

The following illustration of a question and answer in criminal law may show this.

Question: A fire-engine driven at full speed to a fire knocks down and kills somebody. Discuss the criminal responsibility of the driver.
Student's answer: "If the driver has been careful he is not responsible.

(1) It is a well-known custom that as soon as the siren of a fire-engine is heard, other vehicles should pull up at the side of the road, in order to afford free passage. It is therefore safe for a fire-engine driver to

proceed at a higher speed than would be possible for other drivers. Further

(2) it is reasonable for a fire-engine to proceed quickly to a fire, for life and property may be in danger. But I do not put much weight on this second ground, for great as may be the importance of putting out a fire, it is not sufficiently great to justify the driver in leaving a trail of destruction behind him."

Upon reading this answer the examiner may well comment: "A commendable effort by an intelligent student who has not read the textbooks and knows no criminal law". The answer, to be complete, should have stated the crimes for which the driver may be prosecuted (manslaughter, causing death by dangerous or careless driving); it should have stated the requirements of each crime so far as relevant; and it should have pointed out that the burden of proving these requirements beyond reasonable doubt lies on the prosecution. It should also have discussed the possible defence of necessity, referring to it expressly by that name, not vaguely as the last two sentences of the answer do. Put into this legal setting the answer would have been altogether more satisfactory.[6]

It is bad style to begin an answer to a problem by citing a string of cases. Begin by addressing yourself to the problem and identify at the outset the issues that are raised. If the law is clear, first state the law and then give the authorities for your statement. If the law is not clear, first pose the legal question and then set out the authorities bearing on it.

When citing cases, the mere giving of the name is of limited use. What is wanted is not only the name but a statement of the legal points involved in the decision, and perhaps also a consideration of its standing, i.e. whether it has been approved or criticised subsequently. This is so even though the case directly covers the problem. Still more is this so when the case is not on all fours with the problem.

New points often occur in the law, and the lawyer in advising a client must, in effect, predict the probable decision of the court. So also in examinations: a problem is often set upon some point of law that is not covered exactly by authority. No candidate who fails to

---

[6] The point may also be made that firemen on duty are by statute exempt from adhering to speed limits.

see this point can get a first class on that question, and you should pay the examiner the compliment of searching for the point of the problem. Ask yourself what is the point it raises that is not precisely covered by authority.

Failure to follow this common-sense rule is a frequent error of the tyro. Take again, for instance, the "mountaineering" problem already given (p.154). Most raw beginners think that they have adequately solved this problem if they quote *R. v Dudley and Stephens*[7] and declare that necessity is no defence. But if they paused to reflect, they would discover several differences between *R. v Dudley and Stephens* and the facts of their problem. It cannot be asserted with confidence that every, or even any, of these distinctions would find favour with a judge, but at any rate they are possible distinctions which would certainly be made much of by an experienced counsel for the defence, particularly in the light of later decisions, such as the (civil) case of the Siamese twins *Re A (Children) (Conjoined Twins: Surgical Separation)*.[8] They are as follows:

(1) In *Dudley and Stephens* there was a choice as to who was to die. It will be remembered that *Dudley and Stephens* was the case where three men and a cabin-boy were compelled to take to an open boat after the wreck of their yacht *Mignonette*.[9] On the twentieth day after the wreck two of the men killed the boy for food; four days later they were rescued. The two men were convicted of murder. It may be said that these facts are materially different from those in our problem, for in our problem there seems to be no choice as to who is to die: it is simply (one supposes) a question of some or all. It is true that in *Dudley and Stephens* the jury found that the boy was in a much weaker condition than the others and was likely to have died before them. But the jury did not find that the boy might not have been revived had one of the others been killed to provide food for him. So long as the boy was alive and had a chance

[7] (1884) 14 Q.B.D. 273.
[8] [2001] Fam. 147.
[9] Professor A.W.B. Simpson has written an engrossing account of the background to the case, explaining how the accident occurred, against the background of maritime conditions and practices of those days; *Cannibalism and the Common Law* (1993).

of survival he was as much entitled to retain that chance as the others; whereas in our problem it may be that the men who are cut away have no chance of survival at all.

(2) It is not certain on the facts of *Dudley and Stephens* that the two defendants would have died had they not killed the boy. All that the jury found was that had they not done so they would probably not have survived to be rescued. It may be that on the facts of our problem the death of the leader is certain, not merely probable, if the rope is not cut. But it must be admitted that this is not a very strong distinction, for in *Dudley and Stephens* the jury also found that "at the time of the act there was no sail in sight, nor any reasonable prospect of relief"; and it would seem that if the law recognises necessity as a defence it should proceed upon the facts as they appeared to the defendant at the time.

(3) In *Dudley v Stephens* the cabin-boy was not by his own conduct, voluntary or involuntary, bringing the others nearer to death. In our problem the men whom the defendant presumably sends to death are themselves dragging the leader to what will otherwise be his death. It is true that they cannot help it; but does that matter? If an insane person attacks me I am surely entitled to defend myself, even though he is not criminally responsible for his conduct. Also, I am entitled to defend another. Is not our problem a case of defending another (and possibly oneself)?

All of these distinctions are also to a degree present in the case of the conjoined twins. The medical evidence was that one of the twins was very much weaker and more dependent than the other, and that if no action were taken, both of the children would die before very much longer. In one sense, the weaker child was acting as a threat to the life of her sibling, although there was no question of her thereby being at fault. But might it be suggested that, if life-ending action were to be taken it was on the basis of some form of self-defence rather than through a newly found defence of necessity?[10]

---

[10] See the analysis to this effect by J. Rogers in [2001] Crim. L.R. 515.

Another illustration this time from the law of contract, is as follows:

A writes to B offering to sell his horse Phineas for £1,000. B posts a letter accepting, but misdirects it and in consequence it is a week late in being delivered to A. Meanwhile A has sold Phineas to C. Discuss.

The ordinary beginner answers this problem simply by quoting *Household Fire Insurance Co v Grant*,[11] or some other authority to the same effect, and saying that by our law an offeror can be landed with a contract even though he never receives an acceptance, since the contract is held to be complete on the posting of the letter of acceptance. But the whole point of the question is whether *Grant* applies to a *misdirected* letter of acceptance. The examiner cannot help thinking that the candidate who appears completely to miss the point of the question is often being pusillanimous and actuated by some hidden (and mistaken) motive of self-preservation. The candidate really scents the difficulty but thinks it too hard for discussion and so conveniently pretends not to have seen it. More marks will be gained by posing the legal difficulty, even though no solution is suggested, than could be secured by ducking it completely. If, in addition to posing the difficulty, the candidate could say that there is no authority in point or that *Grant* is distinguishable, and could also suggest some reasons why on these facts it ought to be distinguished, the answer would get a first class on that question instead of a very doubtful pass.

One of the techniques of argument is to take an extreme case. "'I took an extreme case,' was Alice's tearful reply. 'My excellent preceptress always used to say, When in doubt take an extreme case. And I was in doubt.'" The technique need not always result in tears. To make the problem into a more extreme case: a week's delay in a letter does not sound inordinately long, but to isolate the question of principle let us make it longer. Suppose that the misdirected letter of acceptance had taken two months on its way, or had never arrived. Had it been properly directed and yet not have been delivered, there would have been a good contract, and A would have been liable in damages to B for not delivering the horse. That is a harsh rule from A's point

[11] (1879) 4 Ex.D. 216.

of view (arguably, a stupid rule, and the hope may be expressed that if you are the reader of this book who is destined to become Lord Chancellor you will get it changed), but it would be even worse if the same rule were applied where B has carelessly misdirected the letter, resulting in gross delay or loss. The rule in *Grant* cannot possibly apply to such circumstances. This would dispose of the main part of the problem and score reasonably good marks. But a perceptive student should be able to make more of it; for example by continuing:

> "However, even if B's letter is not to be treated as an effective acceptance at the time when it was posted, there is the alternative possibility that it might take effect when the letter was actually received by A a week later. In this case, if the lapse of a week is not held to be an unreasonable time, and A has not in the meantime revoked the offer, A will be liable for breach of contract if he does not deliver the horse. If the lapse of time is held to be unreasonable, there is no contract."

The general lesson from this is: in all legal problems use your brain and *have the courage to argue.* Examinations are designed in part to test your ability to apply what you do know to the unfamiliar fact situation. If a problem falls midway between two authorities, this may indicate that there is a fundamental conflict of principle between the two authorities, and that it is necessary to hold that one of them was wrongly decided. Alternatively, you may come to the conclusion that there is a real distinction between the authorities, and in this event the problem must be looked at from the point of view of general legal principle or public policy to decide whether it should be brought under the one head or the other. The situation was characterised by Paley, an eighteenth-century divine, as the "competition of opposite analogies".[12]

To sum up, when the problem is possibly distinguishable from the authority or authorities nearest in point, a careful analysis of the possible distinction or distinctions should always be given. This is particularly important if the authority in question has been doubted by judges or criticised by legal writers. It may be that the student does not feel competent to discuss the various distinctions, but even so the existence of the possible distinctions should be pointed out in the answer. Moreover, distinctions should be pointed out even though in

---

[12] *Moral and Political Philosophy*, vi. VIII.

the opinion of the student they are not material, if it could conceivably be argued that they are material: of course the student should express an opinion that they are not material.

If there is a possibility of the authority in question being overruled, it is more important than ever to mention its status in the judicial hierarchy, as well as stating any objections that have been urged against it.

When you have a number of cases to quote, it is generally best to quote the nearest authority first and to allot it the most space; the other cases can be brought more casually into the discussion, as you have time. When you have read a case in the reports or in a case book, do your best to convey this fact by referring to some apposite passage in the judgment or some other relevant detail of the report which will indicate that you have not merely relied on a textbook.

If you know that there is no case bearing directly upon the problem, say so. The fact that the problem is not covered by authority is in itself a valuable piece of information. If the authority for a proposition is a statute, say this also, even though you may have forgotten the name of the statute.

DOUBT

Where the law is doubtful, a categorical statement that the rule is one way or the other will earn few, if any, marks. This is particularly important in answering problems. If the answer to the problem is doubtful, say so, and then suggest what the answer ought to be. It is a mistake to simulate confidence where you have no certain knowledge.

After discussing a problem full of "moot" points, try to avoid the weak conclusion that "A is perhaps liable". Your conclusion may be that if the facts are so-and-so, he is liable; if they are such and such, he is not. Or, if the court follows *Smith v Jones*, then A will be liable, but if it follows *Robinson v Edwards*, which is to be preferred for reasons previously given, then A will not be liable.

PROBLEMS ON STATUTES

A problem may be set on a statute as well as on a case. If you do not have the statute with you, you must then recall the words of the statute as best you can, apply them to the problem and, as in all problems, look for the "catch". Here is an illustration from constitutional law:

Aikenhead J., a judge of the High Court, is convicted of driving under the influence of drink. Can he be dismissed from judicial office, and if so by whom?

The attitude of students towards a problem like this varies. Some, though knowing the terms of the Act of Settlement, or of the similar statute now in force,[13] steer clear of the problem because they are afraid of it. Others write down simply:

"By the Act of Settlement 1701, 'Judges' Commissions [shall] be made *quamdiu se bene gesserint*,[14] but upon the Address of both Houses of Parliament it may be lawful to remove them'. Aikenhead J. can be removed under this provision."

This is not a bad answer and would be given a pass mark. Had the candidate added that dismissal was actually effected by the Crown this might have risen to a second class. To obtain a first class, one needs to do a little thinking. Aikenhead J. was appointed "during good behaviour". He has been convicted of crime, and we shall assume for the moment that he has not behaved himself within the meaning of these words. Clearly he can be dismissed if both Houses present an Address to that effect. But can he not, in this case, be dismissed even without an Address? What the examiner is evidently after is the correct interpretation of the words of the Act of Settlement, or rather of the Act now in force replacing the Act of Settlement. Do these words mean that judges can be dismissed by the Crown only upon an Address of both Houses (with a direction to the Houses that they are not to present an Address unless the judge has misbehaved himself)?

Or do the words mean that judges can be dismissed by the Crown either if they have not behaved themselves (for example, been convicted of crime) or on an Address of both Houses? In other words, are the Houses the sole judges of the correctness of the judges' behaviour, or not? The second interpretation can be arrived at by reading the

---

[13] The Constitutional Reform Act 2005, s.33.

[14] "For as long as they behave themselves."

provision in two parts: (1) judges' commissions are to be made for as long as they behave themselves, implying that if they misbehave they may be dismissed by the Crown; (2) they may be removed by the Crown on an Address of both Houses, even though they have not misbehaved themselves. The first interpretation can be arrived at by reading the provision as a whole (judges are appointed during good behaviour, and the two Houses are the sole judges of bad behaviour).

A good lawyer, who reads carefully, ponders meanings and is prepared to discuss difficulties, might be able to see this point in the problem without having read anything upon it. When one studies the literature one finds that, surprising as it may seem, the weight of legal opinion is in favour of the second view; and it is not even clear what is the proper legal means that the Crown should use to establish misbehaviour before dismissing a judge.[15] A further question that arises (and that might be perceived on the face of this problem) is whether dismissal by the Crown can only be for misbehaviour in office or whether it can be for an offence not related to judicial office or affecting judicial ability.

If the latter, can it be for any offence or only for a serious one, and is the offence in the problem sufficiently serious? In practice the Crown would now be unlikely to dismiss a judge without an Address, and it would be for the two Houses to decide whether the misbehaviour justified dismissal. This example shows how it is possible to display the qualities of a good lawyer without knowing much law.

Here is another problem in constitutional law to reinforce the point.

At a time of national emergency, a statute is passed giving power to make Orders in Council for the public safety and defence of the realm. Would it be a valid objection to an Order made under this statute that it imposes a tax?

The type of answer to be expected from the Painful Plodder would be as follows:

"A statute similar in terms to that in the problem was DORA,[16] passed in the First World War. By Regulations under this statute the Food Controller

---

[15] A.W. Bradley and K.D. Ewing, *Constitutional and Administrative Law* (16th edn, 2015), p.328; W.P.M. Kennedy, "Removal and Tenure of Judges" (1945–46) 6 U. of Tor. L.J. 464–465.

[16] Defence of the Realm Consolidation Act 1914.

was empowered to regulate dealings in any article. Under these powers the Food Controller ordered that no milk should be sold within certain counties except under licence. In *Att.-Gen. v Wilts United Dairies* (1922) the question arose whether the Food Controller was entitled to charge for the granting of a licence under this Order. It was held by the HL that he was not. This case was approved by the Court of Appeal in *Congreve v Home Office* [1976] in connection with the power to levy an additional charge for a television licence. The answer to the question is therefore—'Yes'."

This answer exhibits a common defect: it cites a case without explaining the legal principle involved in it, i.e. the legal ground on which the case was decided. Plodder says that in *Att.-Gen. v Wilts UD*[17] it was held that the Food Controller could not charge for the licence. This is true, but we need to know why. The facts of the case contained three elements: (1) DORA, giving power to make Regulations for the public safety and defence of the realm; (2) the "daughter" Regulations made under DORA allowing the Food Controller to regulate dealings in any article; and (3) the Food Controller's Order ("granddaughter" of DORA) that no milk should be sold without licence, coupled with the grant of a licence on condition of receiving payment. Now the decision was that the money promised by the dairy company could not be recovered by the Crown, for the reason that (a) any prerogative power to tax had been taken away by the Bill of Rights 1689, and that (b) as for the statutory powers of DORA, the Regulations under which the Food Controller was acting did not on their wording enable him to impose a tax. The Regulations enabled him to regulate dealings in an article, but regulation of dealings is one thing, taxing another. Order (3) was therefore *ultra vires*[18] the Regulations (2). Had the candidate understood these reasons it would at once have been apparent that the decision in *Att.-Gen. v Wilts UD* did not conclude the question asked. All that the case decided was that the Food Controller was acting outside the Regulations since the Regulations did not give the power to tax. The question whether a Regulation that expressly gave the power to tax would itself be *ultra vires* DORA was not decided.

Now here is the answer of a candidate who may be called the Discerning Dilettante. Such a person knows virtually nothing about

---

[17] (1922) 38 T.L.R. 781.

[18] i.e. "outside the powers" conferred by the enabling provision.

the Bill of Rights or the decision in *Att.-Gen. v Wilts UD*, but addresses the question and employs intelligence.

"It may be that the Order is *intra vires*[19] the statute. The statute gives power to make Orders for the public safety and defence of the realm: in other words for the waging of war. Obviously you cannot wage war without taxing. Money, it is said, makes the sinews of war. To this it may be objected that although it is necessary to tax in order to wage war, it is not necessary for the Executive to tax without a statute. Parliament is still in being; why not leave taxation to Parliament?

A valid reply to this objection would be that it is a political objection to the passing of a statute worded in this wide way, not a legal objection to the validity of the Order, if a statute worded so widely has been passed. If the objection were legally valid it could be used to defeat almost all Orders made under this statute, which would be absurd. Suppose that under this defence statute the Government makes an Order requisitioning land for anti-aircraft missile sites. It would obviously be no valid objection to such an Order that the Order is not necessary for public safety because Parliament could have passed it. The object of the defence statute is to delegate to the Executive what in peacetime would be the function of Parliament. Surely the question whether Parliament could have passed the particular legislation is logically irrelevant to the question whether the legislation is for the public safety and defence of the realm.

However, it seems unlikely that a court would take the view that is being expressed here. The English tradition that it is for Parliament to do the taxing is so deep-seated that the court would probably assert a legal presumption, as a matter of statutory interpretation, that powers of taxation are not included in a statutory delegation of power unless clear words are used, and that a general formula like that in the statute stated in the question is not sufficient."

Or, as Atkin L.J. (as he then was) put it in *Att.-Gen. v Wilts UD* in the Court of Appeal, and as the very able candidate might wish to paraphrase, "in view of the historic struggle of the legislature to secure for itself the sole power to levy money upon the subject, its complete success in that struggle, the elaborate means adopted by the representative House to control the amount, the conditions and the purpose of the levy, the circumstances would be remarkable indeed which would induce the court to believe that the legislature had sacrificed all the well-known checks and precautions, and, not in express words, but merely by implication, had entrusted a Minister of the Crown with

---

[19] "Within the powers [of]."

undefined and unlimited powers of imposing charges upon the subject for purposes connected with his department".[20]

The point is reinforced by *Congreve*,[21] where the Court of Appeal assumed that *Att.-Gen. v Wilts UD* was an authority on the application of the Bill of Rights. The really good student would have been able to show, therefore, that *Wilts UD* was relevant to but not decisive of the question set. Discussion of more recent authorities in which the courts have restated the proposition that it is for Parliament to do the taxing (as in the cases where it was held that local authorities have no authority to charge for housing in the absence of express authority such as *R. v Richmond upon Thames LBC, ex p. Watson*[22] and *R. v North and East Devon Health Authority, ex p. Coughlan*[23]) round out the answer in a way that makes it first class.

RELEVANCY

When answering a problem, never preface your answer with a general disquisition on the area of law relating to the problem. Start straight away to answer the problem. Problems are set chiefly to test your ability to apply the law you know, and the examiner will speedily tire of reading an account of the law that is not brought into direct relation to the problem. Where the problem contains several persons, say A and B as possible claimants and C and D as possible defendants, the best course is to begin your answer by writing down the heading: *A v C*. When you have dealt with this, write (say) *B v C*, referring back to your previous answer for any points that do not need to be repeated. Then you will deal with *A v D* and *B v D*.

The advice to plunge into the specific problem, on the model of counsel's opinion, applies even where the problem is divided into several parts, all of which are on the same general area of law. For instance, suppose that in criminal law a question consists of a chain of short problems on insanity numbered (i), (ii), (iii), etc.

It is not advisable to preface the answer with a discussion

[20] (1921) 37 T.L.R. 884 at 886.
[21] [1976] Q.B. 629.
[22] [2001] Q.B. 370.
[23] [2001] Q.B. 213.

of *McNaghten's Case*,[24] even though *McNaghten's Case* is relevant to each of the numbered problems. The examiner is impatient to see you answering the problems. You should therefore write the figure (i) at the very beginning of your answer, and begin to tackle problem (i). In the course of doing so you can, of course, set out and discuss *McNaghten's Case*. When you come to (ii), (iii) and the rest, it will be easy enough to put a back reference, if necessary, to your previous discussion of the case.

Although a problem is not an invitation to launch out into a general disquisition on the area of law on which the problem is set, it is important in working out the problem to state all the rules of law that are really relevant to it. A frequent blemish upon an otherwise good answer is that the relevant rule of law is not expressly stated but is left to be implied from the candidate's conclusion. Much the better practice is first to state the rule of law and then to apply it to the facts. Do not write: "D is liable on the contract because he did not communicate his revocation of his offer". It is better style to write: "An uncommunicated revocation of an offer is ineffective. Here D's revocation did not come to the notice of the offeree, so the offeree's acceptance of the offer was valid, and D is liable on the contract".

Sometimes, the examiner asks: "can B sue A?" This formula, very common in law examinations, means: Can B sue A *successfully?* Examinees sometimes answer it by saying: "B can sue A but he will fail". This displays the writer's common sense but also his lack of knowledge of legal phraseology. It is true that there is virtually no restriction upon the bringing of actions: for instance, I can at this moment sue the Prime Minister for assault— though I shall fail in the action. But when a lawyer asserts that A can sue B, what he means is that A can sue B successfully; if he meant the words to be taken literally, they would not have been worth the uttering.

For much the same reason, you should never write a sentence like: "B can argue that . . . but the argument will fail," or "B has committed such-and-such a crime, but he has a good defence." The proper way to put the last sentence would be to say: "If B is charged with such-and-such a crime, there would be a good defence."

When a problem is based on a rule, for example, the rule in

Derry v Peek[25] or *Rylands v Fletcher*,[26] it is usually advisable to state the whole rule in a sentence or two, even though some parts of the rule are not material to the problem. No further details should be given of parts of the rule that are not material.

Where the problem turns on an exception to a rule (for example, an exception to the rule in *Rylands v Fletcher*), there is usually no need to state any exceptions other than the one that is relevant.

QUESTIONS DIVIDED INTO PARTS

Questions are frequently divided into two or more parts, and this division raises difficulties of its own for the inexpert candidate.

Sometimes the problem begins with a common opening part before branching out into its subdivisions. The following is an example:

A writes to B offering to sell him a horse Phineas for £1,000.

   (i) B posts a letter accepting, but misdirects it and in consequence it is a
        week late in being delivered to A. Meanwhile A has sold Phineas to
        C.
   (ii) B, after posting a letter of acceptance to A, sends A a fax cancelling
        "my letter now in the post". The fax is delivered to A before B's
        letter. Discuss.

It should be obvious that in this type of problem (i) and (ii) are alternative possibilities, to be dealt with separately; (ii) is not meant to follow upon and include the facts of (i). Candidates sometimes suppose that this is all a single problem, to be disposed of in a single breath.

Another mistake that can be made with this particular problem is to suppose that the opening sentence is itself a question, inviting a general disquisition on the legal nature of an offer. Since you are clearly told that A has made an offer, this would be superfluous.

A different type of two-part problem is one in which the second part commences: "Would it make any difference to your answer if . . . ?". This means that the second part of the question is the same as the

---

[25] (1889) 14 App.Cas. 337.
[26] (1868) L.R. 3 H.L. 330.

first part, except for the variation expressly stated. An illustration is as follows:

(i)   A is firing with an air gun in the garden at a target on a tree. The shot glances off the tree and hits A's gardener, B. Can B sue A?

(ii)   Would your answer be different if the shot had been fired by A's daughter, C?

Most students assume that (ii) is a question as to the liability of C. Clearly on its wording the question is the same as in (i) namely, as to the liability of A.

Sometimes a problem is so worded as to involve two successive questions, but the second question logically arises only if the first is answered in a certain way. Suppose that the student has answered the first question in the other way; what is to be done about the second? The answer is that the question should be attempted, and for the purpose of answering the second part of the question the candidate should state that the question is being answered on the assumption that the answer to the first part may be incorrect. An example from the law of contract:

Pickwick, who manufactures cricket bats, affixed a signboard on the boundary of the field belonging to the Dingley Dell Cricket Club, stating that if any batsman hit the signboard with a batted ball during the course of a match Pickwick would pay him the sum of £500. Bothers hit the board whilst batting in a match between Dingley Dell and Muggleton, and afterwards orally requested Pickwick to pay £500 to Mrs Jingle, to whom Bothers was indebted for board and lodging. Mrs Jingle demands payment of the £500 from Pickwick but is refused. Discuss the rights of the parties.

This problem involves two issues: (i) whether there is a contract between Pickwick and Bothers, resulting in a debt owed by Pickwick to Bothers; and (ii) whether Bothers has validly assigned the debt to Mrs Jingle. Issue (i) turns on the difficult distinction between consideration and the performance of a condition precedent to a gratuitous promise,[27] or if you like on the equally difficult question of intent

---

[27] See G.H. Treitel, *The Law of Contract* (14th edn, 2015); J. Beatson, *Anson's Law*

to contract. It may well happen that the student in considering this comes to the conclusion that there is no contract between Pickwick and Bothers. If this view is correct, issue (ii) does not really arise. All the same, it should be dealt with. It may be that the examiner disagrees with the candidate's answer to (i), and although that may not affect the candidate's marks on (i), marks will lost on (ii) if the issue is not dealt with. Even if the examiner agrees with the candidate's answer to (i), the examiner must have meant (ii) to be dealt with, or else it would not have been included.

A fourth kind of two-part question consists of an essay question followed by a problem. The difficulty here is often that it is not clear whether the problem is meant to bear any relation to the essay question or not. No universal rule can be stated, because examiners differ in their practice, but nearly always there is meant to be a connection, at least if the two parts of the question are not subdivided by numbers or letters. I am conscious that this may not sound very helpful advice. But some examinees fail to search for a connection between the essay question and the rider, thus missing the point intended by the examiner, while other examinees, finding no connection between the two, avoid the question altogether, thinking that they must have missed the point. The student must be left to steer a course between this Scylla and Charybdis. A similar potential problem for the candidate when the question is a multi-header is whether all parts of the question carry equal marks. In my view (but it is only my view, and you should check as to the understanding within your own institution) a candidate is entitled to assume that this is the rule that all parts of questions should be treated equally, and that if the examiner wishes to accord marks according to some other scheme, the rubric at the beginning of the paper should alert the candidates to this fact.

The overlapping of subjects

In real life, legal issues do not present themselves as involving problems pertaining only to tort or contract or the criminal law. But for examinations purposes, examiner and examinee alike have

of Contract (30th edn, 2016); Cheshire, Fifoot and Furmston, *The Law of Contract* (16th edn, 2012).

to pretend that they do. Hence, in a problem on the criminal law, make no statement as to the law of tort, unless exceptionally the question whether a crime has been committed involves a question of tort. Similarly, in a problem on tort make no statement as to the law of crime.

ANSWERING PROBLEMS IN CRIMINAL LAW

There is no one correct format for answering a problem question in the criminal law. But as a check list, you could probably organise your thinking around a four-point check list, such as:

(1)   the name of the offence;

(2)   the *actus reus* of the offence;

(3)   *mens rea*;

(4)   possible defences.

   Always consider all the possible crimes that may have been committed, by all possible persons, and all the possible defences open. By "possible" I mean "seemingly possible to an ignorant person". If you consider that such-and-such crime has not been committed, or that such-and-such defence is not available (though an ignorant person might think it is), do not pass it by in silence but state your opinion expressly. You should also give the reason for your opinion as shortly as the importance of the point seems to require. The reason for this advice is that quite possibly the question was deliberately set, and if you refrain from commenting the examiner may think that you have avoided it by good luck rather than good management.
   Never come to the defences until you have stated the crime for which the defendant is in your opinion likely to be charged. Start with the responsibility of the perpetrator (principal), taking accessories afterwards. If you think that the problem leaves open some question of fact, state the law according to whether the fact is present or absent. If the outcome is clear you can say so; for example "D is guilty of murder". But if the application of law to fact is not clear, you need not state a definite opinion or even "submit" that the position

is so-and-so. For example, the question may state that the defendant shot at a burglar when a bystander was standing dangerously close, and hit the bystander. It is not for you to say that the defendant foresaw the possibility of hitting the bystander: that is for the jury. Never assume that the defendant had a particular state of mind unless the question states that such a mental state was present. Instead, consider whether there is any evidence for the jury (sufficient to require the judge to leave the case to the jury); if there is, explain how the judge would direct the jury, and state whether a verdict of guilty would be likely to be upheld or upset on appeal. It is at these points in a jury trial that the legal opinion is important: a lawyer is not directly concerned with the work of the jury.

When several crimes appear to emerge from the facts of a problem, it is best to start your answer with the gravest crime that seems clearly to have been committed. For it would be absurd to open your answer by considering some summary offence of which the defendant is guilty, and then to wind up with the conclusion that he has also committed, say, murder!

The murder should come first, and the lesser offence as a rather casual postscript. If the defendant is clearly guilty of a crime like wounding with intent, and only doubtfully guilty of murder, it is sensible to start with the clear crime before coming to the doubtful one. Problems in criminal law often start with an inchoate crime—conspiracy, attempt or incitement. Even though the problem shows that the full crime was consummated, the culprits may be convicted of attempt or incitement, so that it may be relevant to mention these crimes—though normally, the indictment would be for the completed crime, not for a mere attempt or incitement. If you mention the possibility of a conspiracy charge, it would be wise to add that the addition of conspiracy counts when the crime is consummated must be specially justified. As for incitement, if the crime is actually committed the inciter becomes an accessory to it. In other words, the difference between (i) incitement and (ii) being a participant in a crime as one who has counselled or procured it is that in (i) the main crime has not been (or need not have been) committed by the person so incited, and in (ii) it has.

ANSWERING PROBLEMS IN TORT

As in criminal law, look for all the possible torts that may have been committed, and consider whether their essentials have been satisfied. Draw into your net all possible defendants, and then turn round and consider all the possible defences open on the facts given.

9 ANSWERING ESSAY QUESTIONS

"He that knows, and knows not that he knows,
is asleep—wake him."

—Anon.

This chapter is chiefly concerned with the answering of questions other than problems, though some of the remarks apply also to the answering of problems. Like the last chapter it is not meant for hasty consumption immediately before the fray. The wise student will, well in advance of the examination itself, look at the examination papers for the past few years, and, whether compelled to or not, will write out the answers to some questions (even if only in brief note form) in order to gain practice in self-expression. Past examination papers will also show the probable lay-out of the paper that the examiner will be expected to follow, and the amount of time likely to be allowed for each question. You should also have access to the regulations according to which the form and conduct of the examination is settled, and the syllabus which the examiner is required to treat as the template. You may even have access to the examiner's report from the previous year or years. Remember, though, that the examiner (and the syllabus) may change from one year to the next, and that questions actually asked may reflect legal change that has occurred since previous papers. "Question spotting"—the practice of revising only selected parts of the syllabus in the hope that these are the areas most likely to be examined—is an examination strategy that carries serious risks.

SUBDIVIDED QUESTIONS

If your question is expressly divided into several sub-questions, answer each sub-question separately; and if the sub-questions are numbered (i, ii, iii) or lettered (a, b, c) number or letter them in the same way in your answer. A question may be divided into parts even though numbers or letters are not used. For instance, the question,

> "Summarise the provisions of, and the changes introduced by, the Unfair Contract Terms Act 1977, Part 1 and subsequent statutory modifications."

invites an answer in two parts: (1) the provisions of the Act; (2) its impact on the previous law. It would be wise to write your answer under these two headings (though there would be no objection to applying the double answer to the Act section by section). Always model your answer to conform to the question: do not, for instance, on this particular question adopt the chronological order of (1) the pre-Act law, and (2) the Act. The reason is that if the examiner is reading your script quickly (and there may be hundreds of scripts to mark) it will cause the reader to be puzzled by your departure from the order of the question. Besides, the question may well have been set like that with the object of seeing whether your mind is sufficiently adaptable to vary the order of what you have learnt.

RELEVANCY

In answering a question you should, of course, give as much detail as you can within the limits of the question. It is sometimes possible to answer a question literally in a couple of sentences, but this will not always impress the examiner. The extreme example of this kind of answer is the story told by Mark Twain, in his *Life on the Mississippi*, of his piloting lesson.

> "Presently Mr. Bixby turned on me and said: 'What is the name of the first point above New Orleans?' I was gratified to be able to answer promptly, and I did. I said I didn't know."

Not many candidates would attempt this frankness in the examination room, but they often do suppose that an accurate answer directed to the very words of the question is all that is required. This is frequently a mistake. For instance, in the law of contract the question,

> What is the difference between void and voidable contracts?

could be accurately answered by stating that a void contract is an apparent contract that is in truth no contract at all, while a voidable contract is a contract that is capable of being avoided at the option of one party. This, though correct, would not score many marks. It is an accurate statement of the difference of *definition* between void and voidable contracts, but it says nothing of their different *effects*. The candidate should, therefore, add, as a minimum, a discussion of such cases as *Cundy v Lindsay*,[1] *Lewis v Averay*[2] and *Hudson v Shogun Finance Ltd*[3] in order to illustrate the effect of each kind of contract (or apparent contract) upon third-party rights. To put this advice generally, if you are asked to distinguish between two legal concepts or institutions, you should give not only the difference of definition but also the difference of legal effect. It need hardly be added that the examiner *always* wants reasons and authorities for the answer, even though a question does not expressly ask for them.

To say that a question should be answered fully is not to say that irrelevant matter should be introduced into the answer. Questions are often worded to cover only a fragment of a particular subject; in that case the examiner does *not* want the whole of it.

This question of relevancy is often the examinee's greatest headache. Sometimes, it may be necessary to interpret a badly worded question, with no hope of redress if the guess as to the examiner's meaning should turn out to be wrong. My advice is this. If the question is reasonably clear do not wander outside it. If there is a doubt as to its meaning, the question will usually have at least a central kernel of meaning that is relatively clear. Answer this to begin with. Then, as to the doubtful "shell" of the question, if you still have time to write on the question, you should expressly point out the doubt in your mind as to what you are being asked, and proceed to write on the doubtful part of the question for the rest of the allotted time. If, on the other hand, you have no time left for the doubtful part of the question, declare your doubt whether the question was intended to have any further scope, and leave it there. The fact that you have been able

---

[1] (1878) 3 App.Cas. 459.
[2] [1972] 1 Q.B. 198.
[3] [2003] UKHL 62; [2004] 1 A.C. 919.

to spend your whole time on the core of the question is itself some indication that the question was not intended to have any wider scope.

For instance suppose that a question in the law of contract is:

"Where both parties are equally in the wrong, the claim of the defendant is the stronger." Discuss.

Clearly this invites a discussion of the general rule preventing recovery of money paid or property transferred under an illegal contract, and this rule, with its exceptions and quasi-exceptions, should therefore be discussed first. The problem then arises: does the question cover also the general rule against suing for damages for breach of an illegal contract? However you decide this conundrum, you should state your decision in the answer. If you rule this second topic out of order, and the examiner wished it to be included, the examiner will at least see that you have had the point present in your mind, and will probably also be brought to see that the question was at fault in its wording. In any case, the proper limits of time for the question should not be exceeded. If in doubt whether a particular matter is relevant, a good test is to ask yourself whether, if the examiner had wished you to discuss it, it would have been natural to have framed an extra question upon it. If it would not, you are safe to proceed to answer it within the scope of your present answer.

Once the limits of the question are settled, do not canter beyond them. The examiner cannot give credit for irrelevancy, because that would be unfair to others who have answered only the question that they were asked. There is, however, a clever way in which matters otherwise irrelevant may be lightly introduced. This is by the method of comparison. For instance, if in public law you are directed to write about the status of "proportionality" as a ground for judicial review of administrative action, a discussion of judicial review generally would be out of order. But a comparison with the other grounds of review (irrationality, illegality and procedural impropriety) would be admissible, and credit would be given for it.

Many students begin an answer with a prologue. Cut it out. In particular, do not start with the historical background if you are not asked for it, unless you have some special reason for doing this—and if so, state the reason. Sometimes the historical background makes the law more intelligible, or supports one interpretation of the law rather than another. Your lecturer may well have introduced this background for this purpose, but you should not automatically mimic what you hear in the lectures. If you are asked the history of the action of *assumpsit*, do not begin with a paragraph on the medieval precursors of *assumpsit*—debt, detinue and account. If the question had wanted these it would have said so. If you are asked to discuss, say, *Nordenfelt's v Maxim Nordenfelt Guns & Ammunition Co Ltd*,[4] begin by setting out the facts and decision—do not start in the Middle Ages. Having stated the case you may legitimately put it into its historical setting in order to show what advance it made on the previous law; and you may also indicate the trend of development that it started. But all this depends on the time you have left after giving your attention to the centre of the question.

Students (particularly advanced students) are frequently vexed by doubts as to the amount of detail that they should put into their answer. The best advice is: aim at concentrating all your intelligence on the specific question, and bring in your knowledge only so far as it is relevant. If you show that you are a master of the *relevant* knowledge, the examiner will readily give you credit for knowing the rest of the subject. An example would be the question:

"The monarchy is an historical anachronism." Discuss.

This is not an invitation to give the whole history of the monarchy: the question is whether the monarchy *is* an historical anachronism. Are there any features of the modern monarchy that can be explained only as historical survivals, which are out of place in modern society, or has the monarchy been so adapted that it is a truly modern institution?

Again, should you assume that your examiner is an ignoramus and explain everything, or can you assume that the examiner is a lawyer (and very probably, you will know which lawyer, since it will frequently be the lecturer, or one of them) so that a hint is sufficient? The answer lies somewhere between these two extremes. On the one hand, the examiner wants to be told *nothing* that is irrelevant to the question.

---

[4] [1894] A.C. 535.

On the other hand, examiners are suspicious of "nutshell knowledge" and "footnote knowledge" (i.e. the bald statement of a proposition followed by the title of a case), and will want as full an explanation of everything that is relevant as is possible in the time allowed. More specifically, the following rules may be laid down.

(1)   If a legal concept is mentioned in the question, do not attempt a full explanation of it unless explanation is requested or necessitated by the question. For instance, on a question involving the law of wagers, there is generally no need to discuss what is a wager. Had the examiner wanted such a discussion, this would have been asked for in a separate part of the question. On the other hand, a question in the form of a quotation with a request for discussion normally requires an explanation of everything in the quotation. Thus the question, "How far is the continuing existence of the royal prerogative compatible with parliamentary sovereignty?" demands an explanation of the royal prerogative as well as of parliamentary sovereignty, and an explanation of the difficulties that are posed for the former by the latter.

(2)   If the legal concept is not mentioned in the question but is first introduced by the candidate in the answer, it should be explained. Take, for instance, the question: When will the right to avoid a voidable contract be lost? It is not enough, in the course of answering this question to mention that the right will be lost if *restitutio in integrum* (restoration to the original position) ceases to be possible. You must not assume that the examiner knows what restoration to the original position entails. Say what it means, and when such *restitutio* ceases to be possible.

GETTING AT THE POINT

Before unmuzzling your wisdom on any question, ponder the question carefully. Very often the examiner will have worded it in a particular way in order to enable you to show a little originality of treatment. Take, for example, the following question in criminal law.

Discuss the decision in *R. v Dudley and Stephens* from the standpoint of the purposes of criminal punishment.

This is not simply a question on the decision in *R. v Dudley and Stephens*, nor is it simply a question on the defence of necessity in general. It is a question, primarily, on the purposes of criminal punishment. You are requested to set out the different theories of the purposes of criminal punishment (general and particular deterrence, incapacitation, reformation, ethical retribution) and to consider whether any of these theories can be used to support the conviction in *R. v Dudley and Stephens*.

Another "angle" question, this time from constitutional law:

What parallels may be drawn between royal prerogative and parliamentary privilege? Examine, in particular, the attitude of the court in questions concerning (a) their exercise, and (b) their extent.

I have marked hundreds of scripts in which the answer offered to this question was a formless mass of cases and propositions concerning prerogative and privilege. These candidates simply vomited over the page everything they knew upon the two topics; they made no attempt to bring their knowledge into relation with the question, and did not even divide off their answer by the (a) and (b) of the question. The following is a skeleton of the answer that an examiner wants. It should be within the competence of everyone of moderate ability who has worked properly and who focuses attention upon what is being asked.

"Prerogative and privilege are somewhat similar in definition. Prerogative may be defined as the exceptional position of the king (and hence the executive) at common law. Privilege is the exceptional position of the two Houses of Parliament and of their members at common law *and by statute*. There is, however, a considerable difference of content between prerogative and privilege.

Turning to (a) in the question, the traditional rule is that the court will *not* inquire into the *mode of* user of an undoubted privilege. [Demonstration of this by decided or hypothetical cases.] This was originally true of the prerogative, but later developments establish that the exercise of the prerogative can be questioned in accordance with the ordinary principles of judicial review unless the particular prerogative happens to be 'non-justiciable'. [Demonstration.]

As to (b), the rule is that the court *will* inquire into the *limits* of both prerogative and privilege. [Similar demonstration of this.]

Both prerogative and privilege are subject to statute. [Demonstration.]"

Another example.

How has the doctrine of parliamentary sovereignty been accommodated within the Human Rights Act 1998?

This does not invite a discussion of the basic principles of sovereignty; still less is it an invitation to write a general essay on parliamentary sovereignty. It is a question on the difficulties presented by the doctrine of parliamentary sovereignty that faced the framers of the Human Rights Act.

It may seem unnecessary to add: if given a choice, do not attempt to answer a question that you do not understand (unless, of course, your plight is such that there is no other you can do instead). This may seem obvious advice, but it is often ignored. The following, taken from a constitutional law paper, is a good example of the "wrapped-up" question.

"Much of the structure of the Constitution is now mere form; it is tolerated only because in practice its form is no indication of the way it functions." Comment.

What does this question mean? If it conveys no clear meaning to you, avoid it. If you attempt to answer it and miss the point, the examiner may not be able to give you any marks, because you will not have answered the question. Actually the question is on our old friends, the conventions of the constitution. It is an invitation to enumerate the conventions and to contrast them with the law. Once the meaning is penetrated, the writing of the answer is easy.

INTRODUCING CASES INTO AN ANSWER

Some textbooks state a proposition of law and follow it by a case in small type in a separate paragraph. Do not adopt this practice. It may possibly be a good teaching method, but you are not teaching the examiner the law: you are showing that you can use authorities like a lawyer. Therefore, introduce cases into your answer in literary form.

Remember that the citation of cases is not an end in itself; it is a means to the establishing of legal principle. For this reason you should try to avoid making your written work look like a mere bundle of cases. As a matter of style, an essay that sets out the principle involved in the case before mentioning the case is preferable to one that merely blurts out one case after another without introduction. Here are two answers to the same examination question in constitutional law: both are made out of the same raw material, but observe how much more intelligible the second is than the first.

Question: To what extent is Act of State a defence in respect of acts done on behalf of the British Government which would otherwise be torts?

Answer 1: In Buron v Denman[5] the defendant, a British naval commander, had set fire to Spanish slave barracoons[6] on the coast of Africa (not British soil), and his act was ratified by the Crown. It was held that the aggrieved Spaniard, being a foreigner, had no action in England, Act of State being a defence.

In *Walker v Baird*[7] the defendant, again a British naval officer, had trespassed upon the plaintiff 's lobster fishery in Newfoundland. In doing so he acted under the orders of the Crown. The Privy Council held that Act of State was no defence, the reason evidently being that the plaintiff was a British subject and that the act was done on British soil. A similar conclusion was reached in *Nissan v Att.-Gen.*,[8] where the plaintiff was a British subject and the act was done in the Republic of Cyprus.

In *Johnstone v Pedlar*[9] the plaintiff was an alien resident in England. His property was seized by the police with the ratification of the Crown. The House of Lords held that Act of State was no defence.

The foregoing answer sets out the authorities but it does not clearly extract the principles from them.

Answer 2: Act of State is a good defence where the tort was committed by a State servant against a foreigner outside British soil, and the act was authorised or ratified[10] by the Crown. In *Buron v Denman* all these conditions were satisfied. The facts were that a British naval commander

---

[5] (1848) 2 Ex. 167; 154 E.R. 450.
[6] Sheds.
[7] [1892] A.C. 491.
[8] [1970] A.C. 179.
[9] [1921] 2 A.C. 262.
[10] The difference between authorisation and ratification is that the first comes before the act, and the second after it.

fired Spanish slave barracoons on the coast of Africa (not British soil), and his act was ratified by the Crown. The defence availed. The law has, however, been thrown into doubt by the decision of the House of Lords in *Nissan v Att.-Gen.*[11] According to Lord Wilberforce, Acts of State are confined to "acts committed abroad in the conduct, under the prerogative, of foreign relations with other states". It seems that not every act authorised by the Crown will fall under this definition. Could it even be applied to the act done in *Buron v Denman*?

Discordant views were expressed in *Nissan's case* on whether the defence availed in respect of a tort committed to a British subject on foreign soil. It seems that British subjects (or, at any rate, citizens of the United Kingdom and colonies) are fully protected where the act is done on British soil: see *Walker v Baird*, where the Privy Council held that Act of State did not excuse a trespass committed on a British subject's lobster fishery in Newfoundland.

Equally the defence cannot be set up in respect of a tort committed against a person resident on British soil, even though that person is an alien: *Johnstone v Pedlar*, H.L. (property of alien in England seized by the police with ratification of Crown; Act of State no defence).

In writing down the name of a case it is a good habit to underline the proper names of the parties. It is because lawyers do this that the names of cases come out in italics in print. If you happen to be producing an essay on a word processor, you can italicise the case straightaway. For the student the practice has two advantages. It helps in revising, because it makes the names of the cases stand out to the eye; and it makes the examination-script easier for the examiner to read.

THE SUCCINCT WAY OF STATING CASES

A difficulty that is likely to press upon the better student in dealing with cases in the examination room is that of lack of time. If a single question demands the citation of (say) a dozen cases, how can these be adequately dealt with in the time allowed? The answer is as follows: if at all possible, each case should be dealt with fully,

---

[11] It has been said that this decision was "a disaster for students of the law. The decision of the House of Lords lacks any clear *ratio decidendi* . . . Important questions of law were raised but left half-answered or unanswered, and points that once seemed clear were left shrouded in obscurity." S.A. de Smith and R. Brazier, *Constitutional and Administrative Law* (8th edn, 1998), p.156.

giving in due order the principle involved in the case, its name, its facts, (possibly) the argument of counsel, or the losing argument, (possibly) the court before which the case came, the decision, (possibly) the reasons for the decision, and the *obiter dicta* (if any). If time does not allow of this there is another method. This is to state the rule of law contained in the case, and then to put a full colon, followed by the name of the case, (possibly) the court that decided it, and (in brackets) some outstanding fact or facts. This method was used for *Johnstone v Pedlar* in Answer 2 above. As another instance, the case of *Callow v Tillstone*,[12] on participation in crime, could be stated as follows: "Strict liability in crime does not extend to accessories, who are not liable unless they know the facts: *Callow v Tillstone* (vet who certified unsound meat negligently not an accessory to its exposure for sale, since he did not know it was unsound)". An example from contract would be: "Where it is reasonable to accept by letter, acceptance dates from the posting: *Household Fire Insurance Co v Grant*,[13] CA (lost letter of allotment; held, contract to take shares was complete)".

This shows in a minimum of words that the student knows the rule of law contained in the case and also could state the facts more fully if time permitted. But the method should not be used if a more orthodox presentation of the case is possible. Stating the facts and decision in the ordinary way occupies little more time and looks much better.

CRITICISM

When the question quotes a statement and asks for a discussion of it, do not be afraid to criticise the statement itself if you think it is open to criticism. As often as not the examiner will have disagreed with the statement; that is why it has been set as an examination question (though you must not formulate your answer around that assumption without examining the point from both angles—I have known candidates come horribly to grief by adopting that path).

[12] (1880) L.R. 6 Q.B.D. 79.
[13] (1879) 4 Ex.D. 216.

USE OF FORENSIC MANNERISMS

It was said in the last chapter that doubtful law should not be represented as if it were well established. Conversely, to state the law as doubtful when it is not doubtful will also be penalised in marks. Excessive caution is therefore as much to be avoided as excessive dogmatism. This may seem obvious, but I have known students repeatedly use the phrase "I respectfully submit" before some trite proposition or other, which comes across to the reader as affectation. Even words like "seemingly" or "probably" are out of place if the law is clear.

Strictly, a submission ("I submit that . . .") is an argument advanced in court. Counsel will use deferential language in court, particularly in respect of a decision that, it is submitted, was mistaken; the worse the error, the deeper will be the respect that counsel expresses for the judges criticised. Counsel will venture to suggest with the greatest possible respect to Mr Justice Blank, that his Lordship perhaps did not intend those words to be understood in their widest acceptation. Or counsel may suggest, again with the very greatest respect, that a certain decision may perhaps be reconsidered if the point arises again before a court having power to overrule it; meanwhile, it can be distinguished on the facts before the present court.[14] Similarly, a court that feels impelled to depart from its predecessor's decision will do so not only "with the deepest respect" but "with great regret". These punctilios, which help to moderate tempers and maintain the dignity of the courts, are admirable if not carried too far[15]; but legal writings need not be encumbered in this way.

Some writers express humility in a particularly strange way: when they wish to express an opinion but feel that the first person singular

[14] In *Broome v Cassell & Co* [1972] A.C. 1027 a decision in the House of Lords was characterised by the Court of Appeal as being "unworkable" and as having been rendered *per incuriam*; on appeal, the House waxed indignant, but accepted that the Court of Appeal might properly have suggested that the precedent might be reconsidered by the House.

[15] As they can be. Norman Birkett (afterwards Lord Birkett) as an undergraduate used "I submit" in debating. An undergraduate journal took him to task for using this "tiresome formula", and after becoming a judge Birkett commented: "I have paid handsomely for this piece of folly, for I now have to listen every day of my life to a more tiresome formula—'in my respectful submission'—and I confess I weep secret tears of remorse and contrition". (M. Hyde, *Norman Birkett*, p.43).

is too assertive, they use the plural ("we submit"). It is not proposed to discuss the aesthetics of this usage for the text writer[16]; all that I wish to say is that it should not be copied by the student, for in the prose of the young it sounds too grandiloquent. Naturally, one desires to suppress the personal element so far as possible. But if one has an opinion to express there is nothing to offend anybody in a straightforward "in my opinion". Alternatively, expressions like "it is thought that" or "there are good grounds for saying that" or "it follows from the authorities that" can be used. Or you can say "the better opinion is that" (since your opinion is inevitably the better opinion—in your opinion).

THE ARRANGEMENT AND WORDING OF THE ANSWER

Try to make your answer attractive. Examiners are human beings, and they are easily distracted. If a question is capable of being answered in a sentence, answer it immediately in that sentence and proceed to explanation afterwards. Within limits, it is permissible (and often desirable) to divide up the answer into numbered "points", with subheadings underlined. This both saves your time and enables the examiner to see without effort how you have treated the subject. But the process of subdivision should not be pushed too far. An answer that is excessively divided and subdivided may give an unpleasant impression that the candidate has simply learned a crammer or correspondence course by heart.

Lecturers and text writers often indulge in what R.L. Stevenson called "a little judicious levity". The student, who may not be able to distinguish between the judicious and the injudicious sorts, is better advised to avoid levity altogether. The examination candidate should likewise shun all colloquialisms and colloquial abbreviations ("it's", "isn't", etc.). In short, the student should attempt to write the script upon the model of a counsel's opinion or judge's judgment, with gravity and decorum.

A few remarks may be made about citing authorities. Never quote the textbook for an established principle of law. A sentence like

---

[16] But I cannot forbear to record the observation that the use of "we" should be confined to monarchs and editors.

"every simple contract needs consideration to support it, as Treitel points out" is infantile. Textbooks should be quoted only if they express an individual opinion and the lecturer (*qua* lecturer) not at all. Although the examiner is unlikely to be concerned if you strike the wrong note, there is something of a convention that, when quoting authors, an author who is dead may be referred to by surname only, but if still with us it adds some polish to the answer to use a handle, at least on the first occasion of mention—Sir or Dame, Professor, Dr, Mr, Mrs or Ms. As regards judges the customary J., L.J., etc., should be used irrespective of whether they are alive or dead.

If you cross out some words and subsequently wish to restore them, the accepted way of doing it is to put dots underneath the words so deleted and to write "stet"[17] in the margin.

---

[17] "Let it stand".

10 IN THE EXAM ROOM

> "Examinations are formidable even to the best prepared: for the greatest fool may ask more than the wisest man can answer."
>
> —C.C. Colton, *Lacon.*

Previous chapters gave advice that you can act on when practising writing answers before the exam. Those chapters also have advice as to the best ways of answering exam questions, and if you have time, I suggest that you read them. Now some words of wisdom as to revision[1] and the event itself.

You may find it helps to form a "revision syndicate" with two or three friends. Each member revises a different portion of the syllabus, and there is a meeting at which each teaches the others. The process of interchange helps to fix the memory for both sides. You should also, in the weeks running up to the exam, produce some timed answers (in your own handwriting) using papers from previous years and allowing yourself only as much time as the exam will itself permit. But remember in the exam room itself that the question being set this year is not the same as the question that was in last year's paper. Candidates too readily fall into the trap of reproducing an answer that would have been perfect for last year (or, perhaps, an essay produced in the course of the year) rather than addressing the question in this year's paper.

Some students suffer from excessive anxiety, which produces sleeplessness which in turn aggravates the anxiety. If you know from experience that you are the over-anxious type you must confront the fact and take steps to alleviate it. Allot a fixed ration of time for revision, the rest of the day being spent in exercise and other forms of recreation. Another way of reducing end-of-session flap (if you are reading this section of the book early enough in the year) is to spread the task of learning over the whole year. Spend some time each week

---

[1] On the question of how much of the case to remember, may I suggest that you have another look at what was said in Ch.6?

revising the week's material. If your exam starts at 9 am, make sure that you are physically attuned to that time by keeping regular hours and rising sufficiently early for at least a week before.

FIRST READ THE PAPER

Before starting to write, read through the whole of the exam paper and jot down in the margin or on a piece of scrap paper if that has been provided, the names of claimants (or criminal defendants) in any relevant cases you remember, statutes and any other details that are likely to elude you when you come to write out the question. You thus give your memory two chances of recalling the elusive details. Also, if during the exam you think of any fresh authorities that you do not propose to incorporate at once in your script, make a similar note of them. Some candidates leave the exam room complaining that at one stage they remembered a case, but later forgot to cite it. The practice suggested above should obviate this. Most candidates find it useful to make a quick sketch plan of the answer, but you are advised not to spend too long on doing this, since it necessarily consumes time more usefully devoted to answering the question itself. Any student who has worked conscientiously for the exam will be bound to discover that he or she will know far more than can be reflected in the course of the standard three hour exam, and far more than the examiner is able to test. The difficulty in the exam room is to select the relevant material from this memory store.

The most important general piece of advice on exams is that every question in the paper that the student is expected to and can answer should be answered. A candidate should not spend the entire time on only a few of the questions. There is nothing more tedious for the teacher than to hear one of the best students saying, after the exam: "Oh, I did very well, but I only had time to answer half the paper". In nearly all exams the scripts are not judged simply on the questions that the student has answered, where the script is incomplete because the candidate has not attempted the requisite number of questions. On the contrary, the total possible marks are divided equally among all the questions, and no answer can earn more than the maximum allotted marks for that question. The result is that a student may have answered half the paper in a manner worthy of a Justice of the Supreme Court, and yet obtain a third class or fail altogether because the other half has not been answered. Another point to be remembered in this connection is that an examiner is much more willing to give the first 50 per cent of marks on a question than the second 50 per cent, and full marks are practically never given. A candidate may, therefore, get 50 per cent on the whole paper if all the questions are moderately well answered, whereas 50 per cent will not be awarded if the candidate answers half the questions almost perfectly. For the good student, therefore, there is nothing more important in exam technique than dividing up the available time as equally as may be between all the questions.

The same remark applies to questions containing two or more distinct parts. Here the examiner will probably have divided up the possible marks among the component parts (either explicitly, giving an indication of how much is available for each section or in the absence of an indication, by implication). An answer to one part, be it ever so brilliant, can earn only the appropriate total for that part.

It is most important to search for all the possible angles to a question, and this involves reading the question with meticulous care. Pay particular attention to the rubric, making absolutely sure of what it is that you are being asked to do—it should go without saying (but I fear that it does not) that if a divided question is set in either/ or mode, the candidate should not attempt both parts of the question. Equally, if a divided question requires the candidates to attempt both parts, no marks can be given if the candidate does part one, but neglects the second half of the question: read the paper, read the paper, READ THE PAPER.

CHOICE OF QUESTIONS

Most law exams give a certain choice of questions, and most involve a choice as between essay questions and problems (or sometimes the paper will require a candidate to attempt a mixture of the two). It used to be said that the essay questions ("book work" as they were once somewhat disparagingly termed) were set for the weaker students, but I doubt that the modern university lecturer would accept this. A well-directed essay question can be quite as testing as the best-laid problem. That said, there are differences between the two, and some students find (after practice throughout the year) that they prefer attempting the one rather than the other.

Where a choice is given between problems and essay questions, two reasons are sometimes given as to why the better candidate should prefer the problems. First, they are usually shorter to answer, and so save time. Secondly, an examiner may be grudging in giving marks for essay questions where the answer does not display the application of much detailed knowledge in the answering. A good answer to a problem, on the other hand, at once evokes admiration.

There is, it is true, a certain danger in problems, for if the point of the problem is completely missed the result may be catastrophe. But a good student should be able to sense whether the answer is getting the point of the problem or not. If the problem appears "pointless", the candidate had better exercise choice elsewhere in the paper.

Perhaps I should add a corrective to the foregoing paragraph. I said that if the point of a problem is completely missed the result may be catastrophe. This is true. But to give the wrong answer to a problem is not necessarily to miss the point of it. If the point is seen and well argued, the fact that the examiner does not agree with your conclusion will not seriously affect your marks. In legal matters there is usually a certain room for difference of opinion, and even though there be positive authority against your view, the examiner is anxious not so much to test the details of your knowledge as to assess your ability to argue in a lawyer-like way. A safe course to adopt if in any doubt is to present the argument for both sides—to turn yourself successively into counsel for the claimant (prosecutor), counsel for the defendant, and finally the judge. If then the examiner disagrees with your judgment, it will hardly matter because you will have presented (even though you have also rejected) the argument for the alternative point of view.

NAMES OF CASES

A question frequently asked by law students is as to remembering names of cases. The questioner realises, of course, that there is an expectation that cases are to be read and quoted, where relevant, in the answers; but is the poor candidate expected to behave as though learning the telephone directory?

The first and most important reply to the question is this: never refrain from referring to a case in the exam merely because you have forgotten its name. The name is the least important part of the case. Most important is the rule of law contained in the case; next important are the facts; even the name of the court that decided the case (House of Lords/Supreme Court or Court of Appeal) is of more legal value than the proper names of the parties. If the name of the case is imperfectly remembered the approximate name can be given with a question mark in brackets; thus, *Derry v Peek*[2] might be rendered as "*Perry v Deek*(?)". Or the cases can be referred to by the name of the claimant if that only is remembered, for example, "*Derry's case*". Or the name of only the defendant may be given— though in this case it is desirable to make it plain that the name is that of the defendant, for example, "in an action against one Peek", or "in . . . v Peek". Or the case can be identified by reference to some salient fact, for example, "in the case concerning the tramway company's power to use steam". Even if both name and facts are forgotten, the student can at least indicate that there is authority for the proposition by saying, "in one case it was held that . . .".

But although the name is the least important part of the case, it is not altogether without importance. For the immediate purpose of the exam a script in which cases are referred to by name has naturally a more "finished" appearance than one that merely refers to "cases" in the air. Remember too that it is good practice to underline the names of cases, so that the examiner can see at a glance that you are on the right track in your answer. In your professional life (if, indeed, you intend to make the law your profession), you will find that a memory of the names of leading cases will be of help. If you are turning up a point of law in a practitioner's book, and happen to remember a case bearing upon it, you will usually find that, by tracing the case through the index of cases, you will come upon that portion of law in the book more quickly than by any other method.

In order, then, to lay the foundation of a sound legal knowledge, the student should make some effort to remember the names of the outstanding cases. Many of these, the most important, will be acquired simply through pondering over and discussing the cases themselves. For the rest, the amount of energy that is put into the memorising of their names must be left to the individual. Certainly no more than a very small part of the student's time should be devoted to this task, and too

---

[2] (1889) 14 App. Cas. 337.

much should not be attempted. Some students find it useful to compile a wall chart of cases (with an identificatory tag in brackets following the name), which they ruminate upon over the breakfast marmalade. Or a short recital of the cases can be recorded on tape. Another suggestion is to tabulate the cases on postcards, carrying a selection of them in the pocket and revising them from time to time at odd moments.

The precise date of a case need not be committed to memory, but if it is a very old case the century to which it belongs may be mentioned, for extreme old age sometimes weakens its authority. And it may be important to say that a case was decided before the passing of a particular statute.

HANDWRITING, ORTHOGRAPHY AND GRAMMAR

Some people write atrociously. If you feel apprehensive on this score, give a page of your notes to a friend and ask which letters or words in your handwriting give difficulty in reading. You may be penalised if your handwriting is not legible to a examiner (who may be pictured working long into the night under the pressure of a marking deadline). If your handwriting gives difficulty, you may not be given the benefit of the examiner's generosity if, even after several attempts at re-reading your efforts, they remain indecipherable. Make a special effort to improve the appearance of what you write.

Some people cannot spell and do not care about it, knowing that they can for most of the time rely increasingly on automatic spell-checkers. But if you want to make a good impression on examiners, prospective employers[3] or clients, the mastery of our unreasonable orthography is a necessity. Test yourself with the following passage, which contains misspelt words taken from exam scripts. Some of the words are correctly spelt. Others incorrectly. Pick out the words that you think are misspelt and write your own version. Compare your effort with the key at the end of this section.

---

[3] And may I direct the attention of those who think that insistence upon accurate spelling is pure pedantry to a passage from C Harrison, *From Student to Solicitor: The Complete Guide to Securing a Training Contract* (2nd edn, 2015) at p.179: "Employers are looking for candidates who care about their work and can demonstrate attention to detail; they do not want people who cannot be bothered to proof read their own CV, or who do so and miss the mistakes".

"The Homocide Act does not effect this problem, for the Act has not superceded the common law on the point. The question that ocurrs here is whether responsibility is deminished because there is a likelyhood that the provokation would have lead a reasonable person to loose self-control and inflict this grievious harm. The affect of provocation in cases of this catagory is always difficult to gauge. An analagus case is *Brown*, where something like these facts occured. The acussed alledged that he could not forsee the harm he would do, and proceeded to argue that since he acted inavertently, he did not committ the offence. The prosecution tried to rebutt this defence by offerring evidence of a statement made by the defendant to the police in which he inferred that he wanted to get rid of the person he attacked. After legal arguement the confession was ajudged to be admissable. The defendent appealed, argueing that he had been lead to make the statement by being promised bail, and had been mislead by being falsely told that a companion had confessed; but the judgment of the court was against this. On the principle question in the case, the concensus of the judges was that the authorities against the existance of the defence were irresistable, but perhaps this payed too little regard to the paralell rule for the priviledge of self-defence. I believe it would be indefensable to assert that the court leant it's authority to the test of reasonableness. In any case, it is permissable to observe that one cannot regard the same problem as occuring here. As to the wife. she is now treated seperately from her husband, and her responsability is independant of his. Her ommission to help the victim definately does not mean that she abetts the crime, or is an accessary to it. In the absense of other facts, she is not guilty."

The proper spelling is "homicide". The word comes from the Latin *homo* (stem. *homin-*), a man, or rather a human being of either sex, +*cidium*, killing. Contrast the word *homosexual*, where the prefix comes from the Greek *homos*, meaning "the same"; a homosexual is a person who is sexually attracted within his or her own sex. Classically, the first *o* in both words was short, but both are sometimes lengthened in English.

Effect is wrongly used in the first sentence of the passage. The Homicide Act can affect (have an influence or bearing upon) a problem, or it can effect (bring about) a result. But we would not speak of "effecting" a problem. If these two words bother you, try to remember that affect is always a verb (something affects something else), while effect is nearly always a noun "the effect of X was disastrous").

The rule for verbs ending in the sound -*er*, such as *offer, prefer, occur,* is to double the *r* for the -*ed* and -*ing* endings if the accent is on the -*er* syllable, but not otherwise. Thus *prefer, occur, transfer,* make *preferred, preferring, occurred, occurring, transferred, transferring,* but *offer* makes *offered, offering.*

The spelling of words derived from *appeal* is confusing. Whereas *appellant* and *appellate* have two *l*s, *appealed, appealing* are like *sealed, sealing, peeled, peeling,* and have only one. The "seed" words are also troublesome. Some are spelt "cede" as in *accede, concede, precede, intercede, recede.* Others are spelt "ceed": *exceed, proceed, succeed.* So you must write *preceding, proceeding:* yet *procedure* is so spelt. *Supersede* is exceptional, being derived not from *cedere* but from *sedere,* and means to "sit upon"; remember this, and you will remember the spelling.

The word *consensus* (agreement) is spelt with an *s* because it is derived in the same way as consent, from the Latin *sentire,* to feel. (*Census* is spelt with a *c* at the beginning because it is derived from the Latin *censere,* to rate.) To express the sound *ee,* the rule is: *i* before *e,* except after *c.* So: *achieve, believe, grievous*; but *deceive, receive.*

The word *foresee* takes an *e* in the middle, but you can write either *forgo* or *forego.*[4] *Judgment* is spelt correctly in the above test, but an alternative spelling is *judgement.* The rule generally followed in dictionaries is that mute *e* is dropped before suffixes beginning with a vowel (for example, deplorable, desirable, likable, movable, notably, ratable, sizable, unusable, milage, suing), but not before suffixes beginning with a consonant (*statement*). Statutes do not altogether follow the former rule: "rateable value" is an established statutory spelling. Mute *e* is generally retained after soft *c* or *g* (for example, *unenforceable, changeable*): so *judgement* should really be the preferred spelling though *judgment* is far more commonly encountered.

English has no clear rule on the *-ent* and *-ant* endings, but the former is the commoner. All you can do is to notice the spelling when you read. One special peculiarity: the adjectives *dependent* and *independent* take an *e* in the final syllable, but the noun *dependant* (meaning one who is dependent on another for subsistence) takes an *a.* The difference of spelling in the endings of *appellant, respondent,* derives from Latin.

The word *inferred* in the passage is correctly spelt but wrongly used. The correct word in the context is *implied. Inference* is what

---

[4] But "foregoing" in the sense of "preceding" must be so spelt.

Sherlock Holmes did: one fact is deduced from others. A person may *imply* something in what he or she says, without actually expressing it.[5] Implication is an indirect way of conveying one's own meaning; inference is a process of discovering a fact outside oneself. Dr Watson implies what he or she means, and Sherlock Holmes infers what Dr Watson means. It is nonsense to speak of a person inferring what he himself means.

Note that *criteria, data* and *dicta* are plural words: the singulars are *criterion, datum* and *dictum*. Say "this dictum", not "this dicta". Treating *data* as singular (as people are coming to do) makes it difficult to speak clearly of "this particular datum" as opposed to "the rest of the data".

Although not referred to in the passage, a common error is the mixing-up of "it's" and "its". To avoid this, it is helpful to remember that "it's" as a statement of fact ("It's a nice day") is the contraction of two words ("it is"), so necessitating an apostrophe (*à la* "don't", "can't", etc.) whilst "its" as a statement of possession ("the dog is in its basket") is only one word.

Key to spelling test Homicide affect superseded occurs diminished likelihood provocation led lose grievous effect category ["gauge" is correct] analogous occurred accused alleged foresee ["proceeded" is correct] inadvertently commit ["offence" is correct] rebut offering argument adjudged admissible defendant ["appealed" is correct] arguing led misled principal consensus existence irresistible paid parallel privilege believe indefensible lent its permissible occurring separately responsibility independent omission definitely abets accessory absence.

The commonest grammatical error (if it is an error) is the split infinitive. A split infinitive occurs when a word (usually an adverb) is placed between the word "to" and a following verb, as in "to boldly go". Fowler divided the English-speaking world into (l) those who neither know nor care what a split infinitive is; (2) those who do not know, but care very much; (3) those who know and condemn; (4) those who know and approve; and (5) those who know and distinguish.

---

[5] There is also legal implication, where one statement is deemed by law to include another (whatever the person making the statement may have meant). A contract of sale, for example, contains certain terms implied by law, even though the parties knew nothing about them.

Most examinees belong to the first class, many examiners to the third, though their numbers may be dwindling and even drifting towards category (4). Fowler's successor advises:

"Avoid splitting infinitives whenever possible, but do not suffer undue remorse if a split infinitive is unavoidable for the natural and unambiguous completion of a sentence already begun."

Whatever the merits of the dispute, the safe course for the student, as for every writer who does not wish to risk offending the readers' susceptibilities is to avoid splitting infinitives.

THE PRESSURE OF TIME

Abbreviations of technical words and expressions should be used only very sparingly in an exam. Where the examiner indulges in the fancy of using fictitious names, you are perfectly entitled to abbreviate them to the initial letter—unless two parties in the same problem have the same initial letter (which the examiner ought in good practice to avoid). If, however, you find that time has run short for the last answer, the best course is to reduce the answer to bare note form, using as many key headings as possible and abbreviating freely. You may head such an answer with the words: "in note form". This course should be adopted only in case of absolute necessity, and you should be able to plan out your time so that it is not necessary.

It is no use writing "unfinished" at the bottom of your answer. If anything this will simply irritate the examiner. Some candidates send in meagre scripts in which every answer is carefully labelled "no time to finish". Let me assure them that the phrase has no mark-getting capacity whatever. There is all the difference between an *incomplete* answer labelled "no time to finish" when marks can be given only for what is written down and a *complete* though condensed answer labelled "in note form" when the examiner may out of charity overlook defects of style, excessive abbreviation and lack of full detail.

The legitimate way to save time in an exam is normally not by extensive abbreviation but by omitting windy phrases such as "first it is necessary to consider whether". Long before the exam the student should have practised and perfected a clear, incisive style in which every word is made to count. On no account should you write out the question itself *verbatim*, or, if you have with you in the exam materials such as a statute book, long extracts from the relevant legislation. Selected words or phrases should be quite enough to make your point. You must make every effort to avoid giving any appearance of playing for time because you are reluctant to confront the questions set.

SELF-CONTRADICTION

There is a story of a party of tourists who stood by the Porters' Lodge at King's College, Cambridge. One of them pointed north and said: "That's the chapel". They turned round and another pointed south. "No, that's the chapel". "No", said a third, pointing west, "that's the chapel". "Anyway", they said, as they turned to go, "we've seen the chapel". Many exam scripts are guided by the same philosophy. The candidate will start with one version of the law and then gradually veer round to a contradictory version—thus making sure that the right rule is there somewhere, even though the candidate cannot pick it out. Perhaps the candidate hopes by this means to get the best of both worlds; actually, of course, if you engage in such a practice, you get the worst. If you find yourself changing your mind in the course of an answer, either cross out what you have written and start afresh, or, if there is no time for that, say frankly that you have changed your mind. You must show not only that you have seen the chapel, but that you can identify it.

FURTHER READING

Michael Dummett, *Grammar & style for examination candidates and others* (1993) is the work of an Oxford Professor of Philosophy exasperated by what he had read in examination scripts. On grammar and style in general, R.W. Burchfield, *The New Fowler's Modern English Usage* (Re-revised 3rd edn, 2004) is the modern version of an established classic. Another useful guide is J. Whitcut's edition of Eric Partridge's *Pocket Guide to English Usage: a Guide to Good English* (Penguin, 2001).

11 MOOTS, MOCK TRIALS AND OTHER COMPETITIONS

"In my youth, said his father, I took to the law,
And argued each case with my wife;
And the muscular strength which it gave to my jaw
Has lasted the rest of my life."

—Lewis Carroll, *Alice in Wonderland.*

MOOTS

MOOTS are legal problems in the form of imaginary cases, which are argued by two student "counsel" (a leader and a junior) on each side, with a "bench" of "judges" (more usually, perhaps, only one judge) representing the Court of Appeal or sometimes the Supreme Court (or another tribunal which is the product of the organiser's imagination). Much stress is laid by educationalists on literacy and numeracy, but we hear little about the importance of being articulate. Footballers practise passing and shooting; pianists, singers and clowns also practise assiduously. Why is it supposed that speaking comes naturally and needs no effort or concentration? Fluency and clear enunciation are particularly important for the lawyer, when our forensic practice is largely oral. Although you will be given training in this at the professional stage, there is no reason why you should not participate in the activities of public speaking well before then. Taking part in moots will help you in these respects, giving you experience in the art of persuasion, and of putting a case succinctly and intelligibly. Mooting not only gives practice in court procedure but helps to develop the aplomb that every advocate should possess.

In some universities and colleges, mooting may be a formal part of the curriculum, although the arrangement of the moots is usually the responsibility of the students' law society (which may well have a mooting officer on the executive committee). A law teacher or practising lawyer can usually be persuaded to assist by setting the moot and presiding on the "bench". In the unlikely event that no one else is arranging them, organise one yourself.[1] There are also an increasing number of nationally organised moots[2], such as *The Times* Mooting Competition arranged in conjunction with a leading set of Chambers, and a rather more specialist competition, the Jessup International Law Moot Court Competition. Your student law society should have the details of these, and quite possibly several others.

The precise details of the conduct of the moot might vary somewhat; the organiser of your moot should let you have well in advance details of the rules according to which the contest will be held. Typically though, the proceedings will be conducted as follows. The moot should ideally have two separate points for argument, one for each of the two pairs of counsel. Counsel should notify opposing counsel of the main propositions (a skeleton argument, in fact) and of all the authorities on which they rely. This mirrors practice in the superior courts, and has the merit of identifying the issues somewhat more precisely in advance. A copy should also be made available for the judge, since it will save time that might be spent in transcribing your argument. Ideally, the volumes containing the reports of cases to be cited should be produced at the moot and the Master/Mistress of Moots or other organiser should be informed of the authorities to be cited, in order that arrangements may be made for such reports as are available to be brought to the courtroom. If this is not possible it is not uncommon for the mooters to prepare in advance both a list of the authorities to be cited, and photocopies (or printed downloads) of the judgments upon which it is intended to rely, including if necessary a copy for the judge—particularly if the moot is being conducted in a place where there is not ready access to the law reports themselves.

---

[1] An extremely useful source of information on mooting in general may be found at *www.mooting.net* which affords very useful advice on such matters as research, organisation, the development and articulation of arguments and offers practical guidance as to the judging of moots, competition rules and so forth. It also has links to other mooting websites.

[2] Details of which can readily be found online.

Since the moot is attended by an audience it is important to confine the proceedings to a reasonable length. Between half an hour and 40 minutes for each side (to be divided between leader and junior as they think fit) is enough time.

The presiding "judge" begins by referring to the case (he need not read it out if copies have been made available to the audience); then he says, "I call upon Mr/Miss X" (the leading counsel for the appellant, who sits upon the judge's left—that is to say, what the judge sees as his left). Junior counsel for the appellant is then invited to address the court, followed by the two counsel for the respondent (or Crown). The appellant is supposed to have a right of reply, but this may have to be sacrificed if it has grown too late. Alternatively, the speaking order can be: leading counsel for the appellant; both counsel for the respondent; junior counsel for the appellant (who thus has the last word).

Both counsel and judges follow the punctilios of court procedure and conduct, and a few words may be said on these. Counsel rise to their feet when addressing or being addressed by the court. If your opponent interrupts, resume your seat. If you have occasion to refer to your colleague, you refer to your "learned junior" or "learned leader", as the case may be, and your opponent is "my learned friend", or occasionally, informally, "my friend" (not "the opposition"!). "It has been argued on the other side that" is permissible.

Do not interrupt anyone if this can possibly be avoided. If you must interrupt, do so as gently and courteously as possible. Beginners sometimes get confused between the two polite ways of addressing a judge—"my Lord" and "your Lordship". The difference is that "my Lord" is the mode of addressing a judge in the vocative case, i.e. as a polite way of drawing the attention of the judge to yourself and what you are about to say, while "your Lordship" is the mode of referring to the judge in the course of a sentence, i.e. as a polite substitute for "you".[3] The formula for opening a case is: "May it please your lordship(s), I am appearing with Mr/Miss for the plaintiff

---

[3] As in Richard Bethell's famous piece of rudeness to the judge who after hearing the argument, said he would reserve the point in order to turn it over in his mind: "May it please your lordship to turn it over in what your lordship is pleased to call your lordship's mind?". (It is said that the nearest approach Bethell ever made to politeness was in his reply to a judge who corrected him: "Your lordship is quite right, and I am quite

(prosecution) (appellant), and my learned friends Mr __ and Miss __ are for the defendant (respondent)(Crown). The claim (charge) is . . . ". Other counsel will begin by saying: "May it please your lordship(s)". Female judges are addressed as "my Lady", "your Ladyship".

In referring to the Queen as prosecutor in the course of a case one speaks not of "the Queen" but "the Crown".

The most common breach of etiquette committed by the enthusiastic beginner when arguing a moot case is the expression of a personal opinion on the merits of the case being presented. Counsel may "submit" and "suggest" strongly, and may state propositions of law and fact, but should not express a personal "belief" or "opinion". You should also avoid the expression "I think", however natural it may seem to employ it. It is regarded as being disrespectful to the Bench to say: "My Lords, in my opinion the law is so-and-so", still more to say: "My Lords, in my opinion this man is innocent". As an advocate you are paid to present your client's case, not to offer a sincere opinion on how you would decide if you were the judge. It is only by maintaining this rule that the advocate can be kept free from any possible charge of hypocrisy.

Begin your address to the court by stating quite briefly what you wish to show. Enumerate the points to be made, and state what part of the argument is being left to your junior (if you are acting as leader). This will enable the court, if it so wishes, to express particular interest in one point, in which case you should of course respond by devoting yourself chiefly to it. Take any hint the court drops: if the presiding judge indicates that as at present advised the court is with you on a particular matter, leave it alone—do not insist upon reading out your argument merely because you have come prepared upon it. State your main point as impressively as you can. After stating it, pause to give time for it to sink in. Speak slowly, and get as soon as possible to the core of your case. Your time is much more limited than it would be in a real case, and you cannot afford to waste it; on the other hand, it is no use gabbling what you have to say, for then it will not be understood. Establish eye contact with the judge, and make sure that you can be heard. Do not read out your argument if

wrong— as your lordship usually is".) His customary rudeness did not prevent him from becoming the 1st Baron Westbury, Lord Chancellor of Great Britain in 1861.

you can possibly avoid it, but in any case do not mumble into your notes. While you must consistently keep your voice at a level at which it can be easily heard, you should try to put expression into it, avoiding a dull monotone. It is probably unwise to permit yourself a joke in arguing a moot, at least until you are sufficiently experienced to know when one is allowable. Members of the legal professions do not lack a sense of humour, but there is an ever-present danger that the levity might be interpreted as being deployed at the expense of the litigants.

When citing cases the reference should always be given; and it should be pronounced in full, not in abbreviated form.[4] For instance, [1944] A.C. 200 is, "reported in the Appeal Cases for 1944 at page two hundred", and 2 B. & Ald. 6 is: "in the second volume of Barnewall and Alderson's Reports at page six". You should be prepared to be able to recite the facts of the case, since the judge may not be familiar with them or wishes to check that you are aware of them. It may be sufficient to read the headnote and the passage you want; but if the case is an important part of your argument you would, in court, read what you consider the essential facts in full. When you read an authority, do so slowly, with proper periods and emphasis.

Refer to judges by their full and proper titles (see pp.91–92).

Citing cases, though usually a necessary part of the moot, tends to take a long time and to be boring for the audience. Try, therefore, to pick out the cases that are most apt for your argument, and rely on them. In professional practice it is the duty of the advocate to call the attention of the court to all decisions that are in any way against the submissions made; but this may not be possible in moot conditions. The other side can be relied upon to cite any decision of importance, and you must have mastered those cases too as part of your preparation, being prepared to distinguish them if called upon to do so. Purely for the purposes of keeping the exercise with the bounds of practicality, it is not a bad plan to have a positive rule that not more than, say, six cases shall be cited on each side. The object of a moot is to provide practice in developing an argument, and while the reading

---

[4] There is an old tale of a junior who cited the Law Reports to Lord Esher M.R. as "2 Q.B.D.". "That is not the way you should address us", said Lord Esher. The learned counsel protested that he merely meant to use the brief and ordinary formula for the second volume of the *Queen's Bench Division Reports*. "I might as well", retorted his Lordship "say to you, 'U.B.D.'."

out of decided cases is often the necessary foundation of an argument, it should not constitute the whole of it. Remember that your primary object as an advocate is to persuade: the citing of cases is only a means to this end.[5]

Just as you should not overload your argument with cases, you should not load it with too many separate points of law. "Mooty" as the case may be, it is unlikely that there are many good points to be made for your side. All first-class advocates concentrate on what they consider to be their good points; they do not run the risk of alienating the judge's affections by producing obviously bad ones. If you must add indifferent points to good ones, at least put the good ones first.

A frequent fault is to read out passages from textbooks as though they represented the last word on the law. Although textbooks and treatises are not taboo in court, they should be used sparingly and cautiously. What the judge principally wants to hear about are the relevant cases (and, of course, statutes). It is always desirable, at least in the superior courts,[6] to refer the court to the cases cited by the writer for the propositions.

As will have appeared previously, judges do not take kindly to abbreviations in speech. Always use the official longhand. The Royal Air Force, for example, should be so referred to, and not simply as "the RAF".

All moot court judges may and should give counsel a hot time by interjecting questions and objections to the argument presented. (In this they will not behave quite like real judges, who interrupt only occasionally.) The objection need not represent the judge's

---

[5] The observation of Lord Greene on this matter is worth quoting. If one compares, he says, the student arguing a moot case with the experienced practising lawyer arguing in court, "it will be found (at least that is my own experience) that the student builds up his argument on authorities which he refers to in great profusion whereas the experienced advocate builds up his argument out of his instinct for legal principle and only uses his authorities to substantiate his points or to convince a judge who declines to accept a proposition unless it is supported by authority. Some of the best legal arguments which I have heard on points of difficulty and complication have been conducted with surprising economy of reference to authority. And the reason is that the advocate's instinct for law and its principles has enabled him to present in an attractive and logical way an argument which convinces by its own inherent strength and does not require at every point to be propped up by references to authority": [1936] J.S.P.T.L. 12.

[6] In magistrates' courts a treatise may be used as an authority in itself: *Boys v Blenkinsop* [1968] Crim.L.R. 513.

real opinion; this is done in order to see how the student counsel responds.[7] If you are counsel and recognise that the judge's objection is valid, concede the point gracefully by saying, "I am obliged to your Lordship". If you think you have an argument, stand up for yourself and say, "with great respect, my Lord", and so on. It does not matter how convinced or dogmatic the judge appears to be: keep at your point as long as you think you have some hope of success and the judge is still willing to listen to you.

When you think that the judge has got your point, do not go on repeating it. If you have presented your case to the best of your ability, and the judge is evidently unconvinced, accept defeat and sit down. All this advice applies equally to argument in real cases. If the judge intimates that you should take a certain course, say, "if your Lordship pleases".

The judge may have tried to throw you with an interruption partly because you were reading your argument in a monotonous way. In answering the judge you will have had to abandon your notes. Try to continue your argument without them, referring to them only in order to read out an authority.

In a moot, you should keep punctiliously to your allotted time. In real life you will not have this limitation, but it will still be important not to ramble and repeat yourself.

After counsel have concluded their arguments the presiding judge may invite members of the audience to express their opinions upon the legal problem as *amici curiae*. The members of the court may then confer, and may deliver their judgments in turn. If there are two student members on the bench they may be asked to deliver their judgments before the senior member. (My own opinion is that, owing to the pressure of time, it is best if the senior member alone gives the judgment without consulting the other members. The main function of the other members of the court is to assist in putting possible objections to counsel.)

The organiser of a moot should consider its timing. Half an hour is the minimum for each side; so if the moot starts at 8.30 pm, and if three judges each take 10 minutes to give judgment, it is 10 pm even

[7] If the student counsel fails to make an answer that was open, it is good training for the judge to suggest the answer, and then judge how well the speaker can respond to that.

if not a minute has been lost—and this does not allow time for the presiding judge to invite the audience to comment before judgment is given. It would be much better to hold the moot, say, between 2 and 5 pm. The presence of an audience is relatively unimportant. Far better have many moots with a small or even no audience than one moot with a large audience. The moot competition provides a further element of rivalry. At the close of a moot the judge or judges declare which counsel or side performed best; he, she or they then go on to the next round.

Almost all of us can, if we wish, add to the attractiveness of our speech. You will not be at ease speaking in court if you are conscious of defects in this respect. For all who have to speak regularly, money is well spent on lessons in elocution (speech training)[8]; but some blemishes can be cured by self-help. Many experienced speakers mar their conversations as well as their orations with a profusion of "um"s and "er"s which distract attention. Other bad habits are using "I mean" and "you know". The simplest way to cure these defects—which probably exist in your own speech, although you are unaware of them—is to record your conversation with some other person on a serious subject in which you are both interested, and then listen to it critically. Probably you will be surprised at the imperfections in your own expression. Only by means of a recording device can you hear yourself as others hear you. Try to eliminate all the "filled pauses" in your speech: moments of silence are usually far more impressive than meaningless noises.

Poor, slurred speech is another common defect. As a Spanish observer caustically wrote: "To learn English you must begin by thrusting the jaw forward, almost clenching the teeth, and practically immobilising the lips" (José Ortega y Gasset). As things are going, the clarity and music of our language will remain only in the BBC sound archives. Good diction can still be heard occasionally, particularly on Radio 3, so that no one who aspires to self-improvement need lack exemplars; yet many people are content to mumble and fumble their words. If your speech suffers from this defect, your teachers are unlikely to tell you of it. They have not the time (or expertise)

---

[8] Advertisements for speech coaching are often to be found in the classified advertisement sections of the practitioners' journals.

for speech training, and are perhaps afraid to embarrass you, and by criticising your speech to add to your shyness in discussion. (They may themselves have fallen victims to the cult of mediocrity in articulation, as though slovenly speech is a way of expressing radical views.) Lawyers, above almost all others, should be able to express themselves clearly and pleasantly. Do you open your lips properly when speaking, or do you try to talk like a ventriloquist? (If you took singing lessons the first instruction would be to open your mouth, and the same applies to speech.)

Do you need to turn your volume control up? Quite a number of the people you speak to will be getting on in years and have lost their sharpness of hearing. Some people not only fail to speak up but talk with their hands wandering to cover their mouths.

Listen to that recording device again. Do you make distinct sounds for each of the vowels, or do you use pretty well one indeterminate noise for the whole lot? What I am aiming against is the indistinct mutter; it is not a question of regional idiom, which is often charming. Your aim should be to speak clearly and without affectation. Record a good speaker on the radio, play back a sentence and then record your own utterance of the same sentence. Compare. Repeat the effort until you feel that your own speech is as clear as the one you have recorded—and, if possible, as musical! Do not be afraid to mouth your words. And speak deliberately, not fast.

OTHER COMPETITIONS

A number of different sorts of competitions involving the acquisition and display of legal skills such as client interviewing, negotiation and the examination of witnesses are now held. There is also now a formidable list of internationally organised moots, such as the Philip C. Jessup International Law Moot Court Competition (which as its title implies is set around a problem in International Law) which is held annually in Washington, and the Willem C. Vis International Commercial Arbitration Moot which takes place in Vienna and in Asia. A number of these competitions are discussed in the book by C. Kee mentioned in the reading section at the end of this chapter. Participation in such events is expensive, the competition is fierce since the participants come from universities and other institutions the world over, and they are very time consuming. As a result, not all Law schools can afford to send a team, but the opportunities that they afford to the lucky few are considerable.

SPEAKING IN PUBLIC

It is an excellent thing to take part in debates. The skills involved in addressing a jury are common to the skills involved in public speaking. Here are a few hints for speech-making of any kind.

Plan your speech under a number of points so that it has a definite structure. Write it out in full, reflect on it overnight and polish it the next day. Then summarise the main headings on a small card or cards about the size of a postcard. Include in the card any figures, quotations, names, key phrases or other material which you wish to state exactly. Read through the full speech several times, preferably aloud and preferably into a voice-recorder, but do not try to memorise it word for word. You will probably not succeed in being word-perfect, and there is danger in reciting a memorised speech either of appearing unnatural or of forgetting a complete section or even coming to a dead halt. If you play back a recording of the rehearsal, consider whether you spoke at the right pace, and particularly whether you made an impressive pause at the right moment. When on your feet before the audience, have the outline card or cards in your hand and, with this aid, speak naturally in the way you have planned.

The commonest fault among inexperienced speakers (and even many experienced ones) is to speak too fast. All good advocates speak with great deliberation and force. Tell yourself before you begin that you are going to speak slowly, and keep reminding yourself to do so. Don't hide behind any furniture if you can help it, and don't fold your arms or fiddle with your ears, your spectacles, or anything else.[9] Look at the audience as you speak, and turn to different sections of them. You may use your hands to emphasise points— not in too exaggerated a way, but sufficiently to show that you are putting your whole being into it. When you are not using your hands in this manner, keep them at your sides. Don't sidle around; keep your feet still. If

---

[9] If you are sitting around a table in committee, on no account place your hand in front of your mouth when speaking. Don't even hold your chin!

you make a joke, pause before the punch line—and let the audience know that humour is about to enliven the proceedings by enjoying it yourself beforehand.

If you are nervous, console yourself with the thought that the initially nervous speaker often performs far better than the stolid individual with no nerves. And remember that the audience are on your side. They want to be engrossed by your speech; they want the occasion to be a success. They are not there to criticise you, unless you force the criticism on them.

Ask a friend to observe your performance and to report to you on it with ruthless candour. Ask particularly whether you have any irritating mannerisms: scratching yourself, flicking your hair, pulling your clothes, waving your arms unduly, or swaying hypnotically.

MOCK TRIALS

A mock trial differs from a moot in that it is a mock jury-trial, with jury and witnesses, not an argument on law. The proceedings may be somewhat humorous; witnesses may dress themselves up, and court and counsel wear robes (if procurable). The audience may consist of non-lawyers, who, of course, come simply to be entertained. Since the trial is unrehearsed, it requires a high standard of forensic ability on the part of the student "counsel"; and the proceedings should either be leavened by humour or present an intellectual problem of the "whodunit" type.

There are two ways in which the "case" may be got up. It may have been enacted beforehand by the witnesses, so that they testify to what they have actually witnessed; alternatively, the organiser of the mock trial may simply have given to each witness a statement of the evidence, which he or she is expected to remember. The former method requires some effort, but it makes the case more realistic when it comes to cross-examination, and it enables the preliminary proceedings, including the interviewing of witnesses and briefing of counsel, to be done by student "solicitors". The actual trial is, of course, a valuable experience for budding advocates who take part in it as counsel.

It is a good plan to set the scene of the case (for example, the murder) in some place known to the audience (such as the college or law school). Alternatively, the case can be modelled upon an actual case in one of the Trials Series (below, p.276). Try to depart from your model trial just sufficiently to prevent counsel using the same speeches and the same questions to witnesses. Keep the number of witnesses down to five or six. See that the legal participants have attended real trials in order to learn how things are done; the clerk of the court in particular should know what the job involves. If you are at all doubtful about the success of the evening, do not advertise the event outside your law society.

As another diversion from the serious business of moots, the students' law society may like to try one evening the game of "Alibi". The gathering divides into groups of four, each group being composed of two prosecuting counsel and two defendants. It is assumed that the two defendants have committed some crime at a stated time—say between 10 and 11 pm last Wednesday—and have set up an alibi. They go out of the room for not more than 10 minutes in order to prepare their story. They then return, one at a time, for cross-examination by the prosecuting counsel. Counsel's aim is to break down the alibi by asking unexpected questions and so getting contradictory answers from the two defendants. After the two cross-examinations, lasting perhaps 10 or 15 minutes in all, the two counsel put their heads together for a minute, and then one of them addresses the rest of the gathering, who have acted as jury, and submits that the alibi has been broken down because of this and that discrepancy. The jury signify their verdict by a show of hands, the opinion of the majority being taken. A master of ceremonies is needed to dispatch successive pairs of defendants out of the room, in order to keep the game going continuously. Would-be lawyers will find this game not at all a bad test of their powers of advocacy. No training for would-be defendants is intended.

A somewhat similar game is called "False Evidence". Three masked "defendants" are interrogated on their day-to-day lives by two counsel. One of these defendants has assumed a completely false name and occupation, and it is the task for the jury to decide which. Each defendant must submit to counsel a week in advance a couple of hundred words containing a life summary, and this enables counsel to prepare their questions. Each defendant calls a witness who has also submitted a statement with the facts of his or her life, particularly where that life crosses that of the defendant. In the case of the innocent parties they must have known each other for at least two years. The witness is not in court during the interrogation of the defendant, and counsel try to shake the evidence and establish discrepancies between the defendant and the witness. Each defendant and witness are given a limited time—say 15 minutes altogether—in the box. The judge sums up briefly to the jury, who consider and announce their verdict. The imposter then declares himself, and it is interesting to see if the judicial process has succeeded in ascertaining the truth of the matter. It may be mentioned that the written statements do not contain sufficiently specific information to enable counsel to identify who the person is. Two or three trials may be held on the same evening.

Yet another variant is "Third Degree". One member of the party is selected as the defendant: who is told the outline of an alibi defence and has to fill in the details impromptu under questioning. For example, the defendant may be told that the alibi relates to a period between 2 and 5 pm last Thursday, when she left the house after lunch and took a train to a named neighbouring town and visited a friend in time for tea. The defendant on being told this alibi must immediately amplify it under questioning, and can be "gonged" for undue hesitation in answering or for any vagueness in answering (she must not say "I think so" or "that is probably what I would have done"). She can also be gonged for self-contradiction. The object of the rest of the company, who ask questions for 15 minutes, is to establish a self-contradiction. Leading questions may be asked: for example, if the defendant says that she was not carrying a raincoat, she can later be asked whether the host put her raincoat on a peg in the hall or somewhere else? If the defendant is gonged, or runs for the allotted time without mishap, another outline alibi can immediately be supplied to another volunteer defendant. A beauty of this game is that it can be played by two players only, and it may help you to bring out unsuspected ability as an implacable interrogator.

For the procedure at a mock trial, consult any book on criminal or civil procedure. "Counsel" should make themselves acquainted not only with this procedure but with the main rules of evidence, for example, those relating to leading questions.

FURTHER READING

J. Hill, *A Practical Guide to Mooting* (2009); C. Kee, *The Art of Argument: A Guide to Mooting* (2007); G. Watt and J. Snape, *How to Moot: A Student Guide to Mooting* (2nd edn, 2010); D. Hill and D. Pope, *Mooting and Advocacy Skills* (2nd edn, 2011).

12 LEGAL RESEARCH

"First there's the Bible
And then the Koran,
Odgers on Libel,
Pope's Essay on Man."

—Mostyn T. Piggott, *The Hundred Best Books.*

George III is reputed to have said that lawyers do not know much more law than other people, but they know better where to find it. The observation is if anything even more true today, as the sources of the law become more and more diverse, and it is still an essential part of legal learning that the student should know how and where to find the relevant law.

The expression "legal research" as used in the title of this chapter has two rather different senses. It can be used to refer to the task of ascertaining the precise state of the law on a particular point. All lawyers need to be able to do this, and the skill is of particular importance to the practising lawyer, whether barrister or solicitor. Thus, the Joint Statement of the Bar and the Law Society on the foundations of legal knowledge, which came into force in September 2001, says that:

"... the criteria for Legal Research are: The ability to analyse a problem involving a question of law, and through research to provide a solution to it. This involves the ability

I.   to identify and find relevant legal sources and materials;
II.   to extract the essential points from those legal sources and materials;
III. to apply the law to the facts of the problem so as to produce satisfactory answers to the question posed; and
IV.   to communicate the reasons for those answers, making use of legal sources and materials."

All of these basic skills should be acquired in the academic stage of study.

But "legal research" also denotes the sort of work undertaken by lawyers (often but not exclusively academic lawyers) who wish to explore at greater length some of the implications of the state of the law, the end product of which is then made publicly available in the form of books, whether they be treatises, monographs, textbooks, or more encyclopaedic works, periodical articles and case notes. Here, the task is not so much ascertaining the state of the law, but exploring some particular facet of the legal phenomenon that is being placed under the legal microscope—to "analyse, criticise, sift and synthesise", as Professor Birks has put it.[1]

This chapter is written to help the reader to a more intimate knowledge of the law library and the online resources, and also to guide the first steps of the research worker. Whatever you write, remember that one of the prime qualities of a lawyer is accuracy. All your quotations must be verbatim; all your citations must follow accepted forms[2]; all your statutes must be checked to make sure that they have not been amended or repealed; and if there be any doubt, your cases must be checked to make sure that they have not been reversed, overruled, or questioned.

THE ELECTRONIC SOURCES

Many of the tasks described in this chapter can now be undertaken at the computer. The speed of change in this area is astonishing. Much officially produced information is published electronically, and is available (often free) by using the internet. Most important case law in the United Kingdom is now available online, and there is a free Statute Law Database. A great deal of information is available by subscription only, and the ever-improving databases make the material available in increasingly accessible and comprehensive formats. Your library should have a detailed list of what is available to you on this basis, and should be able to let you have the relevant

---

[1] (1998) 18 L.S. 399.

[2] Most reports and periodicals stipulate (generally in the preliminary sections) how they expect to be cited. In the event of doubt, recourse may be had to one of the general manuals of citation, such as the Cardiff Index to Legal Abbreviations which is to be found at *http://www.legalabbrevs.cardiff.ac.uk*.

passwords and identifiers to enable you to secure access to it. Some further guidance as to electronic research is given later in the chapter.

Having sung the praises of the internet, let me utter some words of warning; it will assist your searching considerably if you are familiar with the structure and general contents of the database that you are using; if you know that what you are looking for is a statute rather than a law report, etc. The second point is that not everything that is useful is necessarily on the internet. Much of the periodical literature, not to say the books and works of exegesis, is available only in paper form. Old-fashioned it may be, but you risk overlooking sources of real importance if you suppose that all your research can be undertaken without entering the portals of the library and prowling the shelves.

ASCERTAINING THE STATE OF THE LAW

The principal type of legal research that most practising lawyers need to carry out is into the law relating to a case that they have on hand. The experienced practitioner carries a mental list of the names of the best works on the subjects with which he or she usually deals, and the sooner the student gets to know some of them the better. For example, the criminal lawyer's bible is called *Archbold's Criminal Pleading and Practice*, which appears annually, and is available online on Westlaw UK, or on CD-Rom as part of Sweet & Maxwell's *Crime Desktop*. Sweet and Maxwell's Common Law Library series has major works on *Contract* (Chitty), *Tort* (Clerk and Lindsell), on *Libel and Slander* (Gatley), *Phipson on Evidence* and so forth. These works are regularly updated by way of supplements. There are also many looseleaf encyclopedias such as Sweet and Maxwell's *Environmental Law* and *Local Government Law*. Increasingly, works like this are also being made available electronically, either in CD-Rom format, or over the internet.

A valuable aid to the interpretation of legal expressions is *Words and Phrases Legally Defined* (4th edn, 2007) plus annual supplements, and now available on-line. This is a collection of words and phrases in statutes which have been interpreted by the judges, together with statutory definitions of terms and definitions advanced by legal writers. Another excellent work of the same type is Stroud's *Judicial Dictionary* (8th edn, 2012) updated annually by supplement.

Treatises and other legal works

It may be necessary to turn to a specialised treatise. There are various ways of finding out what is available. One is simply by brows-
ing the catalogue of the library that you are using, or by going to
the relevant shelves. There are also books, such as D. Raistrick,
Lawyers' Law Books: a practical index to legal literature (3rd edn,
1997), which indicate what might be available. An American counter-
part is *Law Books in Print* (8th edn, 1997) (five volumes plus regular
supplements), which covers books in English published throughout
the world. An alternative would be to go online to the catalogue
of a library, possibly one of the major "copyright libraries" such
as the Squire in Cambridge http://www.squire.law.cam.ac.uk/, the
Bodleian in Oxford (*www.bodley.ox.ac.uk/dept/law*) or the Institute
of Advanced Legal Studies (*http://ials.sas.ac.uk/library/library.htm*).
You could use *www.copac.ac.uk* which is a consortium of a number of
United Kingdom university libraries, though for the task in hand this
might be a case of overkill.

The titles of very recent books can be found in the catalogues
produced by legal publishers such as Sweet and Maxwell,
Butterworths LexisNexis and Hart Publishing, which are widely
accessible online either directly, or, for example, via the Cambridge
Law Faculty website (*www.law.cam.ac.uk*) section on legal publishers. Alternatively, a bookseller such as Wildys in London can be
expected to stock the most recent works; its catalogue is changed
every month.

ELECTRONIC SOURCES

It is arguable that the most significant change in the nature of the
study of law in the course of the last twenty years has been the advent
of its availability on line through the internet.

Electronic research

Before you begin, you should become familiar with general search
techniques, such as the use of Boolean operators and wild cards.

There are various ways to get a start:

(1) Using general search engines. I particularly like *www.google.com*. It is astonishing how quickly a few well-chosen words or phrases typed into the search box will produce leads and otherwise elusive internet addresses.

(2) Law faculty home pages. Your own university or college is quite likely to have a homepage with relevant links, but you can use, in addition, others publicly available such as the Cambridge Law Faculty website (*www.law.cam.ac.uk*). From these, it is simple to go to such links as the judgments of the Supreme Court.

(3) Others legal sites such as Delia Venables (*www.venables.co.uk*) have large numbers of extremely useful links.

The principal databases available in the United Kingdom for research purposes are Westlaw UK and its updating service Lawtel, Lexis Library (formerly LexisNexis Butterworths), Justis and Justcite and (for on-line texts of periodical journals), HeinOnline. These differ somewhat in the materials that they make available, and in the formats in which the material is presented, and it is necessary for users to familiarise themselves with these differences. They provide access to legislation, to decided cases and to periodical literature in which these primary sources have been considered.

STATUTES

Until comparatively recently, it had become increasingly difficult to undertake what should in principle be the simple task of ascertaining the state of the statute book. That is, it was very difficult to find the precise, up-to-date text of a statute. This was partly because of the increasing tendency of the United Kingdom Parliament to enact legislation and then delay the date upon which it was to be brought in to force (the usual legislative formulation was that it would come in to force "on a day to be appointed"). Endless time was expended in searching for both amendments to the original statutes and then for the implementing regulation. Fortunately, the position has altered for the better, even since the last edition of this work, since the statute books (including secondary legislation) have become available electronically. Statutes can be summoned up on screen at the touch of a few keys.

There is an official UK Statute Law Database, available free of charge at *http://www.statutelaw.gov.uk*. This is a significant advance on what went before, but it is relatively unsophisticated by comparison with the commercially available search engines. The *Justis* database has the entire statute book online, going all the way back to 1235. Sweet & Maxwell's *Westlaw UK* online service features full text, fully consolidated legislation going back to 1267, and also has a "versioning" facility that shows how the law stood before and after amendments and how the law will stand when prospective amendments are brought in to force. *LexisNexis Library* provides both the current text and a readily accessible legislative history. The interfaces also provide links to related materials, such as the Statutory Instruments made under the legislation, cases citing the legislation and relevant journal articles. These are remarkable facilities, enormously useful. But beware—they are not official publications, and a practising lawyer who failed to check that the information was absolutely accurate might be accused of negligence.

DECIDED CASES AND CASES JUDICIALLY CONSIDERED

The method of tracing the later history of decided cases in the printed sources has been explained in Chapter 2. If you have access to the electronic databases mentioned, however, the task is considerably simpler. If you are trying to ascertain whether or not a case upon which you are proposing to rely (whether for the purposes of writing an essay, an article, a moot or a thesis), you can first bring the case on to the screen (the search engines will generally permit you to do this either by giving its citation in the law reports, or by the use of catch words). From there, you can click on to buttons giving you such information as the cases in which your decision has been cited (either all the cases or the key ones) and journal articles and books in which the case has been discussed. It is then frequently possible to bring up the cases mentioned through the use of the hyperlink, to see for yourself what the other cases have to say. Justis and LexisNexis Library have similar facilities. You need to be aware, though, that since these are commercial providers, there are some limitations upon what each of the services will make available –   they will generally only afford a full-text version of an article that appears in a journal of which they are themselves the publishers. But they will alert you to the existence of an article published by another supplier, and you can then switch between the different databases to obtain what you need.

STATUTORY INSTRUMENTS

Nearly all government orders made under statute are now generically called statutory instruments.[3] They are cited by title, date and number, for example, the Foot-and-Mouth Disease (Amendment) (Wales) (No.12) Order 2001 (SI 2001/3706).

The following is the table of citation drawn up by Parliamentary Counsel and approved by the Editor of the Revised Statutes.

Instrument	First division	Second division	Third division
Statute	Section	Subsection	Paragraph
Bill	Clause	Subsection	Paragraph
Order in Council, or	Article	Paragraph	Sub-paragraph
Order			
Regulations	Regulation	Paragraph	Sub-paragraph
Rules	Rule	Paragraph	Sub-paragraph
Schedules	Paragraph	Sub-paragraph	(None)

The full text of all published statutory instruments is available online (*www.hmso.gov.uk/stat.htm*).

If your particular statutory instrument is comparatively recent, therefore, it can be consulted online with no difficulty provided that you know its date and number.

If you wish to consult a paper version, such instruments can generally best be looked up in *Halsbury's Statutory Instruments*. The *Consolidated Index* is arranged alphabetically by subject, with a supplementary alphabetical index at the end. There is also a looseleaf

---

[3] Statutory Instruments Act 1946.

Service binder, which contains an annual supplement, monthly news sheets, and a chronological list of the instruments. The work is regularly updated by an *Additional Texts* binder.

An alternative source is the Stationery Office volumes. Orders in force in 1948 were reprinted under subject titles in a series of blue-bound volumes, continued in annual volumes (there are several to the year). There is an *Index to Government Orders* that were in force on December 31, 1991, arranged alphabetically under subject-headings, and continued by annual volumes. A *Table of Government Orders* 1661–1990 lists all orders, distinguishing between those repealed and those in force. Continuation volumes called *List of Statutory Instruments* are published annually, with monthly and daily Lists of Statutory Instruments in addition.

Sweet & Maxwell's *Westlaw UK* and Butterworths online services can save you from much of the drudgery involved in searching these voluminous archives to ensure that the version that you are using has not been amended, but the same warnings as were offered earlier in connection with the statutes must be reiterated here—make sure that you also check the official sources.

ACADEMIC RESEARCH

When the courts were disinclined to take much notice of arguments and ideas that were to be found in the exegetical literature, the ordinary practitioner did not normally need to dig much deeper than was required to ascertain the state of the law. But the courts are now much more receptive to such literature, particularly perhaps material with a comparative perspective. Furthermore, since the decision in *Pepper v Hart*[4] permitted the use of background materials as part of the search for legislative intent, the practitioner needs to know how to find and use official information. It is also part of the purpose of this chapter to assist the student who wishes to research more deeply. For these purposes, the internet has made an extraordinary change, and in a remarkably short time. If anything, the problem now is that there is altogether too much material available, and the difficulty for the scholar/researcher is how to manage such a potentially huge flow

---

[4] [1993] A.C. 593. The case and its implications are considered in Ch.7.

of information. Before plunging in with the mouse, therefore, it is important to acquaint yourself at the outset with what is available, both on paper and electronically, using John Knowles, *Effective Legal Research* (3rd edn, 2012), which is particularly good on electronic sources, P.A. Thomas and J. Knowles, *How to Use a Law Library* (4th edn, 2001) or P. Clinch's *Using a Law Library* (2nd edn, 2001). A couple of hours studying these works will prove to be time exceedingly well spent.

Dissertations

Many undergraduate courses now include a research element, which involves the preparation of a dissertation upon some legal question. Masters courses frequently do so, and the M.Phil or Ph.D is likely to be largely dissertation oriented. The purpose of this section is to provide some tips on undertaking this kind of research, which is rather different from the sort of exercise that is envisaged in Chapter 2.

Amount of supervision and contact with supervisor

At the outset, you should establish how much assistance you are likely to be given by your tutor or supervisor. How much advice will you be given as to the choice of topic? What reading guidance will be offered? Will your adviser be able to read drafts?

Size of the dissertation

The number of words that you are permitted to submit has a considerable bearing on how you go about undertaking the task of researching and producing the dissertation. As you will all too soon discover, 5,000 words does not really permit you to say a great deal. A word of general warning to those who are preparing a shortish dissertation as part of a degree requirement. Take care not to allow your time to be taken over by the project. It is altogether too easy to permit such an exercise to consume a quite disproportionate amount of your study time to the detriment of your other studies.

Finding a topic

If the topic is not one that the lecturer provides, you will have to undertake the selection task for yourself. You may well have encountered
a question in the course of previous studies that has excited your
interest. The breadth of the topic will necessarily depend on the length
of the project, and the degree to which you are expected to be innova-
tive in your coverage. What you may find is that, having identified a
particular area in which you wished to work, it becomes necessary to
narrow the topic down to a manageable size. You may still be able to
use much of the preliminary material and work by showing it as the
context in which your particular investigation occurred.

Finding materials

Do not underestimate the sheer amount of material that may exist on
your chosen topic. In addition to the primary sources (statutes and the
case law), it is entirely likely that the subject that is of interest to you
may also have been the subject of study by another author.

It is quite important to record details of what archives you have
visited in the course of your searches, and to compile a bibliography
as you go.

The writing process

Sketch headings as soon as you can. You may well find, as your
reading continues, that the material will need to be re-arranged to
accommodate your research findings. Use headings and cross-
headings liberally, so that you can readily identify for yourself where
you have dealt with a particular point (and the computer will help
you to keep track of these if you use an automated table of contents
facility). If you are using a computer, it is absolutely vital that you
back up your work on a very regular basis. Since you will probably be
expected to conform to a system of citation, you should both find out
what it is, and try to make a point of using it as you write, so as to save
yourself a good deal of last-minute work.[5] Many journals (such as The

---

[5] For citations and cross-references, see Ch.5.

Cambridge Law Journal) publish their own directions as to house style and references which, being entirely conventional, you might like to consult and copy. You will find it at the back of each annual bound volume or November loose part.

Timetable

Make sure that you know when, and in what format (i.e. are you expected to have it bound, or will it suffice in a ring-binder?) your research paper must be filed with the authorities. There will almost certainly be some penalty for late submission, and there is no point in incurring this unnecessarily. Leave yourself time at the end for checking, and for adding the final details (often very finicky ones) such as the bibliography, the table of cases and statutes, and so forth.

Plagiarism

Make sure that you understand the difference between referring to and borrowing from the work of other scholars (which is permitted—expected even) and plagiarism, which involves using the work of another without acknowledging your sources. The latter is universally regarded as a very serious offence in academic circles.

Periodical literature

For periodical literature, consult the *Index to Legal Periodicals* and *Index to Foreign Legal Periodicals*, published for the American Association of Law Libraries. In addition to the paper and the CD-Rom versions, both are available online (on the internet with the use of a password, or through *Westlaw*). This has a certain American emphasis, but you may well find that American scholars have already thought about the topic on which you are contemplating research, and the *Index* is very useful for that purpose. The *Legal Journals Index*, which started publication in 1986, is an extremely useful source for articles and case notes published in the United Kingdom, and is available on both CD and online as part of Sweet & Maxwell's *Current Legal Information* service. The *Current Law Index* is a similar publication started in 1980. There is also an *Index to Periodical*

Articles Relating to Law which is supplementary to the *Index to Legal Periodicals*. See also W.A. Friend, *Anglo-American Legal Bibliographies* (1944, repr. 1996).

Government publications

There is a vast annual output of papers published by Parliament and non-parliamentary governmental agencies. The official publishers are the Office of Public Sector Information – formerly the Stationery Office (TSO) and before that Her Majesty's The Stationery Office (HMSO), which was privatised in 1996. As more and more of this material becomes available electronically, it is increasingly easy to trace such material as House of Commons Papers and Bills; ditto in the House of Lords, and so-called Command papers, important statements of government policy or annual statistics, reports of Royal Commissions and tribunals of inquiry. As the courts become increasingly receptive to the use of parliamentary materials in the interpretation of statutes, it is important to know how to find the relevant documents. The *Official Report of Debates (Hansard)* is published daily, and the full text is available in electronic form from the United Kingdom Parliament website (*www.parliament.uk*).

Command papers

The finding of an undated Command Paper may give trouble unless the following table is known. There are six series.

1833–69	1 to 4222
1870–99	C.1 to C.9550
1900–18	Cd.1 to Cd.9239
1919–56	Cmd.1 to Cmd.9889
1956–85	Cmnd.1 consecutively
1986 to date	Cm.1 consecutively

European Union law

A starting point for beginning to undertake research in the area of EU Law is to be found in Duncan E. Alford's *European Union Legal Materials: An Infrequent Users' Guide* (2011) at *http://www. nyulawglobal.org/Globalex/European_Union1.htm*.

Commonwealth law

Much good work can be done by comparing legal development in the various common law countries. Part II of the *Manual of Legal Citations*, referred to before, explains the mode of citation of Commonwealth material. For Australian law, a good starting point is N. Pengelly and S. Milne's *Researching Australian Law* (2009) *http://www.llrx.com/features/researchingaustralianlaw.htm* or R. Watt and F. Johns' *Concise Legal Research* (6th edn, 2009). So far as the electronic material is concerned, a great deal of material can be secured through *www.austlii.edu.au*.

For Canada online, you should start with T. Tjaden's Doing Legal Research in Canada at *www.llrx.com/features/ca.htm*, followed by Best Guide to Canadian Legal Research at http://legalresearch.org/docs/bookmark.html. M.H. Kerr, *Legal Research: Step by Step* (2015); D.T. MacEllven, N.A. Campbell and J.N. Davis, *Legal Research Handbook* (6th edn, 2013) M.J. Iosipescu and M.E. Deturbide eds, *Legal Writing and Research Manual* (7th edn, 2012).

New Zealand

There is a site similar to the Australian database, *http://www.nzlii.org/databases.html*. It is nowhere near as comprehensive or ambitious, however. A starting point is to be found in the work by Greville, Davison and Scragg, *Legal Research and Writing in New Zealand* (3rd edn, 2006).

American material

Turning to American material, the Middle Temple possesses an excellent collection of American reports, and a certain number of American textbooks. The libraries of the Inns of Court have a duplicated list showing which American reports are in which libraries. The Middle Temple has the American equivalent of *Halsbury*, the *Corpus Juris Secundum*. Copies of the American *Restatement* are fairly common. The Institute of Advanced Legal Studies, already mentioned, also has a substantial library of American law. Useful guides to American law reports and digests are Barkan, Bintliff and Whisner's, *Fundamentals of Legal Research* (10th edn, 2015); R.C. Berring and E. Edinger, *Finding the Law* (12th edn, 2005) and Toni Jaeger-Fine, *American Legal Systems: a Resource and Reference Guide* (2nd edn, 2015).

Libraries

There is a *Directory of British and Irish Law Libraries* (8th edn, 2006), P. Fothergill ed. Many of the libraries mentioned in it (and indeed the libraries referred to above) are private, but non-members of the bodies to which they belong may often be able to obtain permission to use them.

13 FROM LEARNING TO EARNING

> "No wind makes for him that hath no intended port to sail unto."
>
> —Montaigne.

A career in law offers excellent long-term prospects, even though the employment scene is a rapidly changing one. It tends to follow the ups and downs of the economy, and to a lesser extent the fluctuations of fashion. Some pundits predict that the legal profession will contract as more legal tasks become automated. Official attempts are being made to make courts "paperless", and it seems probable that certain laborious and mechanical legal tasks (such as disclosure in the course of litigation) will be automated and handled electronically.[1]

The powers that be are constantly tinkering with the rules and regulations governing access to the profession, which makes it difficult to present a picture that does not become in some respects out of date almost as soon as it has been written. That said, there are some more-or-less constants about which useful advice can be given, and that is the purpose of this chapter.

The profession is undoubtedly crowded and in consequence competitive and tough, especially if the economic cycle is experiencing a recession. The law is as difficult for beginners as other professions are; many give up and leave it each year. If you have a career open to you in another business you may be well advised to enter it; and in that case there is no great point in obtaining a professional qualification as a barrister or a solicitor, particularly in view of the expense that you will incur in the process. If you have specialised in law in your university or college, the knowledge and skills that you have

---

[1] Richard and Daniel Susskind, *The Future of the Professions* (2015) and R. Susskind, *Tomorrow's Lawyers* (2013) have alerted us to the changes that evolving technologies will entail for the legal profession, in particular. They do not claim that this will require fewer lawyers in the next decade or so, but assert that their lawyering will be different.

acquired will give you a useful background in many walks of life. If you are reading this book before starting on your higher studies, the present chapter may dissuade you from studying law at all, or at least from specialising in it. A more general course in business studies, which includes some law, may be better for your career.

These pages are written mostly for those who think they may wish to become qualified as a lawyer. An initial choice must be made between the Bar and the solicitor's profession; a choice that has to be exercised at a time when the aspirant will probably know little of the implications of the choice, or of his or her own potentialities.[2] It would be sensible if we had a common system of training for the two sides of the profession, so that the choice could be postponed until the last; but (with the exception of those who take the Common Professional Examination as part of the transition to law by those without a law degree) this has not been done. There is also, it must be said, a strong desire in the City of London firms in particular to snap up the best people, and this in turn creates a pressure upon students who are thinking of a career in such circles to make their minds up earlier rather than later. It is, nevertheless, becoming increasingly easy for a solicitor to transfer to the Bar and vice versa,[3] and the development of the hybrid "solicitor advocate" may eventually make that process even easier.[4] It is also easier than it has ever been to obtain sound advice and some experience of what life is like in either side of the profession.[5] Quite apart from the help that is available in

[2] A small book devoted to joining the Bar is A. Kramer and I. Higgins, *Bewigged and Bewildered? A Guide to Becoming a Barrister in England and Wales* (3rd edn, 2016).

[3] Any solicitor who proposes to do this can take inspiration from the example of Lord Lane C.J., and of his predecessor in office Lord Widgery C.J., both of whom were solicitors before turning to the Bar. More recently, it has become possible for judges to be appointed from the ranks of solicitor advocates, and Collins J. was the first person to be so appointed to the High Court, having spent the whole of his practising life as a member of one of the leading City law firms. He was the last person appointed to the Judicial Committee of the House of Lords, in 2009 and was a member of the Supreme Court at the time of his retirement.

[4] The Access to Justice Act 1999 introduced major amendments which granted all solicitors the right to appear in all courts as from July 31, 2000 (including the higher courts such as the Crown Court, the High Court, the Court of Appeal and the Supreme Court) if the appropriate qualification is obtained.

[5] A website that you should certainly consult in your search for a career is at *www. lawcareers.net*. Not to forget the printed page. *The Training Contract and Pupillage Handbook*, published annually by the Law Society, is available free of charge from careers

university careers advisory services, careers fairs and informal contacts, mini-pupillages at the Bar and vacation placements in law firms also offer the student the chance to sample life in the respective parts of the profession, and all students should certainly be encouraged to seek these opportunities during the first or second summer vacation of study. I say this with some caveats. Such placements also offer potential employers the chance to make preliminary assessments of potential employees, so they are not to be undertaken lightly. All of this means moreover, that the student is under some pressure from the outset to make life-altering choices, and that cannot be wholly for the good.

I would advise you to acquire at the outset copies of the works mentioned in footnote 5. They are remarkably useful, containing items such as "Leading firms, the true picture", advice on interview techniques, an A to Z of law firms and chambers[6] and much more. Thereafter, a willingness to spend some time on the internet[7] should enable the aspirant to get a very good idea of what is or might be on offer, and what is required to be done by way of preparation and training.

PRACTICE AT THE BAR

Barristers[8] are specialist consultants and advocates, and until the "solicitor advocate" was born, they were given exclusive rights of audience in the superior courts. It is one of the great and continuing strengths of the Bar that this historical arrangement has created a class of specialists whose services are available to all solicitors. The solicitor is in turn able to advise the client as to the most appropriate person (or set of chambers) to deal with a particular legal problem.

---

advice services and Law Faculties. A comparable publication for those interested in the Bar is *Chambers Student Guide to Law Firms & the Bar.* This too is available without charge.

[6] Groupings of self-employed barristers who share premises and various other professional amenities, such as clerks (or practice managers who are increasingly replacing clerks), secretarial facilities and libraries.

[7] Many individual firms and sets of chambers have their own websites, giving details of training opportunities. It is a very useful way of finding out about them.

[8] A good deal of up-to-date information about the Bar, including the requirements as to the vocational qualifications, is now available on the web. See *www.barcouncil.org.uk*.

There are some discouragements to new entrants for practice at the Bar. First, you will need an approved degree[9] (not necessarily a law degree, though that gives you the advantage of providing you with examination exemptions). Then you will have to pass the Bar Professional Training Course (BPTC) at one of the validated institutions. If you have an approved degree but not in law, you will first need to study for a year and pass the Common Professional Examination (CPE) or a postgraduate diploma in law, though this is rather rarer, at an approved institution. If you intend to practise, you will need to be taken on in chambers or by an Authorised Training Organisation, under the guidance of a junior barrister. This is called "pupillage", and the junior barrister (i.e. barrister who has not taken silk, and who may be in reality a quite senior "junior") is termed the "pupil supervisor". A year's pupillage is (in general) compulsory for those who intend to practise in England and Wales. Certain limited exemptions are allowed. Arranging it may present a problem (to be considered further shortly). But the finish of pupillage is likely to be only the beginning of your real difficulty: getting a "tenancy"—a permanent place in chambers—is another real hurdle: "No room in the Inns".

The practising barrister is a member of a group who share a set of chambers. The decision on whether or not to offer pupillage is now generally taken on the vote of the members of its pupillage committee and the pupil supervisors. A set of chambers in London is likely to have many more pupils than it has available tenancies. The situation has arisen largely because of recent large recruitments to the Bar, and there is a reluctance (for perfectly understandable reasons—the Bar does not wish to place itself in a position where it can be accused of running a closed shop) amongst those providers of the BPTC to be particularly selective as to those whom they will admit. Consequently, many of those who complete the BPTC either decide to do something else, or become "squatters"—unhappy beginners who, having no local habitation, are gravely handicapped in building up a practice. They live in hope of persuading some set of chambers to take them on. Women and members of ethnic minority groups have

---

[9] Since 1984 a lower second has been formally required; in reality an upper second is generally looked for, certainly by the better sets of chambers.

unquestionably in the past experienced particular difficulty, and for all the attempts that have been made to eliminate discrimination, may still do so.[10] Even though considerable effort has been made by the Bar Council[11] and the Inns of Court to smooth the paths of those wishing to approach the Bar, you should think long and hard before deciding to join that unhappy throng.

It is not all doom and gloom. The traditional but constricting attachment of the Bar to the Temple and to Gray's and Lincoln's Inns, and the reluctance of established practitioners to colonise new chambers have disappeared in recent years. The chances of the entrant may be enhanced as new chambers are opened outside the ancient purlieus of the law. It is also becoming common for sets of chambers to merge and in consequence seek ever-larger premises, pooling resources such as libraries. But it is unlikely that even these developments will keep pace with the flow of well-qualified new entrants.[12] If you are considering pupillage or a place in newly established chambers, make careful inquiry into the status of the place and the kind and amount of work coming in. Some may not offer good prospects.

The position outside London, attached to one of the seven circuits into which the country is divided,[13] may afford better opportunities. The number of places available may be fewer, but if you obtain pupillage in provincial chambers, and perform satisfactorily, you are much more likely to be offered a place. This is a strong reason for starting in chambers other than in London, especially as the provincial Bar is now as good as London, apart from specialist chambers.[14] Another

---

[10] It is fair to say that the Bar has made strenuous efforts to prevent discrimination. Employment statistics are kept and monitored, and the Bar code provides that "[a] practising barrister must not in relation to any other person (including a lay client or a professional client or another barrister or a pupil or a student member of an Inn of Court) discriminate directly or indirectly or victimise because of race, colour, ethnic or national origin, nationality, citizenship, sex, sexual orientation, marital status, disability, religion or political persuasion".

[11] The Bar's website address is *www.barcouncil.org.uk*. You will find there such useful information as applications for pupillage under the Pupillage Gateway, via in particular *www.pupillages.com.*

[12] You can find the most recent statistics on the Bar Council's website.

[13] The six circuits in England and Wales were, until March 2001: the Midlands, North Eastern, Northern, South Eastern, Wales and Chester and Western. On that date, a European Circuit was added, the first addition for some 300 years.

[14] Provincial Bars (with chambers offering pupillage) are now established in nearly 40 different centres.

argument in favour of the provinces is that the steady decentralisation of justice from London naturally increases the importance of the provincial Bar. We may well be moving towards a situation in which all trials are held in the area in which they arise, and London retains special importance chiefly as the centre of appellate courts. Solicitors in the north and west will no longer brief London barristers except in matters in which such barristers profess particular expertise.

Then there is the question of finance. Local authorities have long since ceased to fund the early stages of practice at the Bar, and during the first six months of pupillage the fledgling barrister is not allowed to accept paying briefs. But the atmosphere that prevailed in former times, when a fee was charged for pupillage, has completely evaporated; indeed, compulsory funding of pupillage was introduced for pupils commencing on or after 31 December, 2002, chambers being required to provide an income of £12,000 for the year of pupillage, which is generally paid as an award of £6,000 in the first six months and an award or guaranteed receipts of not less than £6,000 for the second six. There is some evidence that this development has diminished the supply of available pupillages (particularly in areas such as the criminal law and family law), and the sum involved does not appear to have been increased to take account of inflation since 2002. But many chambers, particularly the commercial sets, now offer substantial (upwards of £65,000) awards.[15] Increasingly, the Inns of Court offer attractive scholarships to particularly well qualified candidates. You can contact them via the internet, and approach the Student Officer for advice.[16] During the second six months paid work is a possibility, but fees can take months or even years to come in, and quite a proportion are never recovered, so that until at least a year after the end of pupillage the fledgling barrister will probably have to live on the good will of a bank manager or other lender,[17] or the income of parents or spouse or partner. In addition to living expenses, there will

[15] Details of which may be found in the *Training Contract and Pupillage Handbook*.

[16] To find the up-to-date position on these, it is only necessary to consult the website of each of the Inns: Middle Temple, Gray's Inn, Inner Temple and Lincoln's Inn. These are all *www.[onewordname].org.uk*.

[17] The Bar Council has an interest-free loan scheme which can assist pupils experiencing financial hardship. Details of this are available from the Chief Accountant, General Council of the Bar, 289–293 High Holborn WC1V 7HZ.

be professional expenses, including rent of chambers (these are not paid by pupils), clerk's commission, travel, etc. The sum remaining from fees will be subject to further deductions for income tax and national insurance. In specialist chambers the time that must elapse before making a living is longer. These points are made, not to discourage the eager, but to illustrate some of the professional shoals that must be navigated (or at least thought about) at the outset.

As to the volume of work available, crime is still a growth industry (though legal aid for criminal work is being increasingly squeezed by a parsimonious Treasury), and the constantly increasing complexity of many parts of the law (such as has been engendered by the passing of the Human Rights Act 1998) inevitably creates a demand for skilled legal advice. The enlargement of the powers and pretensions of government gives administrative law great and still growing practical importance, while tax law creates continual problems for business and industry.

Some work for those joining the Bar has been lost by the gradual extension of county court jurisdiction (where solicitors have the right of audience), and in the Crown Court, where the Crown Prosecution Service has steadily increasing rights of audience. The income limit for legal aid in civil cases has fallen well behind inflation, so that few people are now eligible for it. Account must also be taken of the degree of competition for the work.

It is not easy to get reliable up-to-date figures as to earnings at the Bar. A barrister is self-employed, which means that he or she has to make provision for pension, sickness insurance, indemnity insurance and national insurance contribution. The barristers who make a lot of money are those who are not dependent on fees allowed by the state—for example, those who practise in the fields of commerce, industry, shipping, construction, insurance, planning and banking, all fields that have an increasingly transnational dimension. It may be concluded that practice at the Bar can lead to a very reasonable income and the strong possibility of a judgeship. And having done my best to alert you to the difficulties of starting a career at the Bar, I must add that the public interest strongly requires that the profession should continue to attract a flow of top quality recruits. Those who do not reach this level but are pretty good can aspire to a circuit judgeship. Many barristers who do not succeed becoming established in practice, or who do not find the life congenial, obtain employment in salaried posts, as will be explained later.

Let me assume that you would like to enter for practice at the Bar and are prepared to brave all hazards. Have you the right qualities? For advocacy, obviously, the prime need is the ability to communicate by speech. Judges confess in private that there are counsel now practising whom they struggle to understand. If you habitually mumble or burble, give up all thought of advocacy. Students can best test and foster their powers of advocacy by making full use of debating societies. Not only must you be able to speak up loud and clear, but you should be able to put a case relevantly, neatly, succinctly, and generally in a way pleasing to the tribunal before which you are appearing. The last means that good manners are important. Quickness of thought is a considerable asset. Cases on the common law side are usually won not through counsel's address to the court, which there is usually a little time to prepare in advance, but through the effective examination of witnesses.

Now although the art of cross-examination can be (and is) taught, cross-examinations themselves cannot be fully prepared in advance, because you can never be quite sure what the other side's witnesses are going to say until they are actually in the box. A certain innate nimbleness of wit is therefore essential. Some people are intellectually very sound but can formulate opinions only after prolonged consideration. That type of mind is no use for advocacy.

A good barrister must also be able to assimilate facts quickly. A brief may contain correspondence numbering two or three hundred letters and other documents, and it may be delivered to the barrister one or two nights before the case begins, and all the facts must be mastered before going into court. The best advocates have had prodigious memories, enabling them to retain the details (facts, figures, names and, especially, dates) of one complicated case after another for presentation in court. Lord Alverstone recorded that when at the Bar he was able to read the sheets of correspondence almost as fast as he could turn them over, and he never required to read them twice. Hawkins, one of the most powerful leaders of the common law Bar in the nineteenth century, used to give the following advice. "Never examine or cross-examine from your brief. Know your brief and examine from your head."

A sound constitution is another requirement, as can be realised from the following passage from Gilchrist Alexander's *The Temple of the Nineties*. Anyone who has seen a busy barrister at work will bear out the truth of the picture.

"Few people realise under what pressure successful barristers live . . . The busy barrister is on the *qui vive* all the time. In court he has to be on the alert every moment and is watched by a highly trained expert on the other side who pounces upon his slightest mistake. Out of court he has to work far into the night, night after night, working hard and continuously at a mass of detail. He cannot, like the head of a big business, delegate to subordinates the actual carrying out of his work. His 'devils' prepare for him notes of his material but once he has gone into court he has to take entire responsibility on his own shoulders."

The advocate needs a sound knowledge of the law, especially that of evidence and procedure. If evidence and procedure are among the subjects available to you at university, you should either include them in your course or, if possible, attend the lectures as an extra. These are now taught on the BPTC but necessarily at a relatively superficial level for the demands of practice.

Then again the advocate, like every kind of lawyer, needs accuracy. Your ability to write and argue is of little avail if you get your facts wrong, fail to find the relevant authorities, rely on a statute that has been superseded or a case that has been overruled, or simply misunderstand the authorities. All these mistakes are only too easy to make, and it takes constant effort to keep oneself up to the mark, even when continuing professional development is a mandatory Bar Council requirement.

On the Chancery (non-common law or property) side, the chief qualifications are patience and thoroughness. There is not so much advocacy to be done; much of the work is non-litigious (such as drafting documents and advising on title), and the cases that do get into court tend to turn upon technicalities of company law, taxation, property and wills, or upon questions of company finance, rather than upon controversial questions of fact. Also, a good deal of litigation work is disposed of not in open court but before a judge or master in chambers. To some types of mind work at the Chancery Bar appears dull and repellent, because it tends to lack human interest. To compensate the, existence is rather more placid than on the common law side.

It is hardly necessary to emphasise the necessity of probity for all members of the Bar. A barrister must have the confidence of the Bench and professional colleagues. Any kind of sharp practice or dishonest dealing will infallibly ruin a career. Make up your mind that whatever the short-term temptations may be, you will never deviate from the highest ethical standards.

In specialist chambers (such as taxation, administrative law, human rights law, employment law, company law, local government law, town and country planning, commercial law, shipping, restrictive practices, media law, and patent), it is harder for the beginner to get a start and less likely that the barely competent can make headway.

However, prospects thereafter are better than in general practice. The life is likely to be less hectic, and the income distinctly greater. There is no official limit to the fees chargeable to clients who are not legally aided, so that when practitioners in a particular speciality are in short supply their fees rise. For those who have an eye to practise eventually at the Parliamentary Bar[18] a scientific qualification may be a help, and in patent work it is common if not an absolute necessity.

Apart from the fees earned, a practising barrister is not featherbedded in any way. There is no pension (except the national insurance pension and any voluntary pension, both of which have to be paid for), no goodwill to sell, no partner to help earn your money if you are ill, so that insurance in cases of enforced absence from work becomes an essential expense.

Assuming that you decide to take the plunge, you should if possible determine early on whether you are going to practise on the common law or on the Chancery side. You are required to join one of the Inns of Court. As between the Inns the choice does not matter a great deal: you can quite well be a member of one Inn, become a pupil in chambers housed in a second, and in due course attain a seat in chambers housed in yet a third. But the Inns do offer different scholarships, advocacy training, lectures and social events, and you may wish to investigate

---

[18] Members of the Parliamentary Bar are concerned with the passage of private and hybrid Bills through Parliament and appear before parliamentary committees acting either for local authorities or others promoting bills, or for petitioners against them. Most members also do town and country planning work.

these matters before making your choice. Apart from the difficulty of finding chambers, it is perhaps easier to get some kind of start on the common law side, where there is more small work, in county courts and the criminal courts; on the Chancery side there is no criminal work and all the civil work tends to be fairly important. The Chancery side is much more concentrated in London than the common law side, though some Chancery chambers have now been established in the provinces.

The old practice which demanded that the Bar student must, according to the quaint custom, eat dinners at the Inn of Court as well as passing the Bar examinations before call, has been significantly modified. The requirement to dine is now (since 1997) referred to as a "qualifying session", and each student must attend 12 such occasions. Dining in Hall is the usual way of complying with this requirement, but account is taken of the fact that the BPTC course is taken out of London, and certain orientation and educational events held either at the Inn itself or at a Cumberland Lodge study weekend also count towards the requirement.

The total fees up to and including membership of an Inn, call and the cost of qualifying sessions are considerable. Attendance at the course at the Inns of Court School of Law[19] or any other provider of the BPTC, including the practical exercises, is compulsory for those who intend to practise in England and Wales; the fee charged varies from one course provider to another, but they are likely to be somewhere between £7,000 and £12,000. Living expenses (possibly in London) must be added in, with another considerable expense for gown and wig once you have successfully completed the course.[20] If you do not already have one, you will almost certainly want to buy a computer (probably a laptop or notebook).

Finding a pupillage

How does one find a barrister who will accept one as a pupil? Matters have much improved in recent years, as the Bar Council and the

---

[19] In 2001, the long established Inns of Court School of Law became part of the City of London University, and that is where the courses are now taken.

[20] If you are not squeamish about such matters, your Inn may be able to help you find a second-hand (and therefore well-ripened) gown and wig, at a correspondingly reduced price.

Inns have sought ways to ensure that those who have done well in their examinations are given equal opportunity to find a place. Your Inn will have appointed a sponsor to help you by mentoring when you joined, as a source of advice on such matters. In addition to that, one of your law lecturers may be able to help. When a barrister comes to speak to your university or college law society, you should ask for advice on the subject. Each Inn has a Student Officer (who have slightly different titles at each Inn—check before you contact) who may be able to assist. As to the mechanics: most chambers have joined the Pupillage Gateway. If you wish, you should register and follow the online instructions, taking particular care to observe the timetable deadlines. Alternatively (or in addition) you should consult one of the Bar Directories,[21] look at the chambers' website (assuming that it has one, which most now do,) and check the details of pupillages available. You could also try *www.lawcareers.net* filling in the online form allowing you to identify the sort of pupillage in which you are interested. Journals such as *Lex* and *The Lawyer* have special student editions giving details of the pupillages on offer. Write to the appropriate person (taking great care to make sure that you write to the correct person— a letter addressed to "the Pupillage Secretary" when no such person exists in the particular may set get you off on the wrong foot entirely). Keep copies of your CV and covering letters, and retain any replies that you receive. If you have the opportunity of an introduction to a particular chambers, find out as much about them as you can.

The difficulties of arranging pupillage make it rather theoretical to give advice on the assumption that it is possible to pick and choose. There are two dangers to be avoided, if possible, in the choice of chambers: attaching yourself to someone who is too busy, who cannot spare the time to give you instruction, except possibly over a snack lunch, and reading with someone who has not enough work to give you proper experience. The ideal person is the youngish barrister in good practice who is rapidly rising. Someone, in other words, who is likely to take silk, but likely to take it at a time sufficiently far in the

---

[21] *The Bar Directory 2016* (available online at *www.legalhub.co.uk*) contains details of over 600 chambers and over 12,000 barristers in independent practice. See also the *Chambers Student Guide to the Legal Profession.*

future to give you a chance of stepping into part of the practice as a junior. If your pupil supervisor is now above doing the humbler type of work (in the county court or before magistrates or administrative tribunals) with which you will have to start in your own practice, arrangements can be made for you to accompany more junior members of chambers to these lower courts and tribunals.

The twelve-month period may be split in several different ways. You may undertake pupillage for six months in each of two different chambers. It is permissible, for example, to spend six months in London and six months in employed practice or with a provincial barrister if your intention is to join the provincial Bar. Some spend six months in Chancery chambers before turning to the common law side. An incidental advantage of splitting pupillage is that you thereby become known in two places instead of one. Wherever you spend your time, the most important thing to inquire about is the prospect of obtaining a tenancy after pupillage. In addition to the well-established route, other avenues are being opened. For example, the second six months may be satisfied by undertaking a "stage"[22] in the legal departments of the European Commission or with an authorised lawyer qualified and practising in another EU Member State. Organisations other than chambers may be authorised by the Bar Council to offer first and/or second six pupillages. Lesser periods may be spent as a marshal with a High Court or circuit judge (six weeks) or with a solicitor or with a body such as a free representation unit (four weeks).

At the start of your pupillage, you must be given a *Pupillage File*, prepared by the Education and Training Department of the General Council of the Bar. This offers a good deal of advice on such matters as the conduct of the pupillage and the respective rights and obligations of supervisors and pupils. The relationship between pupil and supervisor varies enormously according to the personalities involved. Without being too ingratiating, the pupil is well advised to assist the supervisor (and the clerks) if there is to be any hope of an invitation to stay on. A pupil has the right, which should be exercised to the full, of reading the supervisor's papers and attending court. A pupil may be asked to take notes of the evidence. There is a temptation on both sides for the pupil to spend time doing this, but it soon becomes

---

[22] Pronounced in the French manner, with a long "a" as in mirage.

rather profitless. The pupil's day is perhaps far better spent drafting a pleading or researching and writing an opinion and then having the work critically appraised afterwards by the supervisor.

If possible, the cases you attend should be those in which you have been able to read the papers beforehand: the educational value of hearing them is then much greater. When listening to cases in court you should do so not passively, like the spectator of a play, but with active thought, as though you were yourself taking part; framing in your mind during the examination-in-chief the questions you would put to the witness if the cross-examination fell to you. Always attend your supervisor's conferences with solicitors unless, for some particular reason, it is inappropriate for you to do so. It is not usual for the pupil to speak at these, and you should certainly not do so unless invited.

Pupillage in itself does not give experience in the art of advocacy, and you should therefore play your full part in the forensic exercises provided during the BPTC and in the advocacy courses and moots held at your Inn.

Copy the dress of respected members of the Bar. A man should wear a dark suit and sober shirt, and a woman their equivalent.[23] I need hardly add that men should remember the importance of regular haircuts.

If you fail to arrange pupillage you will naturally be very disappointed, but should not feel aggrieved. Far more pupils are taken on than can hope to succeed in practice, and if you have not been able to impress any chambers sufficiently with your qualities to be taken on, it may perhaps be for the best that you are forced to look to a different career at this juncture. You may, for example, become a legal adviser to a firm (see later), or you may transfer to the solicitors' branch. At least when business is buoyant, the City firms are very keen to take well-qualified and ambitious young people.

To go back a little, there is much to be said for spending some time in a solicitor's office before pupillage. You could very well spend one of your Long Vacations in a solicitor's office, and it should not be difficult to arrange; the experience will be of great value whichever branch you

---

[23] For further details see the *Code of Conduct* published by the Bar Council, which is available through the net.

intend to enter, and it could help you to make a wise choice. Work in a solicitor's office can give an understanding of the solicitor's difficulties and requirements which the ordinary barrister often lacks.

Pro bono work

If you have a social conscience you can satisfy it handsomely (and earn useful experience and points for your CV in the process) by taking part in your local legal advice centre or Citizens' Advice Bureau. Some students (including pupil and newly qualified barristers and trainee solicitors) offer their services in a Free Representation Unit for employment tribunals, social security matters and criminal injuries compensation claims, (the office is at 60 Gray's Inn Road, London WC1X 8LU), and via the Bar Pro Bono Unit, 48 Chancery Lane, London WC2A 1JF. Other barristers (as well as solicitors) take salaried employment in a community law centre, providing legal services for poorer people.

Forms of address

A few remarks on addressing your colleagues and the judiciary. Although it is not so long ago that members of the Bar addressed one another by surnames, this practice has more or less died out. Even now, however, barristers do not customarily address one another as Mr, Mrs or Ms X, and the use of first names (and within chambers very probably nicknames too) becomes permissible after short acquaintance. High Court judges and circuit judges are addressed by barristers out of court as "Judge" (not "Judge Smith"), a Law Lord as "Lord Smith", and other judges as "Lord Chancellor", "Lord Chief Justice" (or "Lord Chief X"), "Lord Justice", "Master of the Rolls", "President", "Chancellor", "Common Sergeant", and "Recorder". These conventions are followed both in speech and in correspondence.[24] Members of the public, on the other hand, would speak to a judge as they would to any other knight or peer—Sir John,

---

[24] On the envelope, write "His [or, of course, Her] Honour Judge Smith" (circuit judge), or "The Hon. Mr/Mrs Justice Smith" (High Court judge), "The Rt Hon. Lord Justice Smith", or "The Rt Hon the Lord Smith of Casterbridge", as the case may be.

or Lord Smith. (All judges of the High Court and Court of Appeal are knights, if they are not peers.)

In court, address all judges from the High Court upwards (including both circuit judges and recorders when acting as High Court judges, and including also all judges sitting at the Central Criminal Court) as "my Lord/Lady". Otherwise, circuit judges and recorders and company court and bankruptcy registrars are called "your Honour".[25] Masters are called "Master", magistrates are called "Sir/Madam" (or "your Worship"), and all other judicial officers (like registrars) are called "Sir/Madam".

Taking silk

Even if you succeed in building up a good practice as a junior your troubles will not be at an end, because at that point in your career you will have to decide whether to apply for silk. These expressions need a word of explanation. A "junior" means any barrister who has not taken silk; and some highly successful barristers (especially on the Chancery side) remain juniors all their lives. "Taking silk" means obtaining the right to wear a silk gown by becoming a Queen's Counsel (Q.C.) or (to use the language of lawyers) a "leader". Whereas a junior does both advocacy and the preliminary paper work, a leader's work is mainly in advocacy (apart from the giving of oral and written opinions, an activity common to both grades).

Until comparatively recently, one of the less defensible anomalies of practice at the Bar was that the grant of silk was entirely in the discretion of a political officer, the Lord Chancellor; he canvassed the views of various legal eminences including the heads of the judicial divisions. Only about a quarter of the applicants survived the rigorous screening and obtained silk. Complaints about the system[26] by the Law Society and others were such that the Lord Chancellor requested a report on the judicial appointments process and the appointment of Q.C.s.[27] The system has now been taken out of the hands of the

---

[25] See *Criminal Practice Directions* [2013] EWCA Crim 1631.

[26] See Lord Mackay's response to some of these in *Counsel*, October 1993. See also the *Kalisher Report* (1994).

[27] *An Independent Scrutiny of the Appointments Processes of Judges and Queen's Counsel in England and Wales* (December 1999).

Lord Chancellor and is dealt with by an independent panel applying identified (if controversial) criteria intended to act as a guarantor of quality. The system has become more transparent as a result of these changes, and in the 2016 round, there were 237 applicants, of whom 107 were successful.

Anyway, the position now is that if you do not take silk at the right moment, it may mean that you have to continue working much too hard for your time of life; on the other hand some barristers who take silk repent it, for they find too late that their services in the more expensive class of advocacy are not in demand. Once you have taken silk there is no going back to a junior's practice. It seems a perverse arrangement to add this hazard to a profession that is already too full of risks for our comfortable age.

Further reading

On your BPTC, you will doubtlessly be given reading guidance on the arts of the advocate. New books on the topic appear frequently, and you can find the most recent in the excellent online catalogue of Wildys, the booksellers. A lighthearted collection of stories is to be found in David Pannick's book, *I Have to Move My Car: Tales of Unpersuasive Advocates and Injudicious Judges* (2008). A recent addition is Thomas Grant, *Jeremy Hutchinson's Case Histories* (2015) giving an account of the significant cases of centenarian Lord Hutchinson Q.C. during a very long career at the Bar.

A lively book of advice which all young barristers should read is Henry Cecil's *Brief to Counsel* (3rd edn, 1982) and Iain Morley's *The Devil's Advocate* (2005). On the critical side, see C.P. Harvey's frank and entertaining little book *The Advocate's Devil* (1958). Older books on advocacy include Leo Page, *First Steps in Advocacy* (2nd edn, 1963); also: Sir M. Hilbery, *Duty and Art in Advocacy* (1946); J.E. Singleton, *Conduct at the Bar* (3rd edn, 1946); F.J. Wrottesley, *Letters to a Young Barrister* (1930) and *The Examination of Witnesses* (3rd edn, 1961); Parry, *The Seven Lamps of Advocacy* (1923); Lord Macmillan, *Law and Other Things* (1937), pp.171 *et seq.*, 200 *et seq.*; J.H. Munkman, *The Technique of Advocacy* (2nd edn, 1991) Richard Du Cann, *The Art of the Advocate* (1993). Some notion of the nature and difficulty of cross-examination may be derived from

E.W. Fordham's *Notable Cross-Examinations* (1950). Finally, the travelling lawyer will be helped by Andrew Goodman's annual *The Court Guide* telling you how to reach the various courts and where to eat when you are appearing at them.

THE BAR AS A STEPPING STONE

In addition to the barristers in practice, a considerable number have used the Bar as a stepping stone leading them on to other things. There is, in fact, a glittering array of dignified and sometimes very lucrative offices open to members of the Bar. I shall proceed to describe some of them, prefacing the list only with the warning that for the more attractive of them there is, of course, considerable competition.

For the brilliantly successful and the politically fortunate there are the offices of Attorney-General and Solicitor-General. There are about 145 superior judgeships carrying very comfortable stipends, plus pensions.[28] As consolation alternatives there are many other posts as Circuit Judges and District Judges. Employment is also to be had as chairmen of one of a large number of tribunals, District Judges (Magistrates' Courts)—formerly stipendiary magistrates, official referees, bankruptcy and company court registrars, and posts as ombudsmen.

Many private concerns also employ a legal staff of barristers and solicitors "in-house". These include the legal departments of transport undertakings and big insurance companies, which deal principally with claims for damages, and the legal departments of large businesses. The legal adviser helps to negotiate the firm's contracts (and may have to travel all over the world in order to do so), keeps it right on matters of company law and employment law, assists with takeovers, etc., and may, on a wider front, advise on what is proper conduct within a system of self-regulation adopted within the industry by means of a Code of Practice. For all these purposes it is necessary not only to be a good lawyer but to have business acumen and an intimate knowledge of the problems of the trade or industry in ques-

---

[28] Arrangements as to pensions are changing rapidly, and it is reported that the Chief Justice of England and Wales reported to the House of Lords Constitution Committee that new arrangements were deterring high-flying lawyers from applying for such positions, *The Times,* 28 April 2016.

tion. Many of these posts carry fringe benefits such as a company car, pension scheme, free medical insurance, and assistance with house purchase.

The big newspapers employ a legal staff to read proofs in order to minimise the risk of libel actions or contempt proceedings,[29] and also to watch the interests of the newspaper generally.

Appointments available are not confined to those requiring professional qualifications or a knowledge of law; men and women not uncommonly read for the Bar or for an external University degree after appointment. But naturally a person who already has these qualifications starts with an advantage. After taking the Bar examination you may obtain employment in the legal department of a commercial firm under the aegis of an employed barrister as a "commercial pupil", and this will give you three months' exemption from pupillage if you afterwards decide to take up practice at the Bar. Unless you are very strongly attracted to private practice you would be well advised to prefer one of these careers in salaried employment.

SOLICITORS[30]

The life of a successful solicitor is rather different from that of the barrister: the range of work that might be undertaken by a practising solicitor is very disparate—it may range from work in one of the "magic circle" of huge City firms to fairly general, private client work in the High Street or to predominantly legal aid work. It is therefore more difficult to generalise about life in this branch of the profession. Although the solicitor may have assistant solicitors, legal executives and paralegals to do some of the work, there is less of the camaraderie of the Bar and the regular exhilaration of forensic battle in the exalted courts. But many solicitors are as affluent as their opposite numbers at the Bar, and they have worked quite as hard and under comparable stress to that experienced by any barrister to achieve their wealth. As between beginners of the same ability, there is better assurance

---

[29] This work is also often done by barristers (sometimes of relatively recent call) in chambers.

[30] The Law Society's own website should also be an early port of call: *www.lawsociety. org.uk*. That too has a comprehensive guide to qualification as a solicitor. The annually published *The Training Contract and Pupillage Handbook* is also compulsory reading.

of reasonable success in the solicitors' branch. Certainly, the salaries for newly qualified solicitors are now such as to make senior partners blench.[31]

Not all solicitors have large incomes: the average income of assistant solicitors in regional law firms who are eight years' qualified would not exceed £50,000, and since that is an average many would be earning a good deal less than that.

The type of work done by a solicitor varies enormously from one practice to another. As in the United States of America, English law practices are now distinctively structured. A few very large, affluent international City firms have adapted themselves to act as the agents and advisers of commerce and industry; they have modern offices with every aid and convenience, and the partners and assistants specialise intensively. They may be asked, for example, to draft and help negotiate important commercial contracts of all kinds. These firms almost invariably have overseas branches, sometimes as a result of merger with (particularly) a French or German firm, and increasingly in the Far East; Hong Kong, Singapore, Malaysia and Australasia. They have been joined relatively recently by American firms, some by way of merger, but some also in competition. The apparently glamorous lifestyle led by many working in these large institutions is not to everyone's taste, in spite of the rewards offered. Trainees (and assistant solicitors and, for that matter the partners) are expected to work at the beck and call of clients, frequently international clients whose requirements can be very demanding, compounded in part by different international time zones. Particularly at the early stages of the career, the work can be rather routine but physically exhausting nevertheless. Anxiety about making progress in one's career, and balancing that against the possibilities of a satisfactory social and family life can lead to stress and burn-out. A person thinking about undertaking work in this sort of establishment must decide whether he or she is prepared to make the sacrifices that such a demanding career choice necessarily entails. That said, a training contract in such a place will leave its subject in excellent standing should he or she decide to go elsewhere

---

[31] In 2013, the leading City firms were setting newly qualified salaries at over £60,000 (some American firms in the City go higher than that – up to £97,000 in one case). This is not far beyond what it was four years ago, and reflects the market in recession. In 2016, the reported salaries on offer were not a great deal higher.

following qualification. There are also some large non-London firms in the larger cities such as Birmingham, Bristol, Leeds, Liverpool and Manchester and possibly others which undertake a large variety of commercial work and which offer both considerable rewards and a somewhat less frenetic pace of life.

Next come medium-sized firms with about 50 partners, mainly in London specialising in some particular field of commerce or industry such as shipping, insurance, intellectual property, IT law, media law or property development, and other smaller but still highly specialised firms.

In the High Street, the solicitor is involved in domestic and commercial conveyancing (investigating title to land, preparing contracts of sale and conveyances, advising on rent reviews), obtaining probate of wills, and frequently acting as executor and trustee. The work entails meeting clients, advising them generally on their legal position, and writing letters. A solicitor pilots company promoters through the legal technicalities of forming companies, and litigation—though some firms prefer not to do the last if they can help it. On difficult questions, the opinion of counsel may be sought, and the solicitor also prepares briefs for counsel in legal proceedings in which counsel are employed.

The qualities required of a country-town solicitor appear clearly enough from the foregoing description of the work involved. These include an ability to interview all types of client in order to ascertain the nature of the problem, a knowledge of human nature and practical wisdom. Naturally the practitioner needs a working knowledge of property and company law and the law of procedure; and the better the knowledge, the better the lawyer. It is a great mistake to suppose that a solicitor can get along without having mastered the legal topics which form the staple of the business. However, the finer points can with relative safety be left to repose in the books of reference.

It is solicitors, not barristers, who conduct much the greater number of cases in the lower courts—county courts and magistrates' courts. What I have written in relation to barristers as advocates applies equally to solicitors. However, even with the advent of the solicitor advocate, a solicitor is unlikely to be able to concentrate on advocacy as a barrister can. There is too much interviewing and paperwork, and advocacy is generally confined to the comparatively small cases.

The continuing spate of new legislation imposes a great strain upon the smaller firm. One client will have a problem under some recent Act relating to divorce or maintenance; another will need advice on setting up a business, capital gains tax, or some aspect of employment law (which, increasingly, requires considerable acquaintance with the law emanating from Brussels), or VAT, or company law, or agricultural tenancies. Another client will be enraged by a refusal of planning permission, or the threat of a motorway through the garden. A constitutional upheaval such as that effected by the Human Rights Act 1998 potentially affects all of these areas of practice. Each of these subjects involves a highly intricate body of law, and it is not to be expected that any one person or even three or four can keep abreast of developments in them all. There is a danger that solicitors (sole practitioners) may fail to give adequate advice, and this is not because of any immediate fault on their part but because they are operating in units that are too small. Competent solicitors are a blessing to their clients and a necessity for the economic life of the country. Unfortunately, firms have had to face discouraging difficulties in recent years. They have been hit by sharply rising expenses, while corresponding rises in income have proved difficult to establish as successive governments have made changes in the distribution of legal aid. To take but one example, criminal legal aid work is now very closely controlled, and the franchisees are required to meet very high standards of administrative and other provision before they will be licensed to carry on the work. At the same time, principals are required to confer the benefits of the various employment protection laws upon their own employees, whilst they themselves are deprived of any such security, and must pay the special tax for self-employed people masquerading as national insurance, in addition to the insurance premiums needed to provide for retirement or illness. Solicitors also complain of the expense of the practising certificate, the contribution to the compensation fund to recompense defrauded clients, the professional negligence indemnity premium, and the contribution to the Law Society advertisements for the profession. These disbursements may not worry the senior partner in a large firm, but they fall heavily upon the less well-recompensed. Those of my readers who are already in training will know the technicalities of becoming a solicitor, and I can therefore address myself to those who have not yet secured a training contract. The law graduate who has gained full exemption proceeds at once to the Legal Practice Course (LPC); this requires attendance for nine months at one of the law schools recognised by the Law Society[32] for this purpose. As with the Bar, local authority grants for maintenance have been virtually abolished which means that, for this branch of the profession also, debt is staring the aspirant in the face. Some firms having offered a training contract will also sponsor students on the Common Professional Examination (CPE), though they will expect in return that the period of the training contract will be honoured.

As is the case with those going to the Bar, a non-graduate, or a graduate (law or otherwise) who has not obtained full exemption because one or more of the "core" subjects[33] is not contained in the degree, is required to take the CPE before the LPC; and this again needs a year's attendance at a law school.

Finding a suitable firm for training contracts can present problems. There is no system of open competition, and there is no obligation to advertise vacancies for training contracts: the grant of a training contract is a highly competitive process. That said, however, the majority of firms are only too happy to advertise themselves; the entrance to any law school is these days littered with give-away literature, sponsored by law firms seeking to recruit. Keep an eye out for special student supplements of *The Lawyer*, the *Law Society's Gazette* and *Lex*. Chambers and Partners' annual publication *A Guide to the Legal Profession: Student Edition* is a mine of useful practical information about such matters as the size of firms, numbers of trainees to which they offer places and areas of work undertaken. Advice may be obtained from the Law Society or the teaching staff of your law school and your university careers service. There is also the *Training Contract and Pupillage Handbook* published annually. Under Law Society regulations which came in to force in August 2000, the trainee solicitor must be paid a minimum salary. Some firms, particularly in London, pay considerably more than the minimum. The Law Society has implemented a requirement that the trainee should receive proper training in at least three areas of practice (from a non-exhaustive total

---

[32] *www.lawsociety.org.uk*.
[33] The seven core subjects are: public law (constitutional and administrative, and human rights); European law; contract; torts; criminal law; property law; and equity and the law of trusts.

of 21 ranging alphabetically from banking to wills and probate, and
even more widely as to subject-matter). There is a standard form training contract which before signing you should read carefully to ensure
that it contains the points about which you have agreed in preliminary
discussions. In the course of the period covered by the training contract, you must also take and complete the Professional Skills Course
(either full-time as a fast track course over 12 consecutive days, or
part-time). Some of the bigger firms offer this course in-house, but if
not, separate arrangements must be made, the firm being obliged to
give paid leave to attend, as well as paying the fees for the course itself.

Let me now assume that you are being considered by a prospective
employer and are having your first interview. A number of important issues need to be addressed, though some of them may be best
resolved by informal means, such as discussion with a trainee already
with the firm or in the many informal contacts that are offered in
vacation placements, or in the recruitment literature distributed by
the firm. How often can you expect to sit in with your principal
or another solicitor? Will you be expected to do your own word-
processing or will the office provide that service? What courts will you
be able to attend? How wide will be the experience you will receive
in the firm? Before the new regulations were introduced it was found
that most prospective solicitors gained some practical experience of
registered and unregistered conveyancing, landlord and tenant, matrimonial causes, probate and succession, family law, criminal law, accident claims, litigation generally and briefing counsel. Most of them
never had experience of town and country planning, administration
of trusts, company law, partnership law, tax planning, book-keeping
and accounts, commercial law, or (doubtless) advocacy. The law has
become so complex that it cannot be expected that the solicitor will
be proficient in everything, and the trend is towards the large firm
with specialised partners. All the same, it is important that the trainee
should have as broad a knowledge base as possible, particularly if
uncertain about which field is likely to offer the best opening or is the
most congenial to the individual's temperament.

For this reason, an all-round practice may give better training than
a specialised one—but it may be well worth taking a training contract
in a specialised firm if you are assured that they are looking out for
a bright young person like yourself with the potential to become a

partner. Large firms generally move their proteges around from one department to another—a very satisfactory arrangement.

What about holidays and paid sickness leave? Will you be paid while attending an examination course? What is the attitude of the firm to permitting you to qualify as a solicitor advocate? Can you attend any practical exercises or advocacy training courses provided for trainee solicitors?

The arrangements for becoming a partner vary considerably from one firm to another. In the past, the new entrant was required, in effect, to buy into the partnership, buying out a leaving partner's interest, and it was not unheard of for a person not to be able to afford to become a partner. Those days are long gone, promotion to the top being now a matter of merit and hard graft (however that may be measured). Getting a partnership is not easy, and the new partner who cannot provide capital is inevitably burdened with some form of payment for a share of the business. One practice is to establish a retirement benefit scheme, whereby the younger partners, instead of paying an initial sum as their share of capital, contribute to the pensions of the senior partners as they go. Another plan is for the new partners to be admitted merely on undertaking to contribute their share of the partnership capital, and this may either be raised by borrowing from a bank or insurance company (with periodic repayments) or be left to be paid over a period of years by deduction from their share of the profits. Either way, the new recruit's earnings are greatly reduced.

Instead of going into private practice, or after some years of practice, the solicitor may decide to seek an appointment elsewhere. Within the judicial system solicitors are eligible to apply for high judicial office, and are appointed as masters and registrars of the Chancery Division, taxing masters, the Official Solicitor, bankruptcy registrars, district registrars of the High Court, registrars of county courts, district judges (magistrates' courts), recorders (and, by way of promotion, circuit judges), magistrates' clerks. Current vacancies both in private practice (for legal executives,[34] assistants and partners) and in outside appointments are listed online by the Law Society Recruitment service via the Law Society website, but are perhaps

---

[34] Legal executives have a legal qualification but have not been admitted as solicitors. The website of the Institute of Legal Executives is *www.cilex.org.uk*.

more reliably found in the weekly legal sections of the better quality daily newspapers and professional journals such as the *Law Society Gazette*, the *New Law Journal*, and *The Lawyer*. A number of recruitment agencies specialise exclusively in legal appointments.

Solicitors may be appointed to positions in industry, and remarks made previously in relation to barristers apply equally to solicitors. Most legal departments in industry do the work that would ordinarily be entrusted to a solicitor; sometimes it is largely confined to routine conveyancing and the drawing of contracts but a much wider field may be touched, including the formation of subsidiary companies, company finance, insurance and employers' liability, patents, trademarks—there is, in fact, hardly any limit to the economic activities upon which a large corporation may engage. In addition, all concerns need advice on employment law, and health and safety matters. Some corporations entrust their routine legal work to outside solicitors, but have legal advisers whose task is to give advice at high level within the industry; these advisers organise the legal work which is to be executed by the outside solicitors—perhaps in many countries. The position of legal adviser to a large and growing industry can be of high importance and interest.

Training contracts in industry are not really the best preparation for private practice, and unless you have a fairly fixed intention to make your career in industry or commerce you may find it difficult to settle down even for only two or three years in the atmosphere of a company's legal department.

Solicitors are frequently appointed not only in the legal departments but in the secretarial departments of large concerns (public limited companies are required by law to appoint a company secretary whose function is to ensure corporate compliance with the law; similar appointments are made in other public and private organisations). A person who intends to go for a secretarial department would perhaps be better advised to obtain a secretarial rather than a legal qualification[35] (to have both would, of course, be best of all). To these possibilities must be added miscellaneous positions, not capable of concise description, in building societies, insurance companies and so on.

---

[35] Start at *www.icsa.org.uk* the website for the Institute of Chartered Secretaries and Administrators, for advice as to how to go about this.

A highly specialised profession, open to barristers and solicitors (and indeed to those who are neither) is that of Parliamentary Agent, whose work lies in promoting and opposing Private Bills. They are required to satisfy the Speaker of their expertise in Private Bill procedure.[36]

Further reading

Information on the technical details of becoming a solicitor can be obtained from the Law Society's website, *www.lawsociety.org.uk*. The Society address is Law Society's Hall, Chancery Lane, London WC2A 1PL. Penny Cooper's book *All You Need to Know about being a Trainee Solicitor* (Revised edn, 2011) contains useful information. Or see C. Harrison, *From Student to Solicitor: The Complete Guide to Securing a Training Contract* (2nd edn, 2015).

GOVERNMENT LEGAL SERVICE

Most government departments make appointments from professional lawyers, and there are about 2,000 lawyers in the Government Legal Service. The career is very rewarding in every sense. Details of how and where to apply are available from *www.civil-service.gov.uk/jobs.*

A method of entry has been devised by which legal training is obtained after entry. Those with honours degrees or postgraduate degrees can be appointed as "legal trainees" in the Legal Service, normally after obtaining exemption from passing or obtaining exemption from the CPE An appointment as legal assistant follows admission as a solicitor.

Unfortunately, not many positions are offered (according to the latest information available on the web, only some 20–50 a year), so competition is likely to be keen. Those who have worked in the legal civil service report that it is much more interesting than appears at first sight. The work is not purely legal, and in no department is it narrowly specialist. There are opportunities for foreign travel,

---

[36] There is further information about this somewhat arcane field of work on the House of Commons website *http://www.parliament.uk/about/how/laws/bills/private/ parliamentary-agents/*, including a list of eight firms which have so satisfied the Speaker of their expertise.

as adviser to international conferences, etc., in several departments, including the Diplomatic Service. HM Revenue and Customs service has many problems wholly unrelated to tax law. A barrister who left the Inland Revenue for practice at the Bar summed up his opinion of the service in the following words: "I enjoyed it, they enjoyed me, and I would always consider returning if the Bar did not prove satisfying".

There is no more important, exciting and intellectually rewarding work for a lawyer than that of drafting legislation. The post of Parliamentary Counsel is open to both barristers and solicitors, and candidates of adequate intellectual quality are in short supply. This little book will have performed a useful function if it persuades one or two readers to take up this career. Vacancies are notified by the Civil Service Commission, the broadsheet newspapers and in the professional magazines such as *Counsel*,[37] and further information can be found on the Parliamentary Counsel Office website.

LOCAL GOVERNMENT

Local government offers a highly attractive field for the lawyer. Solicitors in local government take trainees, who are paid salaries, and local authorities are more generous than most private employers in giving paid study leave and assistance for the purchase of books. Lawyers in this field have been conspicuously successful in obtaining the top job of chief executive (the former town clerk or county clerk). The pension rights attaching to these posts must also be considered.

The work of local authorities is wide-ranging; it includes public health in all its branches, education, housing and town planning, environment, public utilities, transport, recreation and social services. It is good practice for a trainee to be given the opportunity to work in more than one department to broaden his or her experience.

A potential drawback of employment in central and local government, to some minds, is that so often you fail to see any

---

[37] For the work of Parliamentary Counsel see Sir Harold Kent's entertaining autobiography, *In on the Act* (1979); Sir Granville Ram in (1951) 1 J.S.P.T.L. 422; Sir Noel Hutton in (1967) 64 L.S.Gaz. 293. The charmed and charming worlds described in those accounts are said by some to be creatures of the past: see D. Greenberg, *Laying Down the Law* (2011).

outcome to your work. You may toil on a project enthusiastically for some years, only to find that it all comes to naught because of a political change of direction. To be a good government officer you must be able to put up with these frustrations. The price of all social improvement is effort, sometimes wasted effort.

Nearly all lawyers in local government are solicitors, and it is better to qualify this way than at the Bar. If, however, you have started at the Bar, there is no reason why you should not apply for any local government post that tempts you. Pupillage is not required.

CROWN PROSECUTION SERVICE

The Crown Prosecution Service (or CPS, as it is known) employs a large number of legally qualified staff (barristers and solicitors) in 13 Areas nationwide. It is the government department responsible for about 80 per cent of prosecutions in magistrates' and Crown courts, conducting the cases in the former courts and briefing the Bar in the more serious cases. It is headed administratively by the politically independent Director of Public Prosecutions, who is accountable to Parliament through the Attorney-General.

Crown prosecutors take independent decisions as to whether or not a prosecution case should proceed, assessing both the weight of the evidence and various identified public interest criteria. Traineeships and pupillages are again now generally available (after being suspended for a period some years ago). The Law Society obligations as to breadth of training are complied with by time spent in other government departments, or with local authorities or private practice. The barrister is expected to have completed the first six months in civil chambers, spending the second six within the CPS itself under an experienced pupil supervisor. For those with a strong interest in the criminal law, the pay and conditions of service are attractive, with options for part-time work, job sharing and career breaks.

The first point of contact is: CPS Headquarters, Rose Court, 2 Southwark Bridge, London SE1 9HS. A careers booklet is available.

CIVIL SERVICE: GENERAL CATEGORY

For the man or woman with a first-class academic brain the administrative posts in the Home Civil Service have great attraction, above all because they give the satisfaction of doing work of paramount social and national importance. There is the interest of being "in the know" when important governmental decisions are being made, and at the rank of Assistant Secretary there is real governmental power. Promotion is not as slow as it once was, the principle of "Buggins's turn" having largely had its day; even so, one reaches the top or near-top only at about the age of 50–55, when one is not far off retirement.

The qualities looked for in a higher civil servant are: intelligence; fluency of mouth and pen, particularly in producing a persuasive argument and in composing a good ministerial speech; the capacity to induce other people to carry out a policy that perhaps they do not much wish to implement; a political "nose"; the ability (in a department or a local or regional office) to organise those beneath; and capacity for hard work (many of those at the top work extremely hard).

Entry into the public Service is now controlled by the Civil Service Commission, established under statute in 2010. There is a Fast Stream Development Programme, which covers most of the departments and agencies through which government is now administered. Otherwise is it necessary to approach individual departments, agencies and management units directly for the employment details.

Selection is by qualifying tests (meant to assess general ability) and interviews.[38] An alternative mode of entry is available for the Inland Revenue and Customs and Excise. If you are undecided whether to apply, you may visit a government department during vacation in order to see what goes on.

The mode of entry described above covers not only the Home Civil Service, but also certain clerkships in the House of Commons and House of Lords (clerks are officers of the Houses of Parliament rather than civil servants). A separate competition is held for the Diplomatic

---

[38] The technique of the Civil Service Selection Board interview is explained in booklets called *Appointments in Administration* and *CSSB: A Guide to the Civil Service Selection Board*, both available free from the Civil Service Commission.

Service, which offers varied experience abroad and a good career structure. Trainees obtain a salary on a par with that obtainable from industry; they enjoy incremental salary scales which ensure progress even during periods of pay restraint, together with near-certain promotion.

BUSINESS MANAGEMENT

Large industrial and business concerns provide many places for arts graduates—an expression which for this purpose includes law graduates. One advantage is that salaries are paid even during training; and a career in the world of manufacture and commerce is attractive to those who want to do something "real", to take part in the basic process of creating wealth, to tackle a variety of problems and jobs and to be able to organise and administer, and perhaps to have a chance to travel. At the same time, the vast output of arts graduates from the universities means that competition for vacancies is acute.

If your ambition takes this line, there are certain basic truths that you will have to recognise. First, your company is out to make money, to provide goods and services at a profit, for otherwise it cannot survive. This does not mean that you should stay in a firm that stoops to fraud or illegality, but idealistic notions have to face an economic assessment. Secondly, whatever knowledge you have acquired before, you are now at the starting-post of your career and have to serve a form of apprenticeship.

This means being ready and anxious to learn, approaching problems with an open mind, and being sensitive to the feelings of others. Success in business requires a knowledge of human nature and an acceptable personality. Seize every opportunity for formal training that is open to you. Do not be afraid to ask questions—particularly, perhaps, questions as to why things are done in the way they are— though you should in the early stages be very restrained in any suggestions you make for improvement.

THE ACADEMIC PROFESSION

If a student aspires to pursue an academic career, there will be no lack of advisers. The rewards are not princely, but there are some lifestyle compensations. University teaching posts are advertised regularly[39]; in spite of the relative lack of financial remuneration, there is competition for these places, and positions at one of the better universities are hard to come by. Ideally, a person seeking to become a law teacher at top level should not only be outstandingly able but also have some practical experience of the profession and some published or approved writings to demonstrate ability in research. But few applicants have all these points to recommend them at the outset; many law teachers are appointed without having had practical experience. If you are such an appointee, it is highly desirable that you should acquire at least some brief experience by being given leave of absence without pay, or by a period of teaching part-time.[40]

Some entrants to the lecturing professions aspire to combine both teaching and practice, as is quite commonly done in America. The demands of both professions are such that there is a real danger that even an extremely able person will excel at neither, and will sooner or later have to choose one or the other course. Even if you secure a foot on the teaching ladder without having demonstrated much research ability (university employers are prepared to appoint on potential), you will rapidly be expected to produce. The "publish or perish" syndrome is, I fear, a reality within the United Kingdom university system. The barrister's clerk will soon forget your face if it is not constantly reminding by its presence. And although you may be able to do a certain amount of consulting with a firm of solicitors, it is unlikely that you will ever reach partner level (at least in a very good firm) on the basis of such a relatively limited commitment.

The usual way of preparing oneself for a teaching appointment (and of securing promotion) is by undertaking research work. This activity can be profitably combined with a visit to other universities, preferably abroad. The United States, in particular, offers varied opportunities of which I would encourage the budding scholar to take advantage. For up-to-date details, my strong advice is that you should use the internet. It is most extraordinary how a few well-chosen words or phrases typed into the search section of the

---

[39] See *www.jobs.ac.uk*. Keep an eye too on the *Times Higher Educational Supplement*, and the Tuesday *Guardian*.

[40] See Professor R.M. Goode in (1979) 129 N.L.J. 1117 for an excellent statement of the reasons why academics should have practical experience.

facility will produce within seconds information of the sort that one seeks. Whereas previous editions of this work have given detailed contact addresses, I shall content myself with a few starting points, and then identify the American schools that I believe to be worth pursuing. For details of American law schools offering postgraduate degrees and an informative booklet *Postgraduate Study in the United States*, contact the United States-United Kingdom Fulbright Commission, 62 Doughty Street, London WC1N 2JZ. This office will also supply details of the numerous scholarships and fellowships available; some are offered by the Commission itself. The list includes Fulbright awards, which do not necessarily cover tuition, but universities are generally ready to allow tuition waivers to Fulbright scholars. You should also consult the American Council of Learned Societies (American Studies Research Fellowships), 633 Third Avenue, New York, N.Y. 10017–6795, USA .

So far as the law schools themselves are concerned, the good law schools include:

Columbia Law School, New York; Cornell Law School, Ithaca, New York; Duke University School of Law, Durham, North Carolina; Harvard Law School, Cambridge, Massachusetts; New York University School of Law; Northwestern University School of Law, Chicago; Stanford Law School, California; Tulane Law School, New Orleans, Louisiana; University of California, Berkeley School of Law (Boalt Hall); University of Iowa College of Law; University of Michigan Law School; University of Virginia School of Law; Yale Law School, New Haven, Connecticut.

Commonwealth scholarships and fellowships are tenable at universities in Australia, Brunei, Canada, Fiji, India, Jamaica, New Zealand, Sri Lanka, Trinidad and Tobago and Uganda; see *www.acu.ac.uk* or write to the Secretary, Association of Commonwealth Universities, 36 Gordon Square, London WC1H OPF. One of these scholarships might well give you the opportunity to take a teaching post.

With our association with Europe, it is vital that lawyers should interest themselves in the law of the European Union and improve their contacts with European lawyers. The European University Institute at Fiesole in Florence and the College of Europe in Bruges in Belgium run postgraduate courses and good scholarships are available to suitably qualified candidates.

There is also a flow the other way: law teachers from "new" Commonwealth countries may apply for research fellowships to the University of London Institute of Advanced Legal Studies, 17 Russell Square, London WC1B 5DR.

The British Academy, 10 Carlton House Terrace, London SW1Y 5AH awards grants and fellowships for research. The Economic and Social Research Council awards studentships for research in socio-legal topics and the Arts and Humanities Research Council in more traditional legal areas. The University of Cambridge offers Humanitarian Trust Studentships in International Law (write to the Secretary, Faculty Board of Law, 10 West Road, Cambridge CB3 9DZ). The British Institute of International and Comparative Law, 17 Russell Square, London WC1B 5DR, offers research fellowships to students from overseas. The Hague Academy of International Law offers a course of study and scholarships (write to the Secretariat of the Academy, 2517 KJ, The Hague, Palais de la Prix, Holland). The Directorate of Human Rights, Council of Europe, Strasbourg offers fellowships for study in the field of human rights.

In addition to posts in the ordinary teaching institutions there are lectureships, tutorships and examinerships, and tutorships, assistant tutorships, and examinerships at the Law Society's College of Law and the other vocational training institutions. Vacancies in the City of London University/Inns of Court School[41] of Law lectureships (which may be part-time) are advertised in the legal papers; they are also announced on the notice boards in the Inns.

There are many teaching opportunities overseas, where you will be paid more highly than in the United Kingdom. Certainly go to a teaching post in Canada or Australia or elsewhere if you can easily return later on to look for your first post here; or go intending to make a new life in a new country; but do not go, severing your connections with the United Kingdom, intending to make this a step to advancement in this country. It is very difficult to transfer to a teaching post in this country from one overseas, because appointments committees

---

[41] In 2001, the long established Inns of Court School of Law became part of the City of London University.

will rarely appoint without interview, and may not be willing to pay travel expenses for candidates who are abroad.

If you wish to work in a university but not as a legal academic, consider taking a course in librarianship. Every law school has a library, and it is difficult to find people who have the double qualification.

ACCOUNTANCY

Quite a number of law students opt for accountancy, and a knowledge of law is useful both for the examinations and for practice. Accountants can become key advisers to industry, and many accountants are to be found on the Boards of large public companies. Some accountancy and consulting firms are setting up their own legal practices, although as yet multidisciplinary partnerships are not permitted—one suspects that it is only a matter of time before this prohibition is relaxed. An important part of the accountant's work is giving advice on tax matters which requires familiarity with the language and legal background of the statute. It should be obvious, therefore, that a law degree combined with a qualification in accountancy is a great advantage. A place to start is the Institute of Chartered Accountants in England and Wales, Chartered Accountants Hall, 11 Copthall Ave., London EC2R 7EF.

LEGAL PUBLISHING AND COURT REPORTING

The Incorporated Council of Law Reporting (publishers of the *Official Reports*, the *Weekly Law Reports* and a great deal more besides) employs a number of qualified lawyers to edit the law reports, deciding what is worthy of report, writing accurate summaries in the headnotes and so forth. Purely commercial legal publishing is another possibility, with firms such as the publishers of this book (Thomson – Sweet and Maxwell) or their competitors.

APPLYING FOR JOBS—SOME GENERAL ADVICE

If you are asked to name referees when applying for a job, always seek the permission of the person concerned before giving name and exact contact details; it is good practice to make a copy of your application (including your CV) available to the referee, these days in electronic form, so that the precise details of your career are readily to hand when the referee comes to write.

Your application for a position should lay out your stall in a curriculum vitae, together with some comments as to why you believe you are well suited to the position advertised. It is important that these documents are well laid out and professional looking – not difficult in these days when you can prepare the application on computer. And may I direct the attention of those who think that insistence upon accurate spelling is pure pedantry to a passage from C. Harrison's book, *From Student to Solicitor: The Complete Guide to Securing a Training Contract*:[42] "Employers are looking for candidates who care about their work and can demonstrate attention to detail; they do not want people who cannot be bothered to proof read their own CV, or who do so and miss the mistakes". With those words in mind, it would pay you to ask a friend to cast an eye over what you have written to see if they can spot any errors that may have escaped your attention.

A few points on the technique of being interviewed. Before the interview, you should closely re-read your own application. Make sure that you know the details of your own career, and can account for anything requiring explanation, such as the reason why you left your previous job. Find out what you can about the firm offering the job by searching on the internet, or reading one of the many Directories available. (Your University Careers Service can help.) How big is the firm; what does it make or do; does it operate abroad? The application process may well involve much more than a single interview, including such practices as role-playing and testing of various sorts. Find out in advance as much as you can about the process.

And what does the job entail? At the interview, remember that you are a salesman for yourself. Do not answer all questions with a mere Yes or No even if they admit of such answers. If you have to answer No, try to follow it with something positive. Some of the questions are likely to be on your past career as evidenced by your application; so be ready to add explanations when you are given an opening. Explain why you continued your studies for longer than usual; why you changed your course, or your university or college; why you took the

---

[42] 2nd edn, 2015 at p. 231.

vacation job. Be quick to mention what the experience brought you. Decide beforehand what are your best points and try to indicate them; make them as specific as possible. What motivates you? What attracts you about the job? What is there in your background or qualifications that make it seem specially suitable for you? Keep your voice up, and your head up. Look the interviewer in the eye (as you should always do when people are talking to you); and if you can manage a smile now and then, to show what a pleasant person you are to work with, so much the better. (A psychological study of non-verbal behaviour in interviews showed that successful outcomes were associated with smiling, eye contact and head nodding by the candidate).

Towards the close of the interview you will probably be invited to ask questions. Consider beforehand precisely what you want to know (it is not a bad idea to jot a couple of points down if your own research has not unearthed an answer). Do not commence with inquiries about the salary, holidays and prospects; it gives a better impression to start with questions about the work itself. What training is provided? What will be your relationship to others in the department? Can you meet them before joining? What are the working conditions and fringe benefits? What are the prospects of promotion, and who decides upon promotion? If you are willing to go abroad, you can lead into this by asking if the firm has openings abroad. One general word of warning. You should not at this point in the interview prolong proceedings by asking questions to which advance research would have provided you with an answer. "How big is the firm?" for example, might indicate to those interviewing that you have not taken the trouble to find out about them and this creates a poor impression. But it would be legitimate to say something like "it is not clear to me from the literature/web what is your approach to . . . ", for example. But just because you are given the opportunity to ask, you need not exercise it for the sake of form, particularly if the interviewers are giving you a signal that the time has run out.

I can say things in print that might naturally give offence (or at least cause distress) if I were speaking to you personally. In print my remarks are obviously indiscriminate. I should not have chosen in a personal conversation to mention the manner of slurred vowels and meaningless noises, as I did earlier. Now here are some words of wisdom, after the manner of Polonius, on the delicate matter of your appearance. It is accepted that students can dress comfortably in jeans and pullovers, or in garb expressing a more extravagant fancy. By the time you are thinking of a career in the law you should be prepared to relinquish these carefree ways. Your acceptance and progress in any walk of life depends upon the judgment of an older generation (to which you will yourself soon enough belong), and they will value conspicuous cleanliness, neatness and absence of undue ostentation in dress and hair style. Much as it may go against the grain, my advice is to remain a conformist when you start your job. It is a folly to let your appearance handicap your career. Neither the Sex Discrimination Act nor the Race Relations Act prohibits discrimination on the ground of dress, and, to most members of selection committees, "dress" means approved business or professional dress. So, if you are a man, buy a suit, dark blue or dark grey, of relatively conservative cut. If your firm has a "dressing down" day, you can perhaps express your personality more freely on those occasions.

If you have some fluency in a foreign tongue, try to keep it up. If the language is French or German, consider studying your law at a university offering a mixed English and French/German law course, as a great many now do; part of your time will be spent in a French or German university, and you emerge with a double qualification. Some universities offer mixed courses in law and languages. Solicitors with an international legal practice (who are to be found not only in London but in some other large cities) will give preference to recruits with linguistic ability. Many City firms have branches in Europe and elsewhere where English solicitors are employed. Recruitment to international legal bodies such as the staffs of the European Union, the Court and Commission requires proficiency not only in law but in languages.

14 GENERAL READING

> "A lawyer without history or literature is a mechanic, a mere working mason; if he possesses some knowledge of these, he may venture to call himself an architect."
>
> —Scott, *Guy Mannering*.

No one wants to read law all the time; some of the hours not spent on serious legal reading may be devoted with profit and pleasure to lighter literature touching upon the law, and to works that set the background in which the lawyer lives.[1] The following, which is hardly more than a list, may be of assistance not merely to the beginner at law but to the practitioner in leisure moments. What is offered is a collection of titles that may come the reader's way at intervals during life, and that are worth reading if they do. Not all the books included are in print but they should be available in bigger libraries.

FICTION

Dickens started life as (among other things) a lawyer's clerk and court reporter, and most of his novels contain legal characters or legal references. The famous trial scene in *Pickwick Papers* (written when the author was only 24) shows the working of the system of advocacy in a common law court at its worst. We have moved far since those days, not least because, since 1851, the parties to the proceedings have been allowed to testify on their own behalf. Students of the reports may like to know that Dickens's Mr Justice Stareleigh was modelled upon the real Mr. Justice Gaselee, while Serjeant Buzfuz was Serjeant Bompas.[2]

---

[1] Such is the pervasiveness of law that the interrelationship between law and literature has become a subject of study in its own right, particularly in the United States. There is even a periodical, *Cardozo Studies in Law and Literature* (1989–). Richard A. Posner's *Law and Literature* (3rd edn, 2009) is a masterly overview. See also (1999) C.L.P. Vol.2, which is given over completely to law and literature. F.R. Shapiro and J. Garry ed. *Trial and Error: An Oxford Anthology of Legal Stories* (1998) contains an eclectic selection.

[2] For a legal study see Percy Fitzgerald, *Bardell v Pickwick* (1902). It is pointed out

Even more engrossing for the lawyer is the description of the appallingly inefficient proceedings of the Court of Chancery in *Bleak House*. Space forbids extended discussion of Dickens's works, but a good commentary is Sir William Holdsworth's *Charles Dickens as a Legal Historian* (1929).[3]

An earlier writer, Henry Fielding, must occupy a special place in the esteem of the lawyer and the law-abiding citizen, for it was he who, with his blind half-brother, sitting as London magistrates, founded the Bow Street Runners, the ancestors of our present professional police.[4] Most of his novels were written when, for want of any other source of income, he was practising at the Bar;[5] but his *Tom Jones* deserves to be read for its own sake, and not merely for the incidental legal allusion. Thackeray entered the Middle Temple (though he did not get much further), and his experience there is pictured in Chapter 29 of *Pendennis*. To legal writers of the nineteenth century belongs the credit of inventing the detective novel.[6] Wilkie Collins, a nominal barrister, was author of *The Moonstone* (1860), which is widely considered to have been the first example of this genre. Galsworthy's *Forsyte Saga* has a solicitor as one of the principal characters, a libel action conducted on somewhat irregular lines,[7] and a will that neglects the Thellusson Act.[8] Someone brought the latter mistake to the author's attention, and in the sequel, entitled *On Forsyte Change*, the point is admitted but ingeniously evaded.[9]

Outside the field of English law there are the works of Sir Walter Scott and Honorè de Balzac—both lawyers, and both prolific in legal allusion. Scott combined novel writing with the practice of a busy Scottish advocate and judicial duties. His more boyish romances do not appeal to all; but the reader may like to know that two novels with

in (1923) 1 Can. Bar Rev. 631 that in *Brooke v Pickwick* (1827) 4 Bing. 753, 130 E.R. 753, the defendant was the coach proprietor of Bath from whom Dickens took the name of his hero, and one of the judges was Gaselee J. The legal purlieus of London as they survive since Dickens's time are described in (1970) 120 New L.J. 492.

[3] See also T.A. Fyfe, *Charles Dickens and the Law* (1910); Sir Gerald Hurst, *Lincoln's Inn Essays* (1949), p.109.

[4] Anthony Babington, *A House in Bow Street* (2nd edn, 1999).

[5] See Jenny Uglow, *Henry Fielding* (1995).

[6] (1975) 139 J.P.N. 572, at 605.

[7] (1929) 5 Can. Bar Rev. 500.

[8] The Accumulations Act 1800, which was replaced by the Law of Property Act 1925.

[9] (1931) 50 L.N. 68.

a strong legal flavour are *Guy Mannering* and *Redgauntlet*. Scott's best
novel, *The Heart of Midlothian*, is also set against a legal background,
and most of the main story is historically authentic. Students of Scots
law will find instruction in *Sir Walter Scott and Scots Law*, by David
Marshall (1932). R.L. Stevenson became qualified as a Scottish advocate, though he never practised. His unfinished *Weir of Hermiston*
gives an arresting picture of a coarse and cruel Scottish judge, Lord
Braxfield (in the story called Lord Hermiston).[10]

It is not only the lawyers, real or nominal, who have written novels
with a legal angle. Trollope is best known for his descriptions of
ecclesiastical life in the *Barchester* series; but lawyers will remember
him for his account of their own profession in *Orley Farm*.[11] Emily
Bronte's *Wuthering Heights* shows an accurate knowledge of the law
of entails 50 years before her own time.[12] George Eliot's *Felix Holt*
has an ambitious legal plot turning on a base fee—though the legal
reader will want to know why the owner in possession of a base fee,
with constant legal advice, did not take steps to bar the remainder.[13]

Modern novelists deserve a paragraph to themselves. The American
thrillers of Scott Turow[14] and John Grisham[15] exploit a rich seam of
public interest in courtroom pyrotechnics, lawyers turned detective
and "innocent" clients. Many of these works have been turned into
hugely successful films. The legal worlds that these characters inhabit
are very different from that found on the other side of the Atlantic,

[10] The number of novelists with legal connections is surprising, and it may be of interest to add a note on two others. Wilkie Collins is notable as one of the forerunners of
the modern detective novelists (see p.266). His novel *No Name* (1862, reprinted by OUP
World Classics in 1988) has a plot depending in part on rules of law: see Sladen in (1980)
77 L.S.Gaz. 1123, and he employed legal themes in many of his later works. John Buchan
started at the Bar and wrote a book on the taxation of foreign income before turning to
fiction. A good many legal texts had their origins in the need for income of tyro barristers.

[11] Those who wish to pursue the legal errors (which do not spoil the tale) will find them
unsparingly attacked by Sir Francis Newbolt K.C. in (1924) 95 *Nineteenth Century* 227,
reprinted in his *Out of Court* (1925). Trollope's views on the ethics of advocacy are discussed in E.B.V. Christian's *Leaves of the Lower Branch* (1909), pp.65–66. See also Henry
S. Drinker, *The Lawyers of Anthony Trollope*; Hugh Cockerall in (1977) 127 N.L.J. 1252.

[12] See C.P.S. [C.P. Sanger], *The Structure of Wuthering Heights* (Hogarth Essays,
1926).

[13] Earlier, Jane Austen had got into trouble on a similar point in *Pride and Prejudice*
(1813). See (1974) 124 N.L.J. 375.

[14] *Presumed Innocent; Personal Injuries; The Burden of Proof; Pleading Guilty.*

[15] *A Time To Kill; The Firm; The Pelican Brief; The Client; The Runaway Jury; The
Partner; The Street Lawyer.*

and there is not really any British equivalent, though lawyers currently writing detective novels include Dexter Dias, Frances Fyfield and Caro Fraser. In a somewhat different genre stands John Mortimer Q.C.'s creation *Rumpole*, who appears in numerous works (translated on to television subsequently; the actor Leo McKern, wig askew, being almost instantly recognisable world-wide as the face of the Old Bailey).

Judge Gordon Clark wrote detective novels under the pseudonym of "Cyril Hare", and the plot of several of them turns on a point of law. Thus his *Tragedy at Law* involves an obscure subsection (now repealed) of an Act of 1934; it is of interest for its detail of contemporary circuit life. *When the Wind Blows* was inspired by a bad old (and long-repealed) rule of the law of marriage. All these novels were reprinted as Penguins, and have subsequently been re-issued by House of Stratus Press as recently as 2001. Another former county court judge, H.C. Leon, wrote under the pen-name of "Henry Cecil". A favourite is his first book *Full Circle*; but he wrote many other humorous best-sellers about judges and lawyers, including *Brothers in Law* which was made into a film. These works too have been reprinted (2001) by House of Stratus Press. A fine recent legal novel, written by an non-lawyer, is Ian McEwan's *The Children Act* (2014) whose subject is a middle aged Judge of the Family Division, Fiona Maye, whose own marriage is falling apart as she struggles to make a life-and-death decision relating to a desperately ill 17 year old.

BIOGRAPHIES

From the many biographies of lawyers one should perhaps put first the lives of two great reformers: C.H.S. Fifoot's *Lord Mansfield* (1936) and Mary L. Mack's *Jeremy Bentham* (1962, Vol.I). The achievement of Sir Samuel Romilly can best be read in Sir Leon Radzinowicz's monumental *History of English Criminal Law*, Vol.1, Pt V. Romilly and Bentham figure, with Beccaria, in Coleman Phillipson's *Three Criminal Law Reformers* (1923). Mention may also be made of Lord Birkenhead's *Fourteen English Judges* (1926), and Catherine Drinker Bowen's biography of Coke C.J. called *The Lion and the Throne* (1957). No fewer than three books have been written about James Fitzjames Stephen, essayist, criminal law reformer and opponent of

John Stuart Mill: K.J.M. Smith, *James Fitzjames Stephen: Portrait of a Victorian Rationalist* (1988); J.A. Coliaco, *James Fitzjames Stephen and the Crisis of Victorian Thought* (1983) and J. Hostettler, *Politics and Law in the Life of Sir James Fitzjames Stephen* (1995). G. Lewis has written biographies of Lord Atkin (1999) and Lord Hailsham (1997). A more general survey is A.W.B. Simpson ed., *Biographical Dictionary of the Common Law* (1984) which affords thumb-nail sketches of the leading personalities of the law.

The interest in these works is largely historical, and many readers will be more attracted by biographies of successful lawyers living nearer to our own time. The apex of success was traditionally until recently the Woolsack, and the careers of those who have reached it are given by R.F.V. Heuston in scholarly detail in his *Lives of the Lord Chancellors 1885–1940* (1964), and a sequel, *Lives of the Lord Chancellors 1940–1970* (1978). Lord Elwyn-Jones, *In My Time* (1983) provides his own account of life leading to and in that office. However, the way lawyers function is of more importance than their biographical details, and a fascinating insight into the House of Lords in action is given by Robert Stevens in his *Law and Politics: The House of Lords as a Judicial Body 1800–1976* (1979) and the same author's work, *The Independence of the Judiciary: the view From the Lord Chancellor's Office* (1993). Alan Patterson for his study *The Law Lords* (1982) persuaded members of the House to reflect upon the way in which the House performed its judicial functions.

Edward Marjoribanks's *Life of Sir Edward Marshall Hall* (1929)[16] may be recommended for its portrayal of the last of the flamboyant advocates, and the same writer's *Life of Lord Carson* (1932) is fit to take its place among the best biographies.[17] Derek Walker-Smith's *Lord Reading and his Cases* (1934) and H. Montgomery Hyde's *Norman Birkett* (1964 and republished by Penguin in 1989) are also worth reading. John Campbell's *F.E. Smith* (1983) affords an insight into the life of the colourful politician/lawyer Lord Birkenhead. E. Heward's *Lord Denning: A Biography* (1997) gives an account

---

[16] Reprinted in condensed form by Pelican Books.
[17] The author had written the first of what were intended to be two volumes when he died, and his work was then published. It was later completed in a further two volumes by I. Colvin; but those who have only Marjoribanks's volume will find that it gives a satisfying account in itself.

of that remarkable man's long life and career, as does Iris Freeman, *Lord Denning: A Life* (1993).[18] Nicola Lacey's work, *A Life of H.L.A. Hart: the Nightmare and the Noble Dream* (2005) is a fascinating account of the life and works of the most central English jurist of the twentieth century. A compendium biography is *Jurists Uprooted; German Speaking Lawyers in Twentieth Century Britain* (2004) edited by R. Zimmerman and J. Beatson, and tells the stories of a number of Jewish lawyers, most of whom were driven from Nazi Germany and who made enormous contributions to the legal life of (primarily) the United Kingdom and the United States of America.

There is a plethora of autobiography, though they are perhaps rather less common now than half a century ago. The late Lord Justice MacKinnon, in his book *On Circuit* (1940), said that most books of legal reminiscence are bad; and he named only two exceptions, in which I hesitate to follow him.[19] Glanville Williams' list of the best legal autobiographies included one by a successful advocate of the last century, one by a judge who made his name on the criminal side, and one by a country solicitor. The first of these is *Some Experiences of a Barrister's Life*, by William Ballantine (1882)—better known as Serjeant Ballantine's *Experiences*. Its gossipy pages are crowded with Victorian personalities who are still alive to students of the law reports. Ballantine was retained on behalf of Orton, the false claimant in the *Tichborne* case, and his book gives shrewd advice on advocacy.

Two generations on comes Sir Travers Humphreys (Humphreys J.), *Criminal Days* (1946). This is an autobiography full of good stories, with reflections upon the criminal law. Reginald Hine's *Confessions of an Un-Common Attorney* (1945) is a revelation of the interest that can be won from life by a country solicitor who observes his fellow creatures and is an antiquarian and litterateur to boot. Lord Denning's *The Family Story* (1981)[20] is the personal testament of our best-known, most popular, most idiosyncratic, most energetic,

---

[18] Lord Denning's work on the Bench is made the subject of detailed analysis by L.J. Jowell and J.P.W.B. McAuslan, *Lord Denning: the judge and the law* (1994).

[19] The two exceptions made by MacKinnon L.J. were *Pie-Powder* by "A Circuit Tramp" (J. Alderson Foote K.C.) (1911), and *As I Went on My Way*, by Arthur J. Ashton K.C. (1924). The former is little more than a collection of anecdotes (chiefly humorous), though the anecdotes have merit.

[20] See also *What Next in the Law* (1982); *The Closing Chapter* (1983); *Landmarks in the Law* (1984); *Leaves From My Library* (1986).

and in some ways most reform-minded judge. Sir Neville Faulks, *No Mitigating Circumstances* (1977) and *A Law Unto Myself* (1978) is another former judge of the Court of Appeal who has put pen to paper, as is Sir Robin Dunn, *Sword and Wig: Memoirs of a Lord Justice* (1993). E. Crowther, *Last in the List: The Life and Times of an English Barrister* (1988) tells the legal story from the perspective of a Metropolitan Magistrate. Two Attorneys-General have also recounted their experiences: P. Rawlinson, *A Price too High* (1989) and Hartley Shawcross, *Life Sentence* (1995). Not one of these is a "must" book, though each is good in its own class. Solicitors have not been tempted to be forthcoming about their experiences to quite the same extent as former members of the Bar. D. Napley, *Not Without Prejudice* (1982) is an exception, as is P. Carter-Ruck, *Memoirs of a Libel Lawyer* (1990) and Lord Goodman, solicitor to the great and the good, published *Tell Them I am on My Way* (1993). A barrister still in practice, G. Robertson Q.C., recounts some of the cases in which he has been involved in *The Justice Game* (1998), and Michael Mansfield Q.C.'s *Memoirs of a Radical Lawyer* (2009) is written by a barrister who was on the verge of retirement.

Finally, it is convenient to mention here the remarkable Pollock-Holmes *Letters* (2 vols, 1942), the correspondence of two men who became the doyens of English and American law, carried on over a period of 58 years. This may well be read with Mark de Wolfe Howe's two-volume biography, *Justice Oliver Wendell Holmes* (1957, 1963), supplemented by G.E. White, *Justice Oliver Wendell Holmes: Law and the Inner Self* (1993) for the later years of Holmes' life.

It may not have escaped your attention that the list just given is exclusively concerned with male subjects. This reflects the subject-matter of this book, which has an almost exclusively male history. That history of the female experience across jurisdictions is ana-lysed in ed. U. Schultz and G. Shaw, *Women in the World's Legal Professions* (2002). The changes that have occurred in the last 35 years or so are not yet represented in legal literature. Books and articles about women and the law that are (painfully slowly) beginning to address the imbalance. Helena Kennedy's *Eve Was Framed: Women and British Justice* (1993) and Clare McGlynn's *The Woman Lawyer: making the difference* (1998) are two important contributions, and the article by Lady Justice Hale, "Equality and the Judiciary: Why Should

We Want More Women Judges?" [2001] P.L. 489 makes a persuasive case. There is an irony in the byline—its author is described as "A Lord Justice of Appeal". Lady Justice Hale (as she then was – she is now the Deputy President of the Supreme Court) is one of 43 biographies to be found in R.M. Salokar and M.L. Volcansek eds, *Women in Law: a bio-bibliographical sourcebook* (1996). Hilary Heilbron Q.C. has given an account of her mother's life and career in *Rose Heilbron: the Story of England's First Woman Queen's Counsel and Judge* (2012). Thomas Grant has produced a remarkable work, *Jeremy Hutchinson's Case Histories* (2015) detailing some of the highlights in the career of a barrister (who recently celebrated his 100th birthday). The incidents that it recounts now seem to belong to a very different legal world, but they give a very colourful account of what life at the Bar formerly involved. The description of the prosecution of Penguin Books for publishing D.H. Lawrence's *Lady Chatterley's Lover*, in particular, is the best account that I have read of that much-discussed trial.

TRIALS

The historian, the devotee of detective fiction, the student of advocacy, and the novelist in search of a plot, should not ignore the very full collection of trials that may be found in some libraries. Cases of historical interest are reported at length in the 34 volumes of Howell's *State Trials*, such, for example, as Coke's virulent prosecution of Sir Walter Raleigh (Vol.2, p.1). A selection from these trials was published in three volumes by J.W. Willis-Bund. Other series are *Newgate Calendars*, the Notable British Trials Series, the Famous Trials Series, and the Old Bailey Trials Series; with the exception of the first-mentioned, these give a full transcript of the cases, so that each step in the evidence can be studied. There are also occasional publications, such as *The Trial of Lady Chatterley (R. v Penguin Books Ltd)*, edited by C.H. Rolph (1961) and Ludovic Kennedy's *The Trial of Steven Ward* (1964). Accounts of libel trials by those who have participated include A. Raphael, *My Learned Friends* (1989) and Alan Watkins, *A Slight Case of Libel* (1990). Professor Richard Evans, *Lying about Hitler* (2001) is an account, by one of the expert witnesses, of the proceedings in a notorious Holocaust Denial libel action.

Perhaps the most remarkable of the nineteenth century *causes célèbres* was that of *The Tichborne Claimant*; Douglas Woodruffe's book under that title is noteworthy. Illustrations of the technique of famous advocates are given in Edgar Lustgarten's *Defender's Triumph* (1951). There is also an inexpensive series of Famous Trials in Penguins, each volume containing condensed accounts of a number of trials. Andrew Rose's *Stinie: Murder on the Common* (1985) and *Scandal at the Savoy* (1991) evoke the past in a vivid way, and M. Friedland's *The Trials of Israel Lipski* (1993) offers a fascinating look at immigrant life in the East End of London. A.W.B. Simpson's grue-somely titled *Cannibalism and the Common Law* (1986) fills in the background to one of the best known of all English criminal cases, *R. v Dudley and Stephens*.[21]

As a matter of interest it may be recorded that R. L. Stevenson's *Kidnapped* is based in part on the famous Appin murder case, *R. v Stewart* (1752) 19 Howell's State Trials 1. This is itself the subject of a study by Sir William MacArthur in *The Appin Murder*, (1960). The *Annesley Case*, retold in the Notable English Trials Series (a series that later became Notable British Trials), supplied material for parts of three novels.[22] Another novelist who used these Trials was Nathaniel Hawthorne.[23]

ESSAYS

It would be possible to compile an anthology of essays bearing upon the law, beginning with Bacon's essay "Of Judicature", and passing through Selden's *Table Talk*, Lamb's "Old Benchers of the Inner Temple",[24] Bagehot's "Lord Brougham",[25] Hazlitt's portrait of Eldon,[26] and several by Maitland, to modern examples such as John Buchan's "The Judicial Temperament" (in his *Homilies and*

---

[21] (1884) 14 Q.B.D. 273. The case is discussed more fully in Ch.8.

[22] Tobias Smollett's *Peregrine Pickle* (1751), Ch.98; Scott's *Guy Mannering* (1815) and Charles Reade's *The Wandering Heir* (1873). See David Marshall, *Sir Walter Scott and Scots Law*, pp.48–57.

[23] See Alfred S. Reid, *The Yellow Ruff and the Scarlet Letter* (University of Florida Press, 1955).

[24] Included among the *Essays of Elia* and republished with notes by MacKinnon L.J. in a limited edition (1927), and again in the same writer's *Inner Temple Papers* (1948).

[25] Republished in N. St. John-Stevas ed., *Collected Works* (1968), Vol.iii, p.159.

[26] Included in his essays entitled *The Spirit of the Age*, first printed in 1825.

Recreations), Lord Justice MacKinnon's *Murder in the Temple* (1935), Theo. Mathew's *For Lawyers and Others* (1937), and Lord Macmillan's *Law and Other Things* (1937). Lord Bingham's work, *The Business of Judging* (2000) is a series of witty and thoughtful essays by the Senior Law Lord who had also been the Master of the Rolls and the Lord Chief Justice. Another selection of his writings, *Lives of the Law* (2011) was published posthumously. The works of another recently retired senior judge, Sir Stephen Sedley's *Ashes and Sparks: Essays on Law and Justice* (2011) is a very thought-provoking read.

Some of the best legal essays are to be found in no other place than the law reports, in the judgments of such men as Mansfield, Bowen, Macnaghten and Sumner. The speech of Lord Macnaghten in *Gluckstein v Barnes* [1900] A.C. 240 at 255 is a brilliant example of pungent wit, which was thought worthy of inclusion in the *Oxford Book of English Prose*; and Atkin L.J.'s judgment in *Balfour v Balfour* [1919] 2 K.B. 571 also deserves honourable mention, as does the same judge's (by now Lord Atkin) brave dissent in *Liversidge v Anderson* [1946] 2 A.C. 206, which is a speech that every student should read. The dissent of Fletcher Moulton L.J. in the Court of Appeal in *Scott v Scott* [1912] P. 262 is quite astonishing for the quality of the prose in which it is couched.[27] Mr Louis Blom-Cooper has published his own selections of best legal writing under the titles *The Law as Literature* (1961) and *The Language of the Law* (1965), as has B. Harris, *The Literature of the Law* (1998), who includes a number of very recent judgments in his selection.

HUMOUR

Collections of anecdotes are usually poor things, but exceptions are Sir Robert Megarry's *Miscellany-at-Law* (1955), and *A Second Miscellany-at-Law* (1973), both including many specimens of judicial wit and wisdom. A *New Miscellany-at-Law* has been edited by Brian Garner and published in 2005. The best book of humorous reminiscence comes from Ireland: it is Maurice Healey's *The Old*

---

[27] I am grateful to Sir David Eady for pointing this out to me, as I am to him for many other suggestions.

Munster Circuit (1939, reprinted by Wildy and Co in 2001). Irish-born Sir James Comyn has produced a series of anecdotal books, under such titles as *Watching Brief* (1993) and *Summing it Up* (1991). W.S. Gilbert's libretto to *Trial by Jury* is a joy to read: but then, Gilbert was by training a lawyer! *The Complete Forensic Fables* by "O" [Sir Theobald Mathew] (reprinted by Wildy and Co, 1999) is well-known. Sir Alan Herbert's even more famous *Misleading Cases* are collected together under the title *Uncommon Law* (1935) with its sequels *Codd's Last Case* (1952) and *Bardot, M.P.?* (1964) reprinted as *More Uncommon Law* (1982). David Pannick's books *Judges* (1987) and *Advocates* (1992) contain much that will amuse, and Michael Gilbert's *Oxford Book of Legal Anecdotes* (1986) also escapes the general condemnation expressed at the beginning of this section.

DRAMA

The number of legal references in Shakespeare has given rise to much argument as to whether he might have been a trained lawyer. The thesis in favour[28] would be more attractive if the internal evidence had not also been used to assign him to a number of other walks in life.

> The bard play-writing in his room,
> The bard a humble clerk,
> The bard, a lawyer, parson, groom,
> The bard, deer-stalking after dark,
> The bard a tradesman—and a Jew—
> The bard a botanist—a beak—
> The bard a skilled musician, too—
> A sheriff and a surgeon, eke![29]

In fact, modern research has shown that there are as many references to legal concepts among the lesser Elizabethan dramatists as in Shakespeare, and that there is no reason to suppose that Shakespeare

---

[28] Propounded in *The Law of Property in Shakespeare and the Elizabethan Drama*, by Paul S. Clarkson and Clyde T. Warren (1942). It is undoubtedly the case that *Twelfth Night* was first performed in the Middle Temple Hall; see A.J. Arlidge Q.C., *Shakespeare and the Prince of Love* (2000).

[29] W.S. Gilbert, *The Bab Ballads* (1869).

possessed any unusual knowledge. Much the best discussion of the plays from the legal point of view is G.W. Keeton, *Shakespeare's Legal and Political Background* (1967). See also the very learned study by Professor O. Hood Phillips, *Shakespeare and the Lawyers* (1972), and Professor Ian Ward's *Shakespeare and the Legal Imagination* (1999). It need hardly be added that, as any commentator will allow, the plays themselves are worth a shelf-full of commentaries; commentaries are for those who know the plays. There is endless fascination in picking out the legal allusions in Shakespeare without the help of commentaries.

Among later dramatists, three of Galsworthy's plays have a direct interest for lawyers: *The Silver Box, Justice* and *Loyalties*, the last involving a strict application of professional etiquette. A performance of *Justice* was witnessed in 1911 by Mr Winston Churchill, then Home Secretary, and he was so moved by it that he made a long-overdue reform in prison administration by drastically curtailing the period of solitary confinement.[30] It is of interest to note that Galsworthy was called to the Bar in 1890; but he never practised. Terence Rattigan's work, *The Winslow Boy* (the tale of a young boy falsely accused of stealing at school) has recently enjoyed a renaissance as a film (screenplay by David Mamet, and available on video). B. Clark's *Whose Life is it Anyway?* is a moving depiction of a person forced to seek legal permission to terminate his own life, which explores the legal and ethical difficulties that surround that predicament.

FILM

Should your taste run to the cinema (and in many cases, the films below are available on demand electronically), I can recommend *12 Angry Men* (1957) in which one juror gradually persuades the others to put aside prejudice and their own preoccupations and consider the evidence against a young man charged with capital murder; incidentally, jurors in England are forbidden under pain of contempt of court from revealing the secrets of the jury room, but in his excellent book

---

[30] He reduced it to one month for all but recidivists. Such a reform had been advocated by a departmental committee in 1895. See S. and B. Webb, *English Prisons under Local Government* (1922), p.223, fn.1.

The Juryman's Tale (1999) Trevor Grove skilfully skirts this law to tell of his experiences as a juror at the Old Bailey. Other films regarded as classics include *Inherit the Wind* (1960); *Anatomy of a Murder* (1959); *To Kill a Mockingbird* (1962); *Witness for the Prosecution* (1957) (though I suspect that some of the detail was legally inauthentic even when it was first produced); *A Civil Action* (1998); *Touch of Evil* (1958); *The Crucible* (1996). These are all essentially works of dramatic fiction. Other works are based, to a greater or lesser extent, on factual events, such as *The Biko Inquest* (1984). *Let Him Have It* (1991) is a recreation of the trial of Craig and Bentley that took place in the 1950s, one of whom (Bentley) was hanged for murder. He was eventually (1998) given a posthumous pardon, and his conviction was quashed by the Court of Appeal. But the law of complicity that underlies the original verdict is probably still good law. *Dance with a Stranger* (1985) recounts the ordeal of the last woman hanged in England, Ruth Ellis, whose plea of provocation was rejected by the court on the basis of what I believe to have been a misunderstanding of the law, namely that an intention to kill is inconsistent with the plea of provocation. Public disquiet at her treatment fuelled the anti-capital punishment movement leading to the abolition of the death penalty by the Homicide Act 1957. *Judgment at Nuremburg* (1961) is not a full-scale account of the trials, but focuses on one judge and one particular defendant. A more recent film, a documentary arising out of the events of the second world war is by a leading academic and Q.C., Philippe Sands, *My Nazi Legacy*, in which the sons of two Nazis take very different views as to the sins of their fathers.

The Accused (1988, starring Jodie Foster) is based upon an event that occurred in America, in which a young woman was raped in a public bar, in full view of the other patrons, some of whom participated in the rape, others encouraged and others were merely present, but doing nothing to intervene. It affords a graphic illustration of the difficulties of attributing liability to witnesses of criminal wrongdoing.

A minor irritant for lawyers watching these legal dramas is that legal verisimilitude is sometimes sacrificed to heightened drama. *In the Name of the Father* (1993), which purports to be an account of the miscarriage of justice suffered by the "Guildford Four", suffered from this. Emma Thompson, the defendants' solicitor (not barrister), is portrayed as giving an impassioned speech to the jury. Marcel Berlins, legal correspondent of *The Guardian*, described the film as "the most ludicrous and wildly inaccurate ever seen on a cinema screen". Similarly, in *Bridge of Spies* which recounts the trial of Russian spy Rudolf Abel,[31] the scenario in which defence counsel discusses the case privately and at the home of the judge rather than in court is utterly implausible.

HISTORY

Legal histories are generally outside the scope of this chapter, but three are so clearly entitled to rank as literature that mention may be made of them. They are Maine's *Ancient Law* (which should be read in Pollock's edition), Maitland's *Constitutional History*, and Holmes's *The Common Law*.

THE CONSTITUTION

Every lawyer will take delight in Sir Alan Herbert's *The Ayes Have It* (1937)—an account of the passage of the Matrimonial Causes Act—and *The Point of Parliament* (1946). If you feel that your knowledge of the working of government is deficient, read E. Barendt's *An Introduction to Constitutional Law* (1998) which is available in paperback. The Constitution of the United Kingdom has altered with astonishing rapidity in the last decade or so, a process charted in successive editions by eds J. Jowell and D. Oliver, *The Changing Constitution* (8th edn, 2015), now joined as editor by C. O'Cinneide, and set in context by V. Bogdanor's *The New British Constitution* (2009). Anthony King's *Does the United Kingdom Still Have a Constitution?* (2001) is a stimulating read, as is the work of two very senior judges, Lord Nolan and Sir Stephen Sedley, *The Making and Remaking of the British Constitution* (1997).

JURISPRUDENCE, LOGIC, PHILOSOPHY AND ECONOMICS

Selection becomes more difficult when one turns to the theoretical treatment of the law. Much has been written on this, but not of a

---

[31] Played in the film by Oscar winner Mark Rylance, who happens to be an Honorary Bencher of the Middle Temple.

character to appeal to the general reader. There is an annual series of lectures, the "Hamlyn" Lectures, whose purpose is to introduce the lay reader to selected aspects of English Law. *Freedom, Law and Justice* by the Rt Hon. Lord Justice Sedley should be read by anybody who supposes that the senior judiciary consists of those whose views are entirely conservative and backward-looking. A simple and readable account of juridical thinking is Lon L. Fuller's *Anatomy of the Law* (Pelican). Judge Jerome Frank's *Law and the Modern Mind* (1930 but reprinted 1951) is a pungent and provocative book, with which may be coupled Thurman Arnold's *The Folklore of Capitalism* (1937). A classic by a great American judge is Cardozo's *Nature of the Judicial Process* (1921).[32] All four of these books are American. Sir Carleton Allen's *Law in the Making* (7th edn, 1964) and Julius Stone's *Legal System and Lawyers' Reasonings* are heavier going, but every lawyer should read them. More introductory are J. Waldron's *The Law* (1990), A.W.B. Simpson, *An Invitation to Law* (1988), Tony Honoré, *About Law: An Introduction* (1995), P. Atiyah, *Law and Modern Society* (2nd edn, 1995). B. Tamahana's book, *On the Rule of Law: History, Politics, Theory* (2004) is a challenging account of a pervasive jurisprudential conception; the author comments in the preface that his intended audience was his father, a non-lawyer, and the book is the more readily intelligible for it. It may usefully be bracketed with a work by Tom Bingham, until 2008 the Senior Law Lord in the United Kingdom. His book *The Rule of Law* (2009) has a more practical orientation – he concludes, for example, that the declaration of war upon Iraq was illegal.

From time to time judges and even Law Lords tell us that logic is not compulsive in legal reasoning. In this they merely betray a lack of understanding of what logic is. A good simple account is Anthony Flew's *Thinking about Thinking* (Fontana, 1975). Other popular expositions of practical logic are R.H. Thouless's *Straight and Crooked Thinking* (1930, later published in paperback) and E.R. Emmet's *The Use of Reason* (1960), Ch.9.

Nineteenth-century Liberalism and economic laissez-faire have moulded the outlook of lawyers more than they themselves realise.

---

[32] Now available in a collected edition including other works of the author: Margaret E. Hall ed., *Selected Writings of Benjamin Nathan Cardozo* (New York, 1947).

In their application to constitutional law the classic is Dicey's *Law of the Constitution* (10th edn by E.C.S. Wade, 1961); on the wider aspects there is the same writer's *Law and Opinion in England during the Nineteenth Century* (reissued as a paperback in 1962). A continuation volume, *Law and Opinion in England in the 20th Century*, was produced by a group effort under the editorship of Morris Ginsberg in 1959. For some time, it has been the fashion to decry Dicey's Rule of Law as well as Adam Smith's economics: before finally subscribing to the current opinion the student should read Professor Hayek's defence of these doctrines in his book *The Constitution of Liberty* (1960), followed by his important trilogy on law, *Legislation and Liberty* (1973). This is an attack upon Socialism, written by a distinguished economist but employing chiefly political arguments which all can understand, whether they agree with them or not. T.R.S. Allan's work has done much to restore the belief in the importance of the rule of law by his two books *Law, Liberty and Justice* (1993) and *Constitutional Justice: a Liberal Theory of the Rule of Law* (2001). Lord Robbins's powerful dissent from Hayek can be read in his *Politics and Economics* (1963). We must not leave the philosophy of Liberalism without mentioning J.S. Mill's famous essay "On Liberty".[33] This is not only a classic but one that can still be read with keen enjoyment. H.L.A. Hart's *Law, Liberty and Morality* is in the same tradition, but should be read in conjunction with Patrick (Lord) Devlin's counterblast, *The Enforcement of Morals*. Essential reading for the modern jurist must include Ronald Dworkin's *Taking Rights Seriously* (1977); *A Matter of Principle* (1985); *Law's Empire* (1986); *Freedom's Law* (1996).

---

[33] Reprinted in Fontana Philosophy Classics (paperback) together with the same writer's "Utilitarianism" and "Essay on Bentham," ed. by Mary Warnock.

Index

This index has been prepared using Sweet and Maxwell's Legal Taxonomy. Main index entries conform to keywords provided by the Legal Taxonomy except where references to specific documents or non-standard terms (denoted by quotation marks) have been included. These keywords provide a means of identifying similar concepts in other Sweet & Maxwell publications and online services to which keywords from the Legal Taxonomy have been applied. Readers may find some minor differences between terms used in the text and those which appear in the index. Suggestions to *sweetandmaxwell.taxonomy@thomson.com*.